QUALITY IN HIGHER EDUCATION

GLOBAL APPROACHES TO IMPROVE SUSTAINABLE QUALITY

QUAMRUL H. MAZMUDER, PHD

University of Michigan–Flint

Copyright © 2017 Quamrul Mazumder
With Darla Nagel

All rights reserved.

No part of this book may be reproduced, stored in a retrieval system, or transmitted by any means, electronic, mechanical, photocopying, recording, or otherwise, without written permission from the author.

Published by

Bloomington, Indiana
(314) 827-6567
info@PenandPublish.com
www.PenandPublish.com

ISBN: 978-1-941799-53-6

This book is printed on acid-free paper.

ABOUT THE AUTHOR

Dr. Quamrul H. Mazumder received his bachelor's degree in Bangladesh and PhD in the United States. He held different leadership positions in engineering for 18 years before returning to an academic position. His research focuses on student learning, motivation, metacognition, teaching and learning styles, quality of higher education, globalization of education, and other related areas. He is recognized as a global leader and expert in the quality and assessment of higher education. He has been providing services and expertise for higher education quality improvement initiatives of Bangladesh, where he has conducted numerous workshops, seminars, and training for faculty, administrators, and students. He served as a Fulbright Scholar in Bangladesh in 2013, where he developed curriculum and assessment processes for a graduate engineering program.

CONTENTS

PREFACE — 7

CHAPTER 1: — 11
Quality Standards in Higher Education

CHAPTER 2: — 43
Global Issues in the Quality of Higher Education

CHAPTER 3: — 51
Globalization of Quality in Higher Education

CHAPTER 4: — 59
European Standards in Higher Education

CHAPTER 5: — 67
Accreditation

CHAPTER 6: — 77
Metacognition

CHAPTER 7: — 89
Motivation in Higher Education

CHAPTER 8: — 99
Learning Styles

CHAPTER 9: — 127
Learning Strategies

CHAPTER 10: — 149
Teaching Styles

CHAPTER 11: — 167
Student Satisfaction

CHAPTER 12: — 185
Ethics

CHAPTER 13: — 209
Quality in Online Learning

PREFACE

This book was motivated by the desire to improve the quality of higher education around the world.

With the wide range of issues faced by higher education institutions around the world, it is critical to address these issues effectively. Quality of higher education has also become an area of great interest in many research fields and higher education communities. Quality can be defined as endurance, luxury, prestige, and conformance to requirements, as well as continuous improvement and added value to higher education. The primary objective of this book is to provide a basic understanding of the issues in higher education systems around the world. The book will include different approaches, methods, and processes that address the challenges in improving the quality systems and processes in an institution or country. This text is intended to provide higher education administrators, faculty, and students with a comprehensive overview of the issues related to the quality of education. The book development process included collaboration and discussion with several faculty members at institutions around the world. This book was written for higher education administrators, policy makers, governmental agencies, faculty, students, higher education communities, and department chairs. This book can be used as a practical guide to improve student learning, assessment processes, and development of policy procedures at department or institution levels.

The book begins with an overview of key elements, such as quality standards in higher education, global issues in higher education, and accreditation and assessment processes used in different countries. Comparative analysis and details of different quality standards with recommendations have also been added. After describing the issues and standards used to manage quality, different methods, tools, techniques, and processes are described. With a focus on student learning as the primary indicator of quality, several topics, such as motivation, learning styles, learning strategies, teaching styles, metacognition, student satisfaction, and ethics in higher education, have been included. Each chapter includes different theories and models and their effectiveness in the socioeconomic context of disciplines that have been analyzed.

This will enable educators to develop an in-depth understanding of different theories and models along with the one that is most appropriate for their discipline, institution, students, or environment. This book concludes with a vision for the future of quality in online higher education around the world.

This book is intended to help higher education administrators or government agencies that oversee quality assurance in higher education and enact regulations to ensure quality. This will also help faculty and students, who are the primary stakeholders of the higher education system. Additionally, programs or faculty that are responsible for ensuring educational quality will benefit greatly from this book, and scholars who have been relentlessly researching education will benefit from its information.

This book can also be used in undergraduate and graduate courses in a plethora of education programs. The following are the distinctions and highlights of the book:

- Quality in higher education has been recognized as a critical success factor by several nations around the world. This is likely because they have realized that economic development depends on a high-quality higher education system.
- All stakeholders in higher education, such as higher education administrators, faculty, and policy makers, can use this book to improve quality.
- This book can be used as a faculty training and development manual to familiarize staff with common quality concerns and the possible solutions to these issues.
- The books that are currently available in the market on the topic of quality in higher education have covered quality in higher education from limited points of view. However, this book provides a comprehensive overview of a wide range of issues and theories in this area.
- The unique perspective and experiences of the author, who has been associated with many organizations working to ensure quality in higher education processes around the world, will create a unique approach to a common global issue.
- This book presents models of quality in higher education from different countries and the models that are most effective in different contexts.

The primary approach used in this book is to improve student learning as a mode of quality improvement because students are the primary stakeholders in the process. A number of tools, techniques, methods, and processes will be presented that include motivation, metacognition, learning styles, teaching styles, learning strategies, and ethics. These tools will be described in detail as separate chapters in the book along with theories, models, application, and effectiveness in improving student learning. Applicability of different theories based on discipline or subject will be analyzed to enable faculty members to select the appropriate theories for their context.

The book also includes different models and policies used to manage the quality of higher education in Asia, Europe, Africa, North America, South America, and Australia with comparative analysis. Additionally, a separate chapter presents a detailed description of ethics, which is very much an important catalyst in quality assurance, though most of the books covering quality in education avoid this topic.

Chapter 1 of this book aims to convey the definition and assessment methods of quality in higher education. Through case studies, the reader will be able to gain a deeper understanding of the criteria that play into establishing quality. The models that are used to address such requirements are described in **Chapter 2**, along with how each model can be used uniquely in different cultures. The advantages and disadvantages are also weighed out in regard to each model. Quality, supply, and value are all analyzed, and their roles in higher education are described when applied in a diverse set of countries, such as Australia, Spain, and Hong Kong. These models are then compared in light of the effects of globalization in **Chapter 3**. Economies and education systems of countries all around the world are changing rapidly. This requires the adaptation of higher education. The specific aspects of quality higher education in Europe are analyzed in **Chapter 4**. Guidelines and regulations often differ from system to system and regulations are not always clear. The standard in European countries was developed to ensure quality within their higher education systems.

A clear way of regulating higher education systems in different colleges and countries is accreditation. **Chapter 5** focuses on the main aspects of accreditation in higher education. Accreditation evaluates higher education programs and can serve as a guideline to those creating curricula and starting new academic programs. There are many types of accreditation depending on the nature of the school or program that is being evaluated. However, all accreditation services have a similar goal of creating the best graduates and higher education systems possible. As discussed in **Chapter 6**, metacognition and student learning are strongly correlated. In basic terms, *metacognition* is "thinking about thinking." Included in metacognition when used as a learning tool are planning, study strategies, as well as monitoring one's progress and adjusting when needed. While focusing on the many aspects of student success, **Chapter 7** focuses on motivation within students in higher education. The transition to higher education can often be difficult for students. This combined with the fact that there sometimes seems to be very little an instructor can do to motivate a student can make motivational learning extremely difficult. Maximizing interest in a student as well as promoting engagement is the key to motivational learning.

The challenge of having a single instructor for many students mainly lies in the fact that every student learns differently. Some students can learn simply by listening, others by seeing written text, and others only by gaining hands-on experience with the material. **Chapter 8** provides a comprehensive overview of the different learning styles and how individual students use them. It is important that students determine what type, or what combination of types, of learning style works best for them to achieve academic success. A person's approach to learning certain material can make all the difference when it comes to his or her success. Within **Chapter 9**, key learning strategies and their success are explained. Many factors play into which learning strategy is the best suited for a situation, such as the specific student, task, and subject. Although student learning lies often in factors that the student can control, such as motivation and study strategies, some factors are out of his or her hands.

Teaching styles, as described in **Chapter 10**, play an important role in the learning process. Different subjects and disciplines often require unique teaching styles based on the material that must be covered. In addition, students often have certain teaching styles they prefer but may not always have the option to partake in a course that is hands-on when the material requires a lecture-based presentation. Each teacher or professor also has preferences for how he or she conveys the material. An effective teacher is able to cater to many learning styles, especially as he or she gains more teaching experience. Many of these discussed factors play into the overall satisfaction of a student during his or her learning experiences. **Chapter 11** defines student satisfaction, discusses how it can be improved, and explains why satisfaction in higher education is important. A case study is also presented within the chapter to further analyze what precise factors contribute to student satisfaction. Quality of higher education, to students, is an extremely important factor because it directly affects their future as well as their current opportunities. Ethical behavior is yet another key factor in the world of higher education, especially in foreign countries. **Chapter 12** discusses not only ethical behavior but also how to incorporate morals and ethical behavior into not only the workplace but also higher education. A person's conduct, whether it is in the workplace or in the classroom, can directly affect the quality of work that is being produced. Several ethical theories are also analyzed within the chapter to convey the importance of ethics. **Chapter 13** applies current understanding of quality in higher education to online learning.

CHAPTER 1:

Quality Standards in Higher Education

CHAPTER OBJECTIVE

The main purpose of this chapter is to define and describe the quality standards of higher education and the assessment of these standards around the world. This will provide the foundation for comparing institutions' quality models and definitions.

1.1 INTRODUCTION

Quality plays a vital role for educational institutions because they have provided assurance to students of effective teaching support and learning opportunities before enrolling in the institutions. Quality can be considered a key measurement to assess the learning opportunities provided to students and how useful they are to reach students' goals. Certain input factors, such as admissions selectivity, faculty credentials, class size, physical facilities, and tuition fee, determine the quality of an institution. The better the institution is in these input measures, the higher its quality. But in reality, using only the input-based measures is not sufficient to define the quality of education. There should be a prominent emphasis on students' learning strategies and outcomes, because actual outcomes matter when analyzing the success of educational institutions (McBride, 2003). It is evident that students need to focus on their skills and knowledge to attain their goals. In workplaces and professional life, what students actually learn and how they can use the skills from their programs actually matter in achieving success. According to Harvey and Newton (2004, as cited in Bollaert et al., 2007), quality of higher education reflects "processes of assessment, accreditation, audit, and external examination" (p. 15). Quality in higher education is a multidimensional, multilevel, and dynamic rational specification where the outcomes are delivered consistently.

1.2 IMPORTANCE OF QUALITY IN HIGHER EDUCATION

Higher education plays an important role in a student's life, both as an individual and as a part of the society in which he or she lives. Higher education aids the students for the growth and the development of a better life. The higher education institutions contribute to society by creating the ideal citizens to make a peaceful society. The transition of students from school to college makes them independent and makes them add to their life experiences. Thus, they learn how to be on their own. If the students truly want to learn during the college years, then the possibilities are unlimited, and they can increase their knowledge through experts in the fields. Thus, we can say that college life teaches necessary life lessons and helps build the right attitude in students. Students get the opportunity to experience life by exploring the world and find themselves. People with higher education are more likely to get jobs with health benefits and pension benefits. Thus, a college degree is the key to a better life with good salaries and to have better partners, parents, and employees.

Due to increased emphasis on developing knowledge-led economies, higher education's quality has been recognized as one of the main agendas of national competitiveness. Higher education institutions around the world, especially in developing countries, are challenged to meet national priorities. Most of the policy makers view higher educational institutions as the economic engines that are necessary to ensure the knowledge production of students through the innovative research and the constant education of the employees (Zaman, 2015).

"To bring about a balance between autonomy and accountability, the role of quality in education has stepped to the foreground, increasing its presence in recent times" (Hénard & Mitterle, 2009, as cited in Zaman, 2015, p. 1). Universities have replaced their focus on daily activities with a focus on strategic direction (Zaman, 2015). "In a handful of countries, different ad-hoc bodies have been established to check the quality of teaching and research within institutions of higher learning" (Organisation for Economic Co-operation and Development, 2003, as cited in Zaman, 2015, p. 2). In the past 30 years, as countries have realized they must act on research, gain specialized skills, and compete with other nations, the higher education workforce has grown to a large degree (Zaman, 2015).

1.3 ASSESSMENT OF QUALITY

"For better performance in higher education, the institutions have to balance their academic mission and executive capacity, and the government needs to maintain the equilibrium between excellence and equity" (Organisation for Economic Co-operation and Development, 2003, as cited in Zaman, 2015, p. 3). Effective governance structures and quality guidelines are vital in creating and ensuring institutional effectiveness. Furthermore, quality guidelines foster an effective culture (Zaman, 2015). By having research centers, educational foundations, and a few nongovernmental organizations perform policy analysis and evaluation, the management of learning in many nations' educational systems has become more effective (World Bank, 1998, as cited in Zaman, 2015).

Dew (2009) sees quality as a broad concept and lists five ways to measure it: endurance, prestige, conformity to requirements, adding value to students, and continuous improvement. He points out people's tendency to doubt a new school's quality and institutions' tendency to spend money making their facilities more attractive. Accrediting bodies, governments, and institutions themselves can define attributes that they must possess to be considered a quality institution, and these attributes can include student ability to contribute to society after graduation. Finally, an institution can attain quality by improving and innovating quickly in all departments, which is how the concept of continuous improvement manifests in higher education (Dew, 2009). Evidence is necessary to assess these five categories. McBride's (2009) evidence examples include alumni and employer surveys, student portfolios, and student results on nationwide subject matter exams.

1.4 REFERENCES

Bollaert, L., Brus, S., Curvale, B., Harvey, L. Helle, E., Jensen, H. T., ... Sursock, A. (Eds.). (2007). *Embedding quality culture in higher education: A selection of papers from the 1st European forum for quality assurance.* Brussels, Belgium: European University Association.

Dew, J. (2009, April). Quality issues in higher education. *Journal for Quality & Participation, 32*(1), 4–9.

McBride, J. K. (2003, June). *A total quality approach to higher education.* Paper presented at 2003 American Society for Engineering Education Conference and Exposition, Nashville, TN. Retrieved from https://peer.asee.org/12193

Zaman, K. (2015). Quality guidelines for good governance in higher education across the globe. *Pacific Science Review B: Humanities and Social Sciences, 1*, 1–7.

CASE STUDY 1.1: ANALYSIS OF QUALITY IN PUBLIC AND PRIVATE UNIVERSITIES IN BANGLADESH AND USA

Mazumder, Q. H. (2014). *International Journal of Evaluation and Research in Education,* 4(2), 99–108. Reprinted with permission.

ABSTRACT

To meet the growing need for increased capacity in higher education, the government of Bangladesh encouraged development of private universities in 1992. Currently, there are sixty private universities, thirty-four public universities and three international universities in Bangladesh. Although the increased number of universities has provided opportunities, a debate has emerged over the quality of education at these institutions due to the significant difference among these institutions. These inconsistencies in quality may be due to the lack of regulatory oversight and inefficiencies of the regulatory agencies of the government. The cost of education at private universities is high compared to the significantly lower cost at public universities that are subsidized by the government. In spite of the higher cost, student satisfaction levels have not been higher at private universities in the past. The work presented in this paper seeks to determine the quality of education in public and private universities in Bangladesh using student satisfaction as a measure of quality. It is well understood that student satisfaction measure may not be the only indicator of quality, but it can be considered as one of the important indicators. The Noel-Levitz student satisfaction index (SSI) survey questions were modified to adapt them to the context of Bangladesh. The twenty-two question survey results from private and public university students of Bangladesh were compared to determine the level of student satisfaction. The results of the current study were compared with the SSI data of US private and public universities. In contrast to past results, results of the current study showed that the students in public universities of Bangladesh had lowest level of satisfaction and the private universities of Bangladesh had highest satisfaction. The results derived from this data can be used by both public and private universities for improving quality in higher education.

RESEARCH METHOD

The survey questionnaires were distributed to all public and private universities of Bangladesh through HEQEP (Higher Education Quality Enhancement Project) sub-project managers. Only five universities responded to the survey because the other universities were unable to see any tangible benefit from this study. This may indicate that most of the higher education institutions fail to consider student satisfaction as a priority. The five universities that participated in the study demonstrated their commitment to making initiatives towards improvement of quality by placing a high value on their students' points of views. The survey questions used a seven point Likert scale to measure students' perceived level of importance and level of satisfaction [15]. The questions were developed using Noel-Levitz student satisfaction index (SSI), a reliable instrument widely used by a large number of universities in the USA to improve student satisfaction. Another reason for using this instrument is the availability of previous data from US universities that can be used in this comparative study. The questions were grouped in four major categories to summarize the results. Questions 1–7 were related to the professor, questions 8–13 were related to curriculum and questions 14–19 related to campus resources and extra-curricular activities.

Data was collected from students at different class rankings ranging from first year to fifth year to assure that the samples were collected from a diverse group of students as shown in Figure 1. The survey respondents included 31% female, 64% male students, and 5% who chose not to respond to the question related to gender. This distribution of male and female students is representative of students at higher education institutions in Bangladesh. Explaining research chronology, including research design, research procedure (in the form of algorithms, Pseudocode or other), one of the previous study discussed how to select statistical test and data acquisition [16]–[18]. The description of the course of research should be supported references, so the explanation can be accepted scientifically [17], [19].

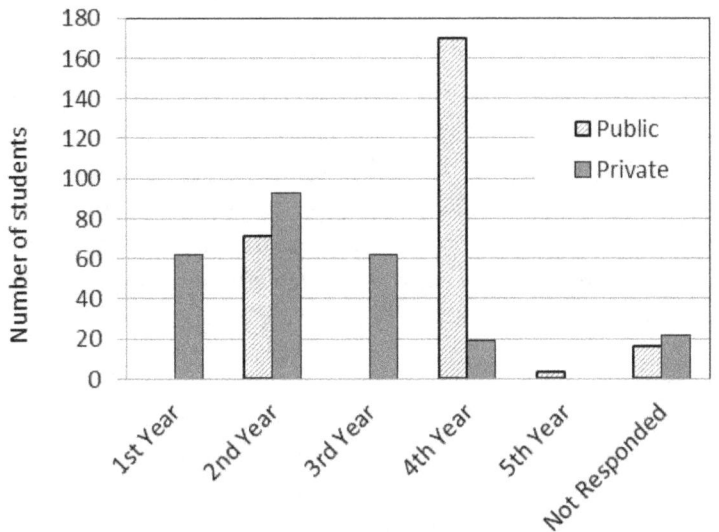

Figure 1. Diversity of Students Responded to the Questionnaire

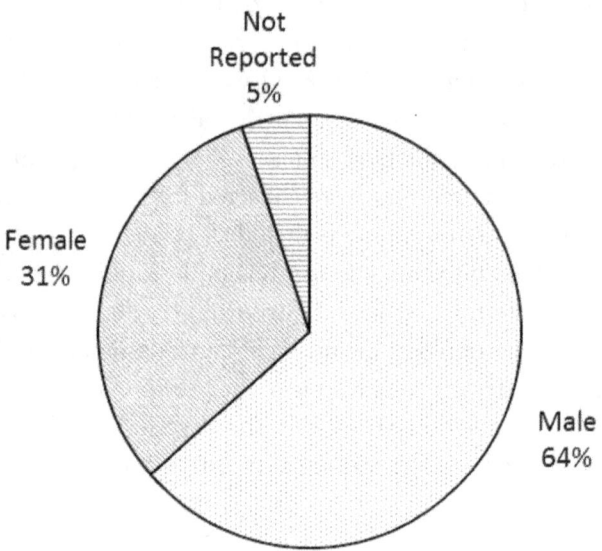

Figure 2. Gender Distribution of Participants

This study used a modified Noel-Levitz Student Satisfaction Inventory (SSI) and expands upon 216 data points in an earlier study [18] to include 518 data points. Three public universities and two private universities were surveyed. An array of geographic locales were surveyed, with two universities from the capital city of Dhaka (IUBAT, AUST), one university from the southeast (CVASU), one from the southwest (KU) and one from the central part of the country (BAU) to provide a representative sample across the country. The importance-satisfaction performance gaps were calculated for both private and public universities of Bangladesh and compared with results from USA universities.

ANALYSIS OF RESULTS

Table 1 shows the results of a t-test to compare between public and private universities. The importance and satisfaction of each category of survey questions were analyzed, as shown in Table 1. The analysis results showed significant differences in importance in professor ($p = 0.001$) and campus resources ($p=0.000$). Significant differences in satisfaction were observed in all four categories ($p < 0.005$). There was no significant difference in how well the universities were able to meet the students' expectations.

Table 1. Importance and Satisfaction in Public and Private Universities (N=518)

Criteria		University Type	Mean	Significance (p-value)
Professor	Importance	Public	5.95	0.001
		Private	5.55	
	Satisfaction	Public	4.31	0.000
		Private	4.29	
Curriculum	Importance	Public	6.03	0.178
		Private	5.71	
	Satisfaction	Public	4.78	0.000
		Private	4.53	
Campus Resources	Importance	Public	6.21	0.000
		Private	5.93	
	Satisfaction	Public	4.53	0.000
		Private	4.5	
Extra-curricular Activities	Importance	Public	5.85	0.170
		Private	5.67	
	Satisfaction	Public	4.25	0.000
		Private	4.48	
How Well Expectations are Met		Public	2.27	0.028
		Private	2.14	
Overall Satisfaction		Public	59.78	0.004
		Private	65.25	

Analysis of importance and satisfaction between males and female students using t-statistics showed no significant difference in any of the four categories, but the mean values indicated female students to be more satisfied than male students. The importance and satisfaction responses for each question were averaged to calculate the performance gap. The performance gap is the difference between importance and satisfaction for each question. A positive gap indicates that the student level of satisfaction is lower than the level of importance.

The survey questions were grouped into four different categories to further evaluate categories that showed largest gap. The questions related to each category were described in the methodology section of this paper. For example, the satisfaction responses of questions 1–8 were averaged to calculate the average satisfaction with professors as these questions are related to professor category. The categorized average responses are presented in Table 2 showing higher performance gaps among public university student responses. Using the performance gap analysis results, the five universities were ranked based on student satisfaction measures. The analysis considered the lowest gap in a category to be highest performance in that category and, therefore, was ranked number one. For example, in the professor category, IUBAT had the lowest performance gap of 0.62 and, therefore, ranked number 1 in Table 3.

Table 2. Performance Gap by Categories in Private and Public Universities in Bangladesh

	Private						Public								
	AUST			IUBAT			KU			BAU			CVASU		
	IMP	SAT	GAP	IMP	SAT	GAP	IMP	SAT	GAP	IMP	SAT	GAP	IMP	SAT	GAP
Professor	5.92	4.0	**1.92**	5.20	4.58	**0.62**	5.83	4.20	**1.63**	5.95	3.61	**2.34**	6.07	5.13	**0.94**
Curriculum	6.02	4.3	**1.72**	5.40	4.75	**0.65**	6.05	5.09	**0.96**	5.78	3.99	**1.79**	6.27	5.27	**1.0**
University Resource	6.37	4.43	**1.94**	5.51	4.58	**0.93**	6.17	4.39	**1.78**	6.28	4.13	**2.15**	6.19	5.07	**1.12**
Extra-Curricular	5.97	4.21	**1.76**	5.38	4.76	**0.62**	5.73	4.61	**1.12**	5.72	3.31	**2.41**	6.10	4.84	**1.26**

Table 3. Relative Ranking of Five Universities Based on Performance Gaps

Category	AUST	IUBAT	KU	BAU	CVASU
Professor	4	1	3	5	2
Curriculum	4	1	2	5	3
University Resources	4	1	3	5	2
Extra-Curricular	4	1	2	5	3

COMPARISON BETWEEN USA AND BANGLADESH

To compare and contrast the quality of public and private universities with those in the USA, the survey responses were further analyzed and presented in Figure 3. Noel-Levitz student satisfaction survey responses from different universities across the USA were used to compare student satisfaction[15]. The survey responses for questions 5, 7, 10, 20, and 21 were not available, as indicated in the table, and, therefore, were not compared. The overall performance gap in public universities appears to be higher than private universities in both countries. Another notable observation was that the performance gaps at the private universities of Bangladesh were higher than private universities in USA. The data indicates similar results for public universities in Bangladesh and USA.

A comparison of public and private universities of Bangladesh and USA is presented in Figure 4. The overall performance gaps are higher at public universities except in a few areas. For example, performance gap at private universities is higher for questions number 11, 13 and 17 that are related to availability of courses to students, cost of education and library resources. Students reported lower satisfaction at private universities in these areas. Students expected better course offerings and library resources from private universities as they are paying a higher tuition rate for their education.

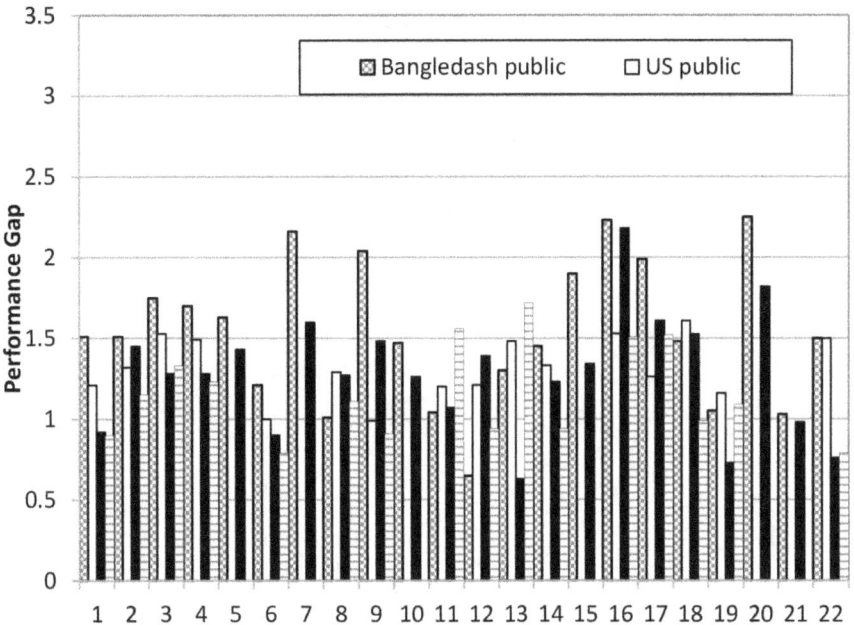

Figure 3. Performance Gap in public and private universities

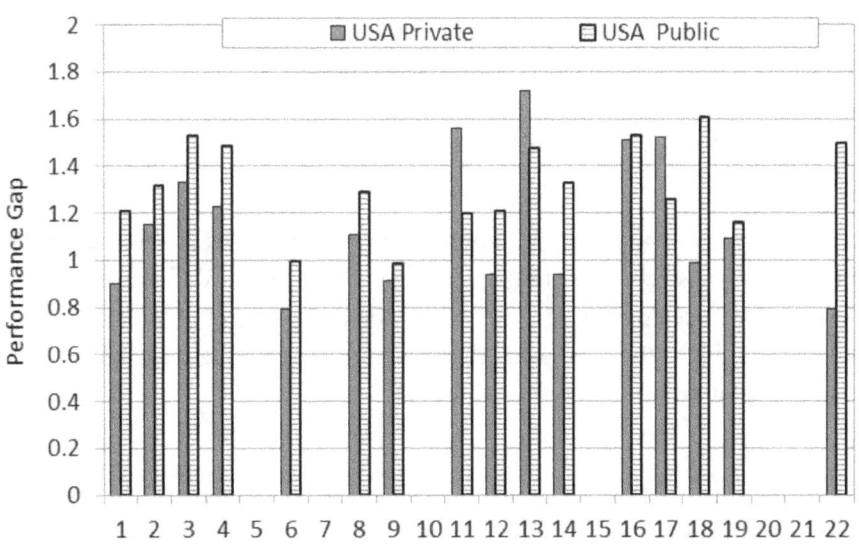

Figure 4. Performance Gap at public and private universities in the USA

Comparison of public universities of Bangladesh and USA showed higher dissatisfaction among students in Bangladesh in all areas except for the amount in which the cost of education influences the students' decisions to enroll. Comparison of gap levels for each question is presented in Figure 5. It must be noted that during this study, the cost of education at public universities in Bangladesh is negligible as these higher education institutions are fully subsidized by government. The difference in gap between Bangladesh and USA are significant in most questions with higher gaps present in data originating from Bangladesh.

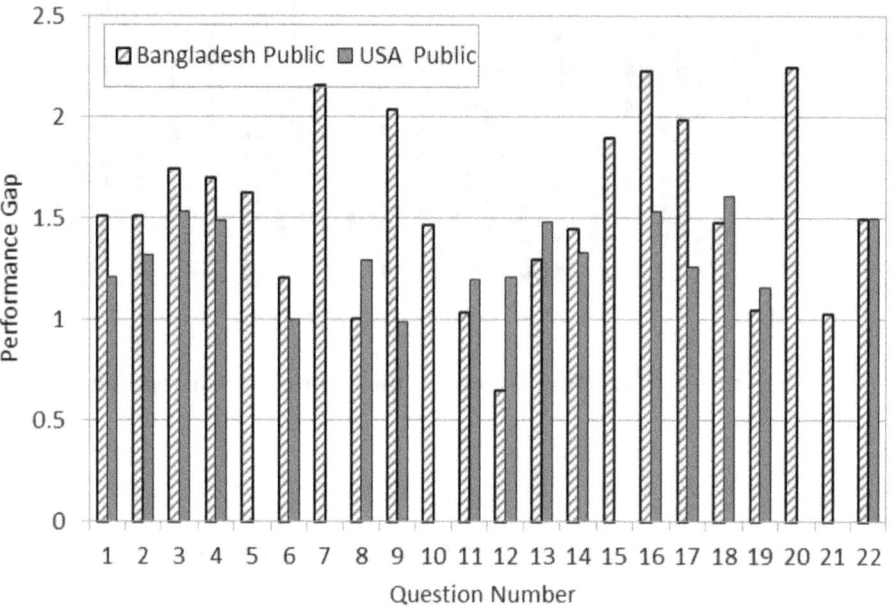

Figure 5. Gap in Public Universities in US and Bangladesh

Further analysis of private universities of Bangladesh and USA showed similar gaps in most of the questions except questions 11 and 13 where higher differences were observed. Question number 11 referred to availability of courses to students and question number 13 referred to cost of education. It appears that students in Bangladesh are more satisfied than USA in these two questions as shown in Figure 6.

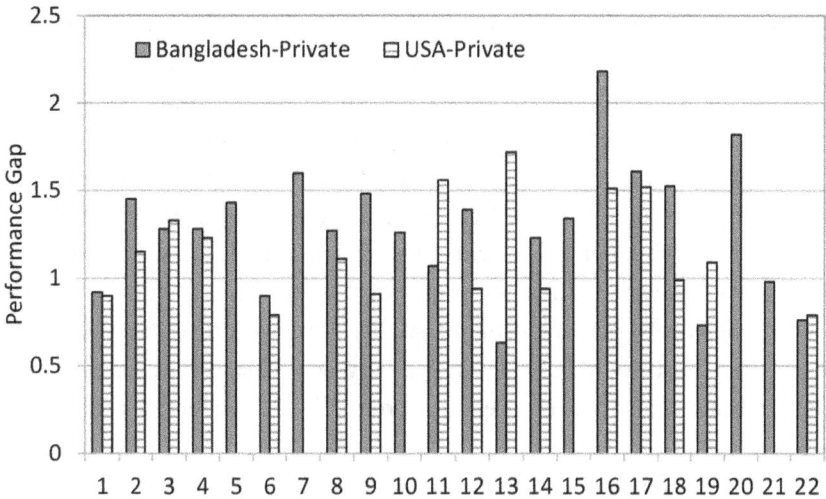

Figure 6. Performance Gap in private Universities of USA and Bangladesh

The results of the survey responses were grouped together in the four categories by averaging the responses of the questions in each category. The summary of the performance gap is presented in Table 4. The largest gap was observed among students of public universities in Bangladesh. The performance gap in private universities of the USA and Bangladesh are similar with a lower gap reported by private university students in Bangladesh.

Table 4. Comparison of Performance Gap in Bangladesh and USA

	Bangladesh Private			Bangladesh Public			USA Private			USA Public		
	IMP	SAT	GAP	IMP	SAT	GAP	IMP	SAT	GAP	IMP	SAT	GAP
Professor	5.55	4.29	1.26	5.95	4.31	1.64	6.37	5.29	1.08	6.38	5.07	1.49
Curriculum	5.71	4.53	0.88	6.03	4.78	1.25	6.46	5.21	1.25	6.40	5.16	1.23
UNIV resource	5.93	4.50	1.43	6.21	4.53	1.68	6.34	5.13	1.21	6.25	4.87	1.38
Extra-Curricular	5.67	4.48	1.19	5.85	4.25	1.60	5.63	4.84	0.79	5.82	4.32	1.50

DISCUSSION

To address an important question about the quality in public and private universities in Bangladesh and compare them with those of USA, a study was conducted using student satisfaction as a determinant of quality. Analysis of the results showed a larger gap in student satisfaction in public universities compared to private universities in Bangladesh in all four categories. This indicates that private university students in Bangladesh are more satisfied. However, smaller gaps were observed between private and public universities of USA indicating no significant difference in student satisfaction. The observations and results of this study is similar to a previous study but contradicts with general view of government and people of Bangladesh who perceives higher quality at public universities. One of the possible reasons for this disparity may be absence of any quality standards or accreditation bodies in Bangladesh and government oversight on quality of universities that may be biased and inefficient.

Due to their reputations and negligible tuition rates, public universities in Bangladesh were able to attract higher quality of students with higher grade point averages. However, the quality of instruction, infrastructures, bureaucratic policies and involvement in political activities results in a poor academic environment. The public universities are resistant to update their curriculum, instructional methods and adapting new pedagogical approaches, such as active learning and assessment techniques. The University Grants Commission of Bangladesh (UGC) has recently developed an accreditation policy that will be only applicable to private universities as public universities expressed strong opposition to be assessed. In contrast, the private universities have been working towards developing new programs, curriculum, pedagogy and assessment to improve the quality of education at their institutions. Incorporating world-class standards and curriculum and attracting faculty members from universities across the world, their recent efforts have been successful in improving the quality. However, the higher cost of tuition in private universities of Bangladesh made them beyond the reach of students from middle-income families of Bangladesh. The higher profit motivation by the private universities is also a deterrent to investment in quality.

The results of this study can be effectively used by higher education institutions and the government to improve quality of education. Potential students, parent and other stakeholders can also use this information to have a better understanding of quality in terms of student satisfaction.

CONCLUSION

A survey was conducted to evaluate the importance and satisfaction of students at five different public and private universities in Bangladesh. The survey was based on a modified Noel-Levitz Students Satisfaction Index questionnaire. The results best exemplifies a study of students in Bangladesh, understanding education and the relationship between the quality of higher education and students' satisfaction in their education at their chosen university. This study included information from each respondent, asking for their importance and their satisfaction ratings toward their professor, curriculum, resources, and other extracurricular activities. It also compared and contrasted the deviations and means between public universities and private universities. Alongside of tested survey results, there are referenced resources that make common claims to this study. The hypothesis states that students attending private universities in Bangladesh are more satisfied than students attending public universities. After analyzing the survey results, the conclusion does in fact support that claim. The data portrays that private universities have the resources and services that meets the needs of their students and that they have a higher satisfaction levels than public universities. The higher satisfaction levels may justify higher costs, and public universities may also be able to improve services, based on private university services.

Comparison of private and public universities in Bangladesh and the USA showed the largest gap in ratings from public universities in Bangladesh followed by public universities in the USA. Performance gaps in ratings from private universities are lower than public universities in both USA and Bangladesh.

ACKNOWLEDGEMENTS

The author would like to acknowledge Dr. Rezaul Karim of Khulna University, Dr. Alimullah Miyan of IUBAT, Dr. Gouranga Chandra of CVASU, Dr. Nazrul Islam of BAU, Vice Chancellor of AUST of Bangladesh for their support in collecting the data for this study.

REFERENCES

[1] T. Bozbura et. al., "A Causal Model of Quality Management Practices and Stakeholder Interests in Higher Education Institutions: Comparison of Public and Private Universities," in *PICMET Technology Management in the Energy Smart World*, 2011.

[2] D. Edens, "Predicting For-Profit Student Persistence Using the Student Satisfaction Inventory," Ph.D. dissertation, Dept. Higher Education, Asuza Pacific Univ., Azusa, CA, 2012.

[3] D. Avison, "Public universities deliver quality," Times Colonist, CanWest Interactive, pp. A13, 2004.

[4] S. Hadikoemoro, "A Comparison of Public and Private University Students' Expectations and Perceptions of Service Quality in Jakarta, Indonesia," Ph.D. dissertation, Dept. Bus. Admin., Nova Southeastern Univ., FL, 2001.

[5] M.A. Ashraf, "Quality Education Management at Private Universities in Bangladesh: An Exploratory Study, *Jurnal Pendidik dan Pendidikan*, vol. 24, pp. 17-32, 2009.

[6] Mazumder Q., "Student Satisfaction in Public and Private Universities in Bangladesh" Paper no. ASEE2013-6265, *American Society of Engineering Education, 2013 Conference*, Atlanta, GA, USA, June 23-26, 2013.

[7] J. Stark and M.A. Lowther, "Measuring Higher Education Quality," *Research in Higher Education*, vol/issue: 13(3), pp. 283-287, 1980.

[8] Welch G., "Studies from G. Welch and Co-Researchers in the area of British Education Research" ISSN 1938-1840, May 2011.

[9] M. K. Roszkowski, "The Nature of the Importance-Satisfaction Relationship in Ratings: Evidence from the Normative Data of the Noel-Levitz Student Satisfaction Inventory," *Journal of Consumer Satisfaction, Dissatisfaction, and Complaining Behavior*, vol. 16, pp. 212, 2003.

[10] M.A. Ashraf, "Quality Education Management at Private Universities in Bangladesh: An Exploratory Study," *Jurnal Pendidik dan Pendidikan*, vol. 24, pp. 17–32, 2009.

[11] A.B. Siddiqui, "Management Education in Bangladesh", *South Asian Journal of Management*, vol/issue: 1(4), pp. 45-55, 1994.

[12] M.Z. Mamun, "Quality of Private University Graduates of Bangladesh: The Employers' Perspective," *South Asian Journal of Management*, vol/issue: 18(3), pp. 48-68, 2011.

[13] G.M. Chowdhury, "Challenges for private universities in Bangladesh," NIAS Nytt, vol. 2, pp. 15-17, 2007.

[14] Mazumder Q., "Student Satisfaction in Private and Public Universities in Bangladesh," *International Journal of Evaluation and Research in Education*, vol/issue: 2(2), 2013, ISSN 2252-8822, DOI: 10.11591/ijere.v2i2.2060.

[15] Levitz, R. S., Noel, L. and Richter, B. J., "Strategic Moves for Retention Success," *New Directions for Higher Education*, pp. 31–49, 1999. doi: 10.1002/he.10803

[16] "List of Private Universities," University Grants Commission of Bangladesh. www.ugc.gov.bd. 3 Dec. 2012.

[17] "List of Public Universities," University Grants Commission of Bangladesh. www.ugc.gov.bd, 3 Dec. 2012.

[18] "List of International Universities," University Grants Commission of Bangladesh. Web. 3 Dec. 2012.

[19] M.A. Ashraf, "Quality Education Management at Private Universities in Bangladesh: An Exploratory Study," *Journal Pendidik dan Pendidikan*, vol. 24, pp. 17-32, 2009.

CASE STUDY 1.2: APPLYING SIX SIGMA IN HIGHER EDUCATION QUALITY IMPROVEMENT

Quamrul H. Mazumder, University of Michigan–Flint
© American Society for Engineering Education, 2014
Indianapolis, IN

ABSTRACT

Quality in higher education became an important issue due to ever increasing demand by stakeholders and competitive environment. Although six sigma has been successfully used in product and service improvement in the business environment, the concept has not been adapted in higher education. To improve understanding of how six sigma can be used for higher education process improvement toward achievement of quality, a number of models are presented. Six sigma principles such as process improvement, reducing waste and continuous improvement aligns closely with the mission of higher education institutions and accreditation agencies. Using six sigma tools such as statistical process control, lean manufacturing, failure mode and effects analysis can help in the development of sustainable higher quality educational process. A process map with SIPOC (supplier, input, process, output and control), cause and effect analysis, FMEA (failure mode and effects analysis) for higher education was developed and presented. These tools can be used by higher education institutions to better understand the higher education process and how it can be improved to meet the desired quality goals.

INTRODUCTION

The concept of Six Sigma was introduced by Motorola in the 1980s to improve their products and maintain quality. The core of Six Sigma lies in the continuous improvement process using the DMAIC (Define, Measure, Analyze, Improve, and Control) method [9]. It has since then been adopted by many other companies to achieve their respective goals both in production of goods and in rendering services. Due to the success of this method, academic institutions attempted to adapt six sigma methodologies to improve the quality of education and services. These concepts have great potential for improving process efficiency and quality of higher education. The improvements can be enhanced by integrating other similar concepts such as lean manufacturing and SPS (statistical process control).

Lean manufacturing was originated as "a philosophy of continuously simplifying processes and eliminating waste"[16]. By streamlining the processes, cycle times for data collection and analysis can be reduced in academic environment due to time constraints faced by students and faculty. The statistical process control (SPC) method uses control charts to analyze variations in a process with predetermined upper and lower control limits (UCL, LCL). Two types of variations are common in any process and are described as follows: (1) random variations, which are the only variations present if the process is in statistical control, and (2) assignable variations, which indicate a departure or deviation from statistical control. The purpose of a control chart is to identify when the process is out of control, thus signaling the need for remedial action. A control chart is a graphical technique in which statistical results are computed from measured values of a certain process characteristic are plotted over time to determine if the process remains in statistical control. Statistical process control charts and run charts are helpful tools fotr large amounts of outputs such as in manufacturing processes or when dealing with a large student body in a university [12].

LITERATURE REVIEW:

According to Freeman, there is an increasing need to improve the quality of higher education because education is becoming a global entity facing challenges with resource constraints [3]. Unlike other organizations, higher education has several stakeholders such as students, parents, future employers and society [7]. Zhang proposed eight important questions to ask regarding a Six Sigma research program. Of these eight, the most relevant to higher education are: "How can the effectiveness of a Six Sigma program be validated?" "How should Six Sigma be customized for different organizational contexts?", "What is the most effective organizational structure for a Six Sigma program?", and "How do leadership development and human resource practices relate to Six Sigma program?"[19]. The answers to these questions center on empirical validation of effectiveness and customization of the program, separating the Six Sigma program from Quality Control.

Adaptation of six sigma approaches in higher education requires careful consideration of differences in stakeholders' requirements and expectations. Unlike business environment, higher education may be perceived by some as non-profit to serve the greater intellectual and societal needs. Decisions in higher education are not always data driven and the need for data is underestimated. An example of a process improvement involves recording scores on the accounting section of the Educational Testing Service standardized test. Additional data such as faculty assignments, textbooks, course design, teaching methods, and course order were collected. To improve average test scores from 42.4% to 46.5%, the input variables were altered. These changes to the program design resulted in an actual increase to 47.3%, above the desired goal[6].

In the study by Razaki & Aydin, different process improvement methods from the business world are analyzed for their usefulness in the academic world. Four different methods were analyzed, including Total Quality Management (TQM), Six Sigma, Business Process Reengineering (BPR), and Lean Manufacturing. "TQM was highly suited to improving the departmental processes to effect a transition to excellence, Lean Six Sigma provided a few but highly effective methods for departmental improvement." The use of Lean Six Sigma was revealed from their analysis of the Kukreja study. It was noticed that the data collection cycle was too long and a great deal of time was necessary to complete the project. Since most students are only enrolled for four years, this did not work well with this required timespan. They propose mixing the appropriate parts of Six Sigma and Lean Manufacturing to make the process more appropriate for the relatively short time available to collect data on individuals. This method uses statistical tools of moderate complexity, with a short cycle time and a focus on elimination of waste [12].

Higher education process can be viewed to be similar to a manufacturing process. In a manufacturing process, raw materials are processed through a series of steps to produce finished products. Similarly, the higher education institutions produce intellectual graduates from incoming students through a series of steps. In higher education, quality depends on several factors such as curriculum, course content, incoming students, teachers, pedagogy, and assessment methods. Since one of the focuses of Lean Manufacturing is reducing waste, it is important to define waste in the higher education system of processes. Examples of educational waste include, "teaching topics already taught in other courses, excessive review of prerequisite materials, unnecessary and redundant introductions, spoon-feeding, teaching obsolete topics, and waiting for unprepared students to catch up" [16]. In order to produce a high quality graduate, efforts to minimize wastes must be undertaken throughout the process with careful consideration of stakeholders' views.

Statistical process control can be a useful tool in the academic environment as the institutional analysis involves a large amount of data such as enrollment trends, graduation rate, retention rates, etc. As every process has an expected degree of variation, it is necessary to determine what constitutes 'normal' variation so that it can be predicted. The more the variation of a process can be minimized or controlled, the more accurately the process results can be predicted." When the process is under appropriate control, the produced variations will be consistent and within the accepted range. The method of SPC can be challenging to apply outside a manufacturing environment, such as a service industry like higher education. In situations where performance parameters are not taken from tangible, measurable products more work is needed. In a study by Roes & Dorr of SPC implementation in the service industry, the key characteristics for process control were defined as the degree to which the service to the customer is indeed intangible, the intensity of involvement of employees in the interaction, and the extent of customer influence on the service provided [13]. For academic environment, the customer would be a future employer, employees would be university faculty, and the service would be the provided education. The SPC approach can be used to improve course instruction, using the following steps:

1. Identify the process to control
2. Determine quality characteristic to monitor
3. Choose the appropriate control chart based on
   a. Type of data
   b. Sample size
   c. Frequency
4. Perform process improvement using SPC tools
5. Implement continuous quality improvement on process [10].

Quality, with respect to higher education has several challenges such as endurance, conformance to requirements, continuous improvement and value added [2]. The process variability not only exists within the students, but within professors as well. For example, grading by professors may be different and the instructional methods may also have variations. In a study by Knight, professors graded unnamed assignments and then re-graded these assignments weeks later to observe the difference in grades received. These grades were then subjected to statistical analysis, finding the average range for each professor. These were then averaged with each other and used to find an upper control limit for the ranges themselves. In future grading, if grades exceeded this range, the assignments would then be re-evaluated. [5]

The application of Six Sigma DMAIC methodology to improve quality in engineering educational had been successful in improving the quality consciousness with students and the management of institution [11]. The Six Sigma method can also be applied within the course to continuously improve its quality. The Statistics department of Florida State University, engaged students in seven different projects throughout a course. The first project involved the students listing two contributions they would like to make to their careers. The next five projects followed the DMAIC process, and the final project requires a report on the overall process. In each project, the students applied the DMAIC principles toward achieving their goal, learning the language and function of Six Sigma as they progress [18]. By applying DMAIC, students were able to achieve their goals and familiarize themselves with the system.

The problems associated with change management is challenging in higher education due to the nature of the environment that promotes academic freedom. Academicians have been accustomed with this environment and have individual views towards different issues as well as departmental politics and inter-departmental acrimony that increase complexities associated with any change in the process. "It is estimated that 70% of organizational change initiatives fail completely. Of the ones deemed successful as many as 75% of these fail to achieve their intended result." Individuals do not always get along in an organization, and, when the success of a program is dependent on collaboration, noncooperation can be a hindrance to achieving an organizational change. Given all these problems, there is a question as to whether there truly is a "best practice" for such change. "It appears that many popular management practices labeled as best practices (such as Total Quality Management, Six Sigma, and Lean) are based on anecdotal evidence rather than empirical data." This perception may be due in part to the fact that "the terms 'organizational change,' 'change management,' and 'best practice' appear to be used in a variety of perspectives and research applications but the search for affinity patterns have not resulted in any stable conclusions"[4]. As with many aspects of management, it would appear that flexibilities must be exercised to implement changes appropriate to the environment. Apart from the students, teachers and the management involved, the infrastructure and educational resources that students access also proves to be vital in achieving a higher quality education [14].

SIX SIGMA METHODOLOGY:

Statistically Six Sigma quality defines limiting the number of defects to 3.4 (parts per million PPM). The term Six Sigma refers to the six standard deviations away from the mean in a normal distribution or bell shaped curve. It uses the measurement of factors in a process and works on improving the output based on continuously improving the system and its processes. The defects in a Six Sigma process are the total area to the right and left of +6σ and -6σ respectively as shown in Figure 1.

Statistically Six Sigma quality defines limiting the number of defects to 3.4 (parts per million PPM). The term Six Sigma refers to the six standard deviations away from the mean in a normal distribution or bell shaped curve. It uses the measurement of factors in a process and works on improving the output based on continuously improving the system and its processes. The defects in a Six Sigma process are the total area to the right and left of +6σ and -6σ, respectively, as shown in Figure 1.

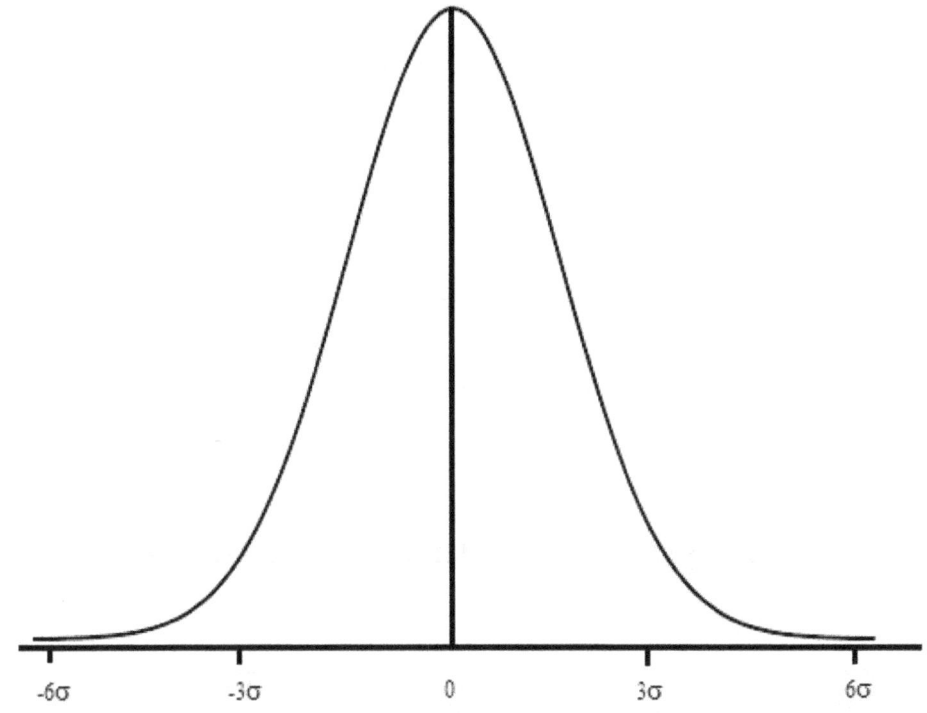

Figure 1: A normal distribution curve with six sigma (σ = 0 at mean)

Among different approaches used toward achieving six sigma level of quality, the DMAIC and the focus is on continuous improvement lies in the heart of six sigma process. DMAIC is an abbreviation for Define, Measure, Analyze, Improve and Control. The following section of the paper attempts to demonstrate how DMAIC methodology can be used to continuously improve the quality in higher education.

DEFINE PHASE:

In the design phase, the goals and the parameters must be clearly identified and defined. Six Sigma methodology can be effectively used in higher education institutions [1]. The first step to understanding the process is to develop a process map for higher education and then construct a cause-effect diagram to evaluate the effect of input variables on output. A process map for higher education is presented in figure 2 and compared to a manufacturing process as shown in figure 3. The potential suppliers of higher education are educational institutions such as high schools, community colleges or universities. The input consists of new first year students, transfer students, K-12 teachers, and high school graduates. The Process involves a sequence of steps from which a student takes various course over a period of time and graduates. The customers consist of employers, graduate schools, society, and others, as some students may be self employed.

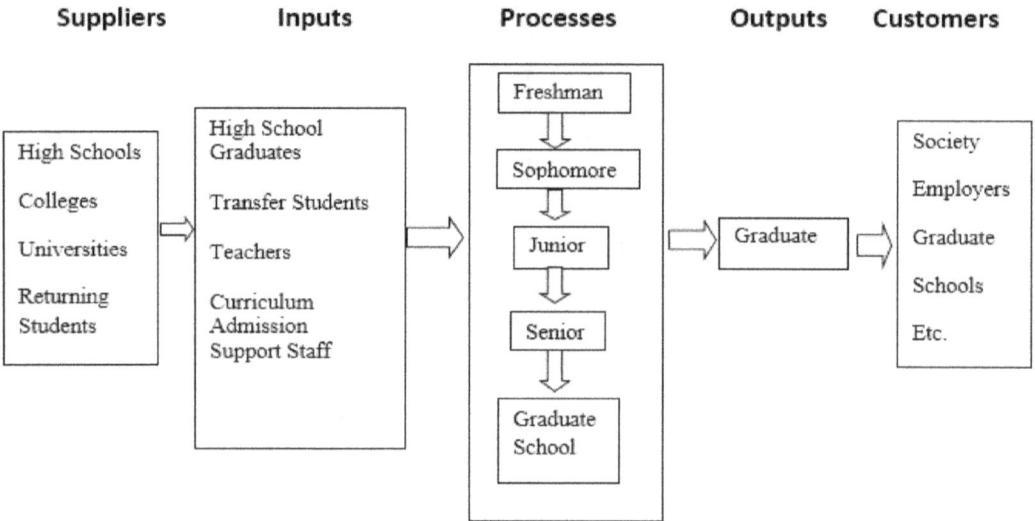

Figure 2: Six Sigma Process (SIPOC) in Higher Education

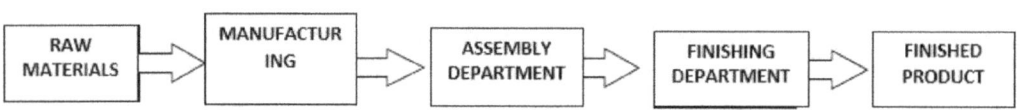

Figure 3: Process flow in a conventional manufacturing process

MEASURE PHASE:

In the measure phase, all measurements related to the process are calculated. Although a number of different measurement tools can be used in this phase, an example of SPC is presented in this paper. Among different factors affecting quality of education process and student performance, the important ones may be GPA, professors' performance, number of students in each class, course materials and course order. The factors used to measure student success are student retention rate, graduation rate, and percent employed in the field related to academic degree immediately after graduation as presented in Figure 4. These variables can be analyzed using SPC to identify which input or inputs have the greatest effect on the outputs. Some of the inputs do have dependencies on each other and this will be analyzed as well to ensure the accuracy of the analysis.

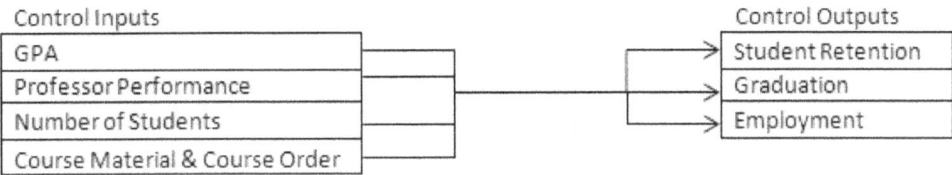

Figure 4: Output Controls and its dependency on Inputs

Both quantitative and qualitative control charts have been developed to monitor the performance of individual student and the institution. The two quantitative charts are the Individual/Moving Range chart (IX/mR) and the Average/Range chart ($\overline{X}$/R). To monitor an individual's performance IX/mR chart was developed using the following steps.

1. Gather the data. (Verify data validity by considering the collection method.)
2. Calculate the moving ranges (difference between each successive data point).
3. Plot the data in time ordered series (Individuals [IX] chart)
4. Plot the moving ranges in time ordered series on the moving range (mR) chart.
5. Calculate the following formulas provided on the following pages:
    a. Average of all the moving ranges ($\overline{\overline{mR}}$)
    b. Estimate of the sigma/standard deviation ($\overline{\overline{mR}}$/d2)
    c. Average of all the data points ($\overline{X}$)
6. Plot the lines representing the averages, LCL's, and UCL's on the IX and mR charts.

Table 1: Courses and GPA in the class with moving range (mR)

Class Level	Course	GPA Received	mR
Freshman	EGR102	4	
Freshman	EGR280	3.3	0.7
Freshman	EGR230	3.7	0.4
Freshman	EGR260	3.3	0.4
Freshman	EGR165	4	0.7
Sophomore	EGR310	3	1
Sophomore	EGR350	3	0
Sophomore	EGR353	2	1
Sophomore	EGR330	3.3	1.4
Sophomore	EGR356	3.7	0.4
Junior	EGR370	2.7	1
Junior	EGR315	2.7	0
Junior	EGR321	2	0.7
Junior	EGR392	1.3	0.7
Junior	EGR380	2.7	1.4
Senior	EGR399	3.3	0.6
Senior	EGR432	3.7	0.4
Senior	EGR410	3	0.7
Senior	EGR465	3.7	0.7

The current study for an individual student was based on the grade point average (GPA) in the courses related to their major. The students' academic progress was considered as a single process for application of SPC recognizing variations in courses, professors, and levels. For example, a student in the Mechanical Engineering program requires five prerequisite courses, eight core courses, and seven elective courses with a total of 20 engineering courses. Table 1 shows the moving range chart for GPA in the engineering courses. The upper control limit (UCL) and lower control limit (LCL) of moving range and individual control chart is presented in Table 2.

Table 2: UCL and LCL of Moving range and Individual Control Chart Moving Range (mR) Chart Data

Moving Range (mR) Chart Data	
Average mR	0.673684
Estimate of Sigma	0.597232
UCL (mR)	2.200963
LCL (mR)	0

Individuals (IX) Chart data	
Average GPA	3.07
UCL (IX)	4.861713
LCL (IX)	1.278287

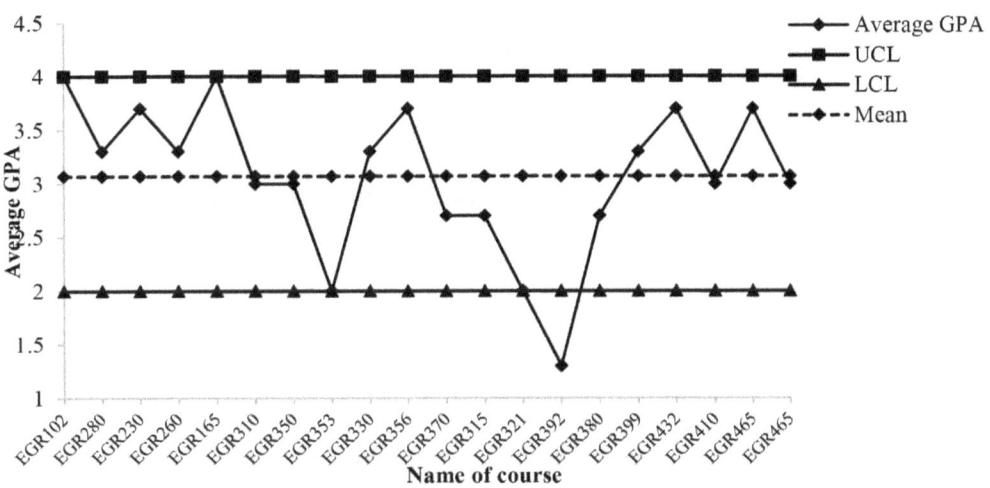

Figure 5: Average GPA of students in each course

A control chart for students' GPA in different engineering courses is presented in Figure 5. The UCL of 4.0 represents the maximum attainable GPA and the LCL of 2.0 represents the minimum required GPA required by the university to be in good standing. Students with less than a 2.0 GPA are placed on academic probation and may be terminated if they fail to improve their GPA. It can be observed from the control chart that the process is not in control for two courses. The average GPA for EGR 353 (Thermodynamics) is at the lower limit of control chart and the average GPA for EGR 392 is lower than the lower control limit. This clearly identifies improvement needs in these two courses, as the success rate of students in terms of GPA is less than expected. Figure 6 shows the moving range showing any significant difference between two successive control points. All the points in the moving range chart are within the control limits and hence there is no control point with significant difference compared to its successive control point.

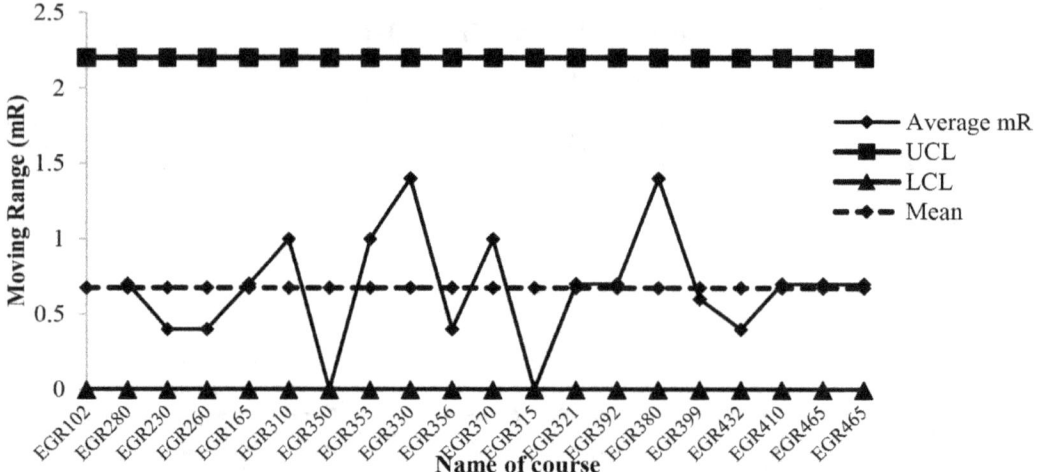

Figure 6: Moving Range (mR) across each course

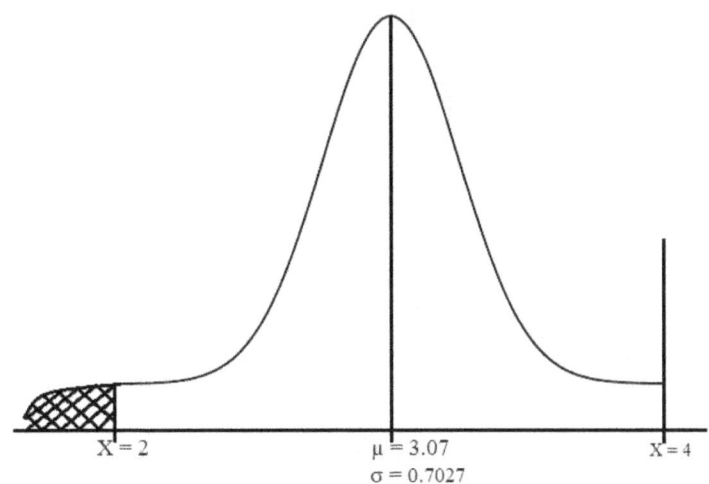

Figure 7: Normal Distribution (Bell Curve) of student's grade (GPA)

Figure 7 shows the normal distribution curve for the student's grade. The right side of the curve has a maximum value of 4 with the minimum value as zero. The average value of GPA (μ) from the current set of data was 3.07 with a standard deviation (σ) of 0.7027. The students with less than a 2.0 GPA may be considered as the defects in the system as shown in the area of normal distribution curve to the left of X = 2. The area to the left of X = 2 was calculated as 0.06392 which means that approximately 6.4% of the students received GPA of less than 2. Therefore, the defects per million is 63,920 that meets 3σ level of quality in the process. To achieve six sigma level of quality the value must be reduced significantly.

ANALYSIS PHASE:

After the development of the process map, it is important to identify the causes for poor quality in higher education. A cause and effect or fishbone diagram is a widely used approach to identifying the root causes and their effects. The sources of poor quality were identified as curriculum, teachers, students, assessment, and the academic and social environment. The possible causes from each of these sources have been schematically shown in figure 8. The fishbone diagram displays the root causes from six different sources that contribute to poor quality of education. Identification of these sources can help in making changes to improve quality of education.

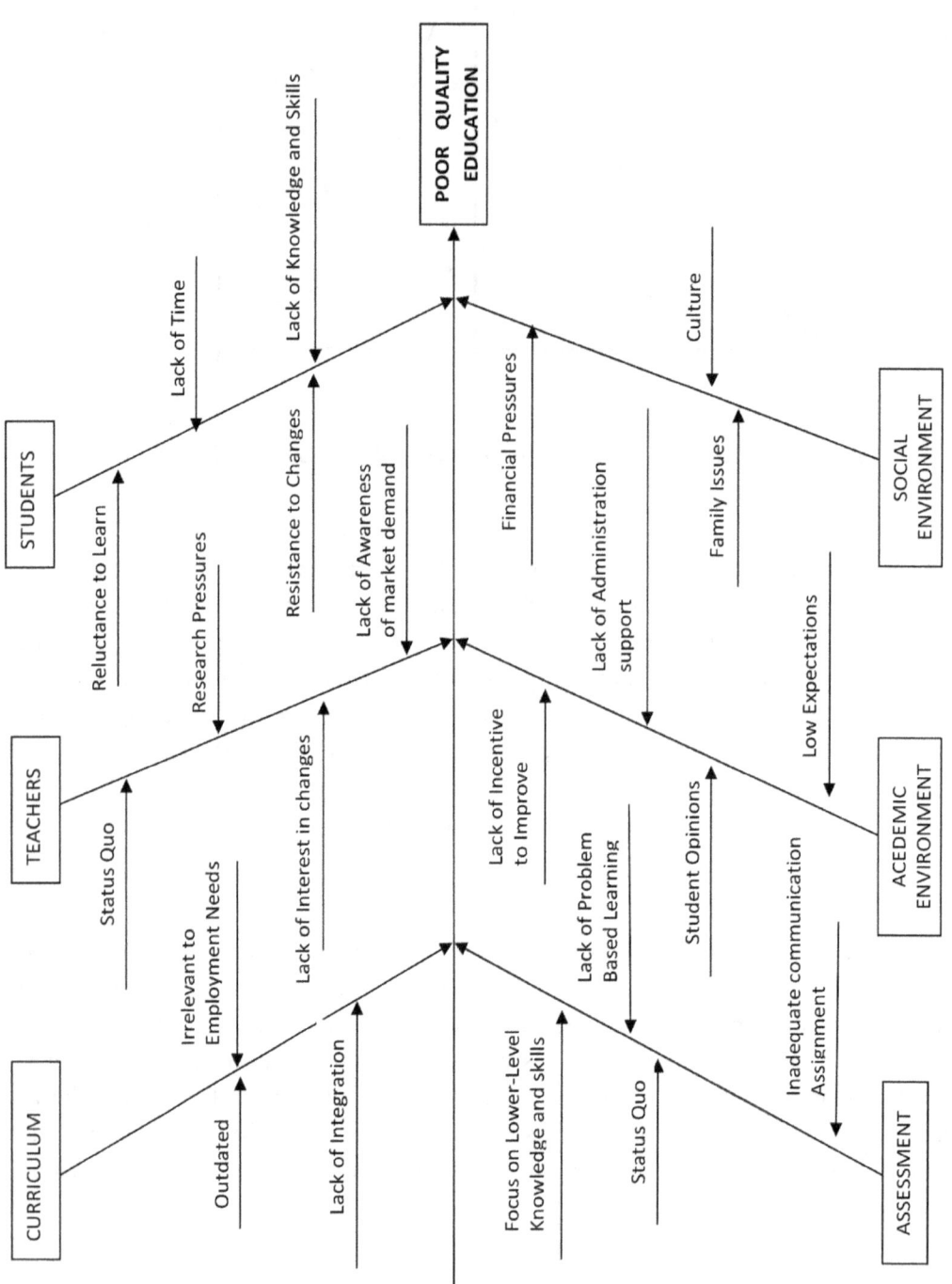

Figure 8: Cause and Effect Diagram of Quality of Higher Education

IMPROVEMENT PHASE:

In the improvement phase, the causes for failure or poor quality must be identified with a solution that will reduce defects in the process. A failure mode and effect analysis or FMEA can be used to improve the process. These quality tools could be very well used for the improvement of organizations and institutions [17]. A step-by-step procedure is used to identify all possible causes of failure and their corresponding effects with recommended corrective actions to avoid the failure modes. Quality needs to be properly assessed with respect to students, teachers, departments and Institutions, which makes curriculum [15]. A FMEA was developed to address the above factors as shown in Table 3.

Table 3: A Failure Mode and Effect Analysis of Higher Education Process

Process step	Failure Mode	Failure effect	Failure cause	Controls/Preventive action	Recommended action	Responsibility
Students	Reluctant to learn		Lack of interest	Internal Assessment	Educate on the importance of education	
	Lack of time	Students having a GPA less than 2/Students skills and knowledge not matching the industry requirements	Bad time management	Personal Assessment	Educate and provide techniques on time management	Teachers
	Resistance to changes		Lack of interest/Unaware of advantages of new changes	Feedback from teachers	Educate on the importance and benefits of change	
	Lack of knowledge/skills		Knowledge and skills not transferred properly	Feedback from teachers	Make sure knowledge is transferred properly from teachers to students	
Teachers	Research Pressures		Concentrating on lot of research work	Number of research articles to be presented	Limit the number of research work depending on the work load each semester	
	Lack of interest in changes	Students having a GPA less than 2/Students skills and knowledge not matching the industry requirements	Lack of interest/Unaware of advantages of new changes	Internal Assessment	Educate on the importance and benefits of change	Teachering fraternity, Management and authorities of the Institution and Curriculum
	Lack of awareness of market demand		Less interaction with industry/No source of update	Educational content up to date	Constantly be in contact with people in industry and latest technology	
	Stauts Quo		Unwilling to change	Open to change	Educate on the importance and benefits of change	
Curriculum	Outdated			Educational content up to date	Constantly be in contact with people in industry and latest technology	Teachering fraternity, Management and authorities of the Institution and Curriculum
	Lack of Integration	Students having a GPA less than 2/Students skills and knowledge not matching the industry requirements		Management Assessment		
	Irrelevant to employment needs		Less interaction with industry/No source of update	Updated curriculum		

CONTROL PHASE:

The control phase requires institutionalization of the improvement results obtained from the Six Sigma process for sustainability. The key to success in achieving quality is to standardize the improvement process and fostering a six sigma or continuous improvement process in the organizational culture. The results of the new standardizations or procedures can be further improved using different six sigma tools and procedures with a goal of reducing variation or defect in the process. Control charts are an effective way of statistically keeping a track of performance and using the data for continuous improvement in Six Sigma methodology [8].

SUMMARY

A number of six sigma models have been developed and presented to improve quality in higher education. The key inputs and output variables were identified in the define phase of DMAIC process. The input and output variables were measured by collecting the data over time. The analysis phase used SPC to identify the variables outside the control limits. After identification of the variable that lies outside the control limits, appropriate corrective actions can be implemented for process improvement. This phase is considered important in academic environment, as it is critical to student success and quality improvement. In the control phase, the input and output variables require continuous monitoring to ensure sustainable process.

CONCLUSION

The higher education process showed a three sigma (3σ) level quality that requires significant improvement to achieve six sigma (6σ) level. The primary objective of higher education is student success through higher quality education where failure of any student may be considered as a defect in the process. Due to variability in the process such as different type of instruction by different professors, a variation of quality exists. Variations of quality may be due to lack of understanding of how students learn and adapting to different learning styles of students. After identification of the issues and defining the problems, a solution can be developed using six sigma approaches and models presented in this paper. A control chart can be used with UCL and LCL along with a continuous improvement plan to improve the higher education process. This will result in higher quality and sustainable process in the institution with higher levels of student satisfaction and success rates such as graduation and retention rates. The information and tools provided in this paper is an attempt to shed some lights on how different quality improvement models can be used in higher education.

REFERENCES

[1] Antony, J., Krishan, N., Cullen, M., & Kumar, M. (2012). Lean six sigma for higher education institutions (heis): Challenges, barriers, success factors, tools/techniques. *International Journal of Productivity and Performance Management, 61*(8), 940-948.

[2] Dew, J. (2009). Quality issues in higher education. *The Journal for Quality and Participation, 32*(1), 4-9.

[3] Freeman, R. (1993). *Quality assurance in training and education.* (p. 176). London: Koogan Page.

[4] Hallencreutz, J., & Turner, D. (2011). Exploring organizational change best practice: are there any clear-cut models and definitions. *International Journal of Quality and Service Sciences, 3*(1), 60-68.

[5] Knight, J. E., Allen, S., & Tracy, D. L. (2010). Using six sigma methods to evaluate the reliability of a teaching assessment rubric. *The Journal for American Academy of Research Cambridge, 15*(1), 1-6.

[6] Kukreja, A., Ricks, J. M., & Meyer, J. A. (2009). Using Six Sigma for performance improvement in business curriculum: A case study. *Performance Improvement, 48*(2), 9-25.

[7] Madu, C. N., & Kuei, C. H. (1993). Dimensions of quality teaching in higher institutions. *Total Quality Management, 4*(3), 325-338.

[8] Maleyeff, J., & Kaminsky, F. (2002). Six sigma and introductory statistics education. *Education Training, 44*(2), 82-89.

[9] Mitra, A. (2004). Six sigma education: a critical role for academia. *The TQM Magazine, 16*(4), 293-302.

[10] Perry, L. (2004). *Instructional effectiveness: A real-time feedback approach using statistical process control (spc).* Proceedings of the 2004 American society for engineering education annual conference & exposition, Utah, USA.

[11] Prasad, K. D., Subbaiah, K. V., & Padmavathi, G. (2012). Application of Six Sigma Methodology in an Engineering Educational Institution. *Int. J. Emerg. Sci, 2*(2), 222-237.

[12] Razaki, K. A., & Aydin, S. (2011). The Feasibility of Using Business Process Improvement Approaches to Improve an Academic Department. *Journal of Higher Education Theory and Practice, 11*(2), 19-32.

[13] Roes, K. C., & Dorr, D. (1997). Implementing statistical process control in service processes. *International Journal of Quality Science, 2*(3), 149-166.

[14] Sasikala, S., & Vincent, G. S. (2010). Infrastructure and learning resources in higher educational institutions (HEIS) using six sigma quality strategy. *Library Progress (International), 30*(1), 97-109.

[15] Stark, J. S., & Lowther, M. A. (1980). Measuring higher education quality. *Research in Higher Education, 13*(3), 283-287.

[16] Tatikonda, L. (2007). Applying Lean Principles to Design Teach, and Assess Courses. *Management Accounting Quarterly, 8*(3), 27-38.

[17] Weinstein, L. B., Petrick, J., Castellano, J., & Vokurka, R. J. (2008). Integrating Six Sigma concepts in an MBA quality management class. *Journal of Education for Business, 83*(4), 233-238.

[18] Zahn, D. (2003). What influence is the six sigma movement having in universities? what influence should it be having?. *ASQ Six Sigma Forum, 3*(1), Retrieved from http://asq.org/pub/sixsigma/past/vol3_issue1/youropinion.html

[19] Zhang, W., Hill, A. V., & Gilbreath, G. H. (2011). A research agenda for Six Sigma Research. *Quality management journal, 18*(1), 39-53.

CHAPTER 2:

Global Issues in the Quality of Higher Education

CHAPTER OBJECTIVE

The primary goal is to provide a brief overview of the challenges to quality in higher education and identify problems in higher education in different countries. This chapter also explores what aspects are mainly responsible for the problems and how countries may address these problems.

2.1 INTRODUCTION

Because the world has changed rapidly over the past two decades, the United States must address new economic, political, and national security challenges. To react to these issues, it is key that higher education institutions' graduates are globally competent, meaning they can add to and comprehend knowledge in the interconnected world (National Association of State Universities and Land-Grant Colleges, 2004, as cited in Brustein, 2007). If graduates cannot do either, they will be inept global citizens and will not be able to contend effectively in the global marketplace or with national security needs (Brustein, 2007). Along with knowing the challenges of higher education in the United States, it is important to know the related challenges Vietnam, Venezuela, Ethiopia, and India face and how these countries are addressing them.

2.2 UNITED STATES

There are real weaknesses in the structure of area and international studies programs, which are colleges' vehicles to global competence. Area study programs typically minimize theory and are extremely broad. These programs habitually take after a cafeteria-style menu: one course from each rack. One way or another, students are expected to pull together the different pieces into some clear understanding. International studies curricula habitually disregard the significance of cultural contexts. Endeavors at applying theory to these contexts are rare. Students repeatedly finish these programs with no competency in a foreign language or culture (Brustein, 2007).

Additionally, Figure 2.1 shows that area and international studies programs frequently skip vital activities, according to Brustein (2007), including:

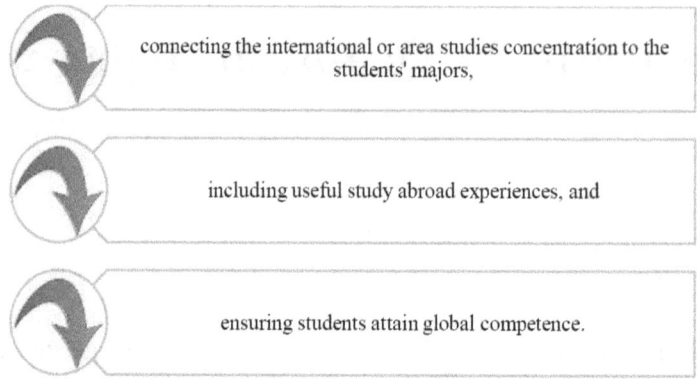

Figure 2.1: Issues in the Area and International Studies of the United States

To address these issues, Brustein (2007) recommends internationalizing education in all disciplines. Comprehensive and well-organized educational experiences will prepare students to wind up globally competent. In an endeavor to build global competence into the educational experience, the University of Pittsburgh, for example, created a bachelor of philosophy degree in international and area studies in 2005 to supplement disciplinary degrees without adding to students' time at the university. The degree is structured to be pertinent to students' disciplinary degrees (Brustein, 2007).

Colleges must not force faculty to confer global competence on students but instead use incentives to encourage faculty to participate, for instance by making internationalization of teaching and research endeavors a requirement for promotions or raises. Appealing to the self-interests of faculty is a method of securing their buy-in (Brustein, 2007).

2.3 VIETNAM

Vietnam's higher education has centralized governance. Reforming it in the past decade has brought about poor results. To comprehend in detail the difficulties confronted by open higher education establishments in Vietnam, Dao (2014) conducted a case analysis. Yin (2003, as cited in Dao, 2014) defines a case analysis, or case study, as research in which a modern phenomenon is considered inside its context, supported by evidence from various sources. Dao investigated a major public university in central Vietnam. The data collected showed challenges concerning poor governance, lack of real quality assurance, and financial shortfall, as shown in Figure 2.2.

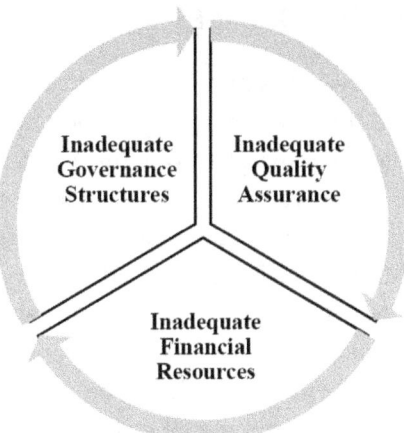

Figure 2.2: Issues in the Higher Education of Vietnam

2.3.1 INADEQUATE GOVERNANCE STRUCTURES

Dao (2014) writes, "The University is one of three large 'regional universities' established in 1994 in Vietnam" (p. 749). It resulted from a merger of two "member universities," but the merger "continues to give rise to significant governance challenges" (Dao, 2014, p. 750). The once independent universities' faculty attempted to operate as they had before and felt they were looked down upon because they now reported to both the university and the Ministry of Education and Training. The Ministry could not improve the governance structure because it is not responsible for compliance with the regulations it creates for higher education.

2.3.2 INADEQUATE QUALITY ASSURANCE

In the same way as other Vietnamese higher education institutions, the university began its quality assurance program after the Ministry of Education and Training executed a quality affirmation system in late 2005 that included 53 quality-related criteria for surveying state-funded colleges. In 2007, a further correction of the system with 61 criteria and 10 standards was implemented by the Ministry of Education and Training. Dao (2014) reports, "The University also had its own Department of Quality Assurance and Higher Education Project Management" (p. 752). Despite quality assurance progress, numerous managers reported it fell far short of expectations. For example, a retired manager explained that ensuring quality for both employees and students was challenging given the specific criteria on working space for professors and for students and the university's overpopulated training programs.

2.3.3 INADEQUATE FINANCIAL RESOURCES

Dao (2014) explains the university's income originated from the state budget "(around 40%), tuition fees (around 40%), and services and cooperation projects (around 20%)" (p. 753). Stores from the state spending plan were furnished every year depending on the university's program profile and enrollment. Allotments for the university were expanding, however not sufficiently quickly to compensate for increased infrastructure needs and enrollment. Therefore, the Ministry of Education and Training worked with the university based on spending plans put together by the member universities through negotiations with the university. These assets went toward mainly base pay and day-to-day operations. Member universities' budgets were normally decided using the quantity of students enlisted. These budgets were insufficient and represented just around 30–40% of member universities' needs (Dao, 2014).

2.3.4 ADDRESSING QUALITY ASSURANCE ISSUES

Dao (2014) concludes, "Regarding quality assurance, the case study suggests that there is neither a proper understanding about nor a real commitment to quality assurance in Vietnam's higher education system" (p. 756). Because of exclusive administration by the Ministry of Education and Training, multiple groups interested in enhancing educational quality of the system lack influence. In fact, the Ministry required self-assessment of the university against standards. Self-assessment is acceptable to most Vietnamese universities but typically centers on inputs, not outcomes, and may be subjective. The approach also discourages institutions from doing what is necessary to fulfill their unique purposes and from innovating to improve their futures. It also reinforces a tendency to focus on past and present achievements, as opposed to encouraging future-oriented improvements (Nguyen, Oliver, & Priddey, 2009, as cited in Dao, 2014). Dao (2014) continues, "Another consideration is that there has not yet been any public disclosure about the quality assurance outcomes for at least 40 higher education institutions that have undertaken institutional self-assessment" (pp. 756–757). A quality assurance agency beyond the Ministry appears necessary.

2.3.5 ADDRESSING FINANCIAL ISSUES

The government's ability to provide more funds to higher education "is widely regarded as being limited and so increased tuition fees seem to be the only option available in order to pay for future growth and improvements" (Dao, 2014, p. 757). However, the National Assembly, not the Ministry of Education and Training, set a flat tuition rate and is hesitant to raise it. Dao (2014) continues, "A key point for reform here is that nothing will change at the University, or at others like it, without there being an improvement in terms of access to increased funds" (p. 757). Without financial resources, along with better institutional accountability and autonomy, the university may not measure up to international standards. It appears to make changes by upgrading facilities and computers but does not improve relationships and processes, so its reform is incomplete (Dao, 2014).

2.4 VENEZUELA

Venezuela's higher education reform is linked with its 21st-century political reform. In 2006, higher education spending comprised about 15% of the national budget (Muhr & Verger, 2006). New content and pedagogies have been introduced. However, they represent the opposite of the global educational trends of increased competitiveness and efficiency (Muhr & Verger, 2006). The new educational system has a clear political (socialist) agenda. A main purpose and evaluation criterion of students' development is their responsible, conscious, and active social participation. In addition, local communities play a role in colleges' governance, and colleges conduct research locally that contributes to societal transformation. In 2009, the Venezuelan government required the provision of baccalaureate education to citizens (Griffiths, 2013). With increased enrollment has come struggles to provide staff, infrastructure, and student resources (Griffiths, 2013). In addition, educational reform has followed an indirect and slow path.

2.5 ETHIOPIA

In terms of management and organization, the public university system in Ethiopia is challenged by a scarcity of resources, poor institutional governance, and lack of autonomy. Dependence on public resources to support higher education is probably soon to decrease (Kahsay, 2012). Federal funding of universities has not increased as quickly as student enrollment has, leading to decreased quality. For example, Jigjiga University had not finished constructing facilities when its classes began. A shortage of resources hinders quality assessment as well. On the other hand, Addis Ababa University bought computers but did not enable students to use them, showing that having resources does not mean they are used effectively. Without proper access to or use of resources, teaching theory is emphasized over experiential learning (Kahsay, 2012).

Resources are not the only mismanaged aspect of universities. Public universities have a lax admissions policy because the government assigns some students to attend. Many students can enroll despite their low entrance exam scores, which leads to their attrition and a waste of schools' limited resources. Mekelle University lacks transparent grading, and some professors grade based on their like or dislike of students. Universities' staff lack the training and motivation to ensure quality, often because of inexperience, even though the Ministry of Education controls hiring. Curriculum design and revision are disorganized despite some government supervision, and programs fail to intertwine theory and application and to reward students (Kahsay, 2012). The government limits what operations universities may manage independently. A 2009 government proclamation established public universities' autonomy in financial, administrative, and academic matters; established academic accountability; and established required internal quality review processes but no accreditation process (Kahsay, 2012).

Formal quality assurance is a 21st-century phenomenon in Ethiopia. It entails a self-evaluation submitted to the Higher Education Relevance and Quality Agency followed by an external audit. The in-depth evaluations consider the quality and relevance of teaching and programs. However, institutions cannot create self-evaluation guidelines, and few of the Agency's staff are qualified to assess higher education because their expertise is in agriculture (Kahsay, 2012). In addition, the Agency lacks autonomy because it is part of the Ministry of Education. Internal quality assurance lacks proper methods and structure, so they fail to cause improved quality. In fact, this process focuses on inputs, not outcomes, and is bureaucratic without follow-up. External quality assurance is also bureaucratic. Kahsay's (2012) study of Ethiopian public universities found that introducing explicit quality assurance has not resulted in its full adoption or in improved education because policies are introduced merely to obtain state legitimacy. These quality assurance failures result from institution-specific and external factors. Staff shortages, leadership incompetence, poor usage of resources, and lack of a quality and professional culture are the institution-specific factors. Lack of a strong leading agency to foster internal quality review processes, of a supportive sociocultural context, and of academically prepared students are the external factors. As a result, graduation rates are low, and students are dissatisfied with and often unable to find meaning in their studies (Kahsay, 2012).

2.6 INDIA

"Indian higher education can be characterized by a sea of mediocrity, in which some islands of excellence can be found" (Altbach, 2014, p. 505). About 20 million Indian students attend at least 574 universities and 35,500 affiliated colleges (Altbach, 2014). Although several universities with direct government sponsorship or without colleges affiliated with them are of high quality, most institutions, especially those with low or no government funding, provide a poor quality of education. However, wealthy philanthropists have founded a few private, nonprofit universities that show great potential (Altbach, 2014).

Decreased quality results partly from great expansion of access to higher education despite students' lack of academic preparation. Relaxed admission requirements have become more so for traditionally disadvantaged groups but without provision of assistance for students from poor-quality secondary schools. These disadvantaged groups, including students from tribes and lower castes, make up nearly half of newly admitted students and hired faculty. A result of this admission and hiring practice is a high dropout rate (Altbach, 2014). Poor-quality higher education also results from lack of planning, politics, and poor investment.

2.6.1 LACK OF PLANNING

Lack of innovation has not caused the problems in Indian higher education. Altbach (2014) writes, "At least a half dozen high-level commissions have issued intelligent reports over the past 40 years" to analyze current conditions and give recommendations for development and reform (p. 506). "Over time, elements of some of these reports have been partly implemented, but in no case at all have any been comprehensively applied" (Altbach, 2014, p. 507). The states have funding for and supervisory power over colleges but are endeavoring to keep up with increased enrollment rather than planning strategically. "The University

Grants Commission—responsible at the national level for funding, innovation, and planning of higher education under the control of the central government—has developed some small-scale programs in curriculum, teaching, and other areas" but has had a small role in macrolevel innovation (Albach, 2014, p. 507). Because governing bodies overseeing higher education do not coordinate their efforts or have the power to change institutions, planning in higher education has been unsuccessful (Altbach, 2014, p. 507).

2.6.2 POLITICS

Altbach (2014) reports, "Indian higher education, much to its detriment, is infused with politics, at all levels" (p. 507). Some political leaders create colleges to give jobs and access to constituents. Altbach (2014) explains, "University and college elections are frequently politicized. National, regional, and local political machines are frequently engaged in campus politics. Student unions are often politicized. Academic decisions are determined more by political than academic considerations" (p. 507). Politics can interfere with academics. As long as politics continues to wield such influence, "India will be unable to fulfill its goals of quality, access, and the creation of a world-class higher education system" (Altbach, 2014, p. 508).

2.6.3 POOR INVESTMENT

University funding remains inadequate. India spent less than other countries with rapid economic growth on higher education in 2011/2012: 1.22% of the gross domestic product (Altbach, 2014). This is despite increased enrollment. Most financial responsibility for colleges has fallen to the states, but many cannot support higher education enough because of the need to spend money on increasing literacy. Without sufficient funds, colleges' gains in quality will not keep up with their gains in student enrollment (Altbach, 2014).

2.6.4 FUTURE CHALLENGES

Altbach (2014) concludes, "Given the realities of contemporary Indian higher education, it is not possible to be optimistic about a breakthrough in quality" (p. 510). A world-class university is not in India's future. If the government were to upgrade and greatly increase funds to colleges, governance reform would be necessary. So far, using the private sector to improve higher education has caused problems. "The greatest challenge is, of course, continued expansion of the system to provide access" (Altbach, 2014, p. 510). India must give attention and resources to maintain expansion. Doing so is necessary to fulfill future labor needs.

2.7 REFERENCES

Altbach, P. G. (2014). India's higher education challenges. *Asia Pacific Education Review, 15,* 503–510. doi:10.1007/s12564-014-9335-8

Brustein, W. I. (2007). The global campus: Challenges and opportunities for higher education in North America. *Journal of Studies in International Education, 11*(3/4), 382–391.

Dao, K. V. (2015). Key challenges in the reform of governance, quality assurance, and finance in Vietnamese higher education – a case study. *Studies in Higher Education, 40*(5), 745–760.

Griffiths, T. G. (2013). Higher education for socialism in Venezuela: Massification, development and transformation. In T. G. Griffiths & Z. Millei (Eds.), *Logics of socialist education: Engaging with crisis, insecurity and uncertainty*. New York, NY: Springer.

Kahsay, M. N. (2012). *Quality and quality assurance in Ethiopian higher education: Critical issues and practical implications*. Enschede, the Netherlands: Creps.

Muhr, T., & Verger, A. (2006). Venezuela: Higher education for all. *Journal for Critical Education Policy Studies, 4*(1). Retrieved from http://www.jceps.com/wp-content/uploads/PDFs/04-01-7.pdf

CHAPTER 3:

Globalization of Quality in Higher Education

This chapter provides a brief overview of the globalization of quality in higher education and identifies different models of quality in higher education in different countries. This also discusses how and why the models differ from country to country and compares those models, focusing on the weaknesses and strengths of each.

3.1 INTRODUCTION

The world has become a global village. This phenomenon, along with the global economy's change to being knowledge based, has changed the higher education process and education's nature around the world (Mok, 2014). Some terms, such as excellence, competitiveness, efficiency, accountability, and devolution, alongside different strategies, such as performance pledges, management by objectives, internal audit, and quality assurance, have been adopted by many governments and institutions as they attempt to improve public services' efficiency (Mok, 1999; Welch, 2003; as cited in Mok, 2005). There are many theories and models regarding quality of higher education in vogue in different countries.

3.2 THEORIES OF QUALITY

There are several definitions of quality we find in business, corporate, and education sectors, including the following: We deem a product or service a quality one when it satisfies a customer's expectations (Guaspari, 1985, as cited in Bogue, 1998). A product or service that conforms to specific designs is a quality product or service (Crosby, 1984, as cited in Bogue, 1998). In essence, "Quality is a multifactor concept involving not only fitness for use but also reliability, durability, esthetics, and so on" (Garvin, 1988, as cited in Bogue, 1998, p. 8).

Despite being an oversimplification for higher education institutions, one can use three perspectives to consider quality. "One of these perspectives assumes that by definition quality is in limited supply—a competitive affair" in which only a few excellent institutions exist (Bogue, 1998, p. 8). The second perspective proposes that quality should align to each institution's mission and goals. The third perspective proposes that "quality is to be found not in resources and reputations but in results, in the 'value added' by the institution (Bogue, 1998, p. 8). Figure 3.1 shows these different theories of quality as they are integral to each other.

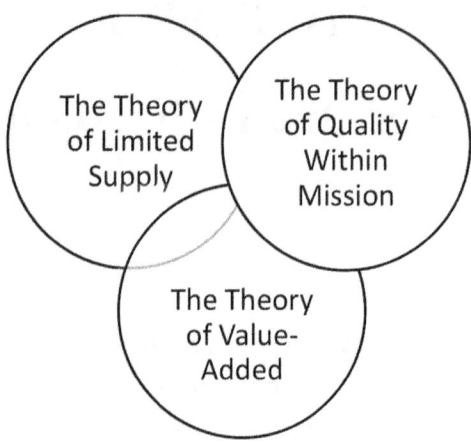

Figure 3.1: Theories of Quality

3.2.1 THE THEORY OF LIMITED SUPPLY

Academics and friends of higher education commonly have the assumptions shown in Figure 3.2 (Bogue, 1998, p. 8).

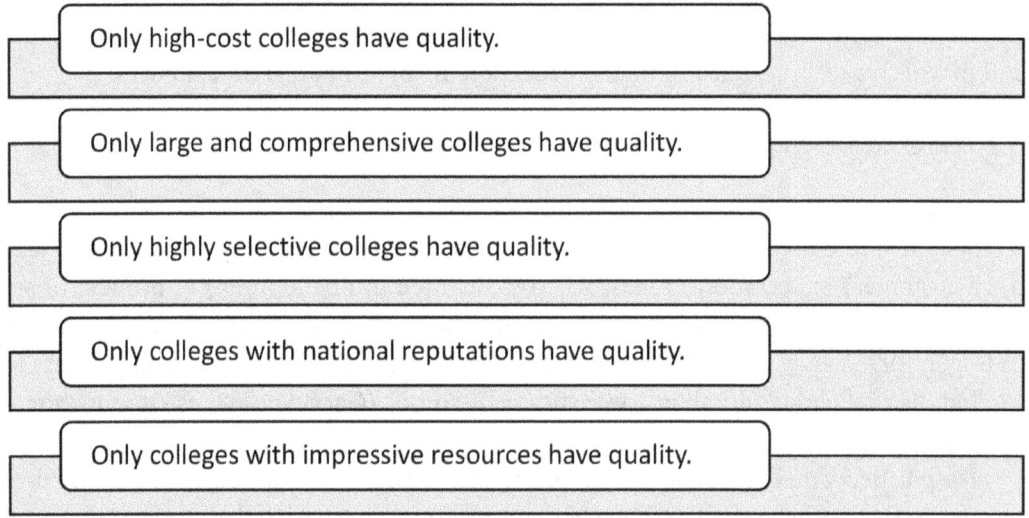

Figure 3.2: Conventional Assumptions about Higher Education

Bogue (1998) asks, "Is collegiate quality in finite supply, a commodity of scarce availability?" (p. 8). The above assumptions can create a pyramid of impressiveness in which less well-known and two-year colleges sit at the bottom whereas larger institutions perch at the top of quality. U.S. annual rankings of best colleges display this theory.

3.2.2 THE THEORY OF QUALITY WITHIN MISSION

Besides the pyramid structure, one could perceive the potential for quality in college missions and request colleges achieve quality according to those missions. This vision of quality conveys the thought that every college ought to show quality in its main goal (Bogue, 1998). U.S. accreditation processes often use the college's mission statement to evaluate its quality, or in other words, its suitability for its own purpose (Westerheijden, 2005). This theory, though sound, makes comparing institutions to one another difficult because of their varying missions.

3.2.3 THE THEORY OF VALUE-ADDED

As opposed to the input-focused theories, Dew (2009) offers a theory focused on higher education outcomes. Not only should students gain measurable knowledge through education, but they also should contribute to society with it, such as by designing buildings, translating, or becoming educators themselves. Students should be transformed, and that should be the measure of quality. In this theory, seeking to define quality in higher education entails a complex philosophical voyage.

3.3 QUALITY IN HIGHER EDUCATION AROUND THE WORLD

Given the increasing interdependence of nations, examining how various countries and city-states' colleges ensure quality can shed light on which policies are effective or ineffective. This section covers quality of higher education in countries from four continents.

3.3.1 SINGAPORE

Recent changes in Singapore's universities reflect the city-state's economic development. Its politicians are thinking creatively to ensure Singapore benefits from being part of the knowledge-based global economy (Olds, 2007). Singapore is endeavoring to become a global knowledge center (Olds, 2007). According to Marginson (2006), this has been successful, because he calls this place an example of brain drain reversal that transforms national research and education roles. In fact, its research reputation is strong relative to its financial resources. Singapore's educational quality model has heavy government influence because, in response to a perceived need for graduates with technology and science skills, the government has implemented structures and funding incentives for higher education. These incentives include those given to foreign universities to found satellite campuses in Singapore (Pusser, Ordorika, & Kempner, 2010). This illustrates the desire for global competence and for educational quality because it is assumed that the invited foreign institutions will establish quality programs. Global competence is a likely outcome of Singapore's education because Singapore is one of the most globalized states if not the most globalized state in the world (Olds, 2007). In turn, this city-state is a desirable place for new universities run by foreign institutions, such as Duke and Cornell, because of its commitment to education, its local high-quality colleges, and its transnational companies. These firms have also lobbied the government to generate better workers and offer lifelong learning to expatriates through enhanced quality of higher education, which has led to improvement of executive education programs in particular (Olds, 2007). The role of government in higher education quality in Singapore is similar to the role of other Asian governments in higher education, as the next section shows.

3.3.2 HONG KONG

Mass access to higher education and the government's plan to make Hong Kong an education center in Asia have given rise to quality assurance. Hong Kong's quality assurance system has been performance based since the 1990s (Mok, 2014). Quality of research performance determines how much government funding each institution receives. Academics also strive to enhance their colleges' quality through effective teaching and community service. In acknowledgment of the theory of quality within mission, the government has institutions generate unique missions and centers of excellence based on their strengths (Deem, Mok, & Lucas, 2008). Whether this quality model achieves the government's goal remains to be seen.

The intersection of governance and quality presents challenges. Hong Kong's universities are under pressure to rank high and increase their global competitiveness (Mok, 2014). At the same time, the government has decreased universities' funding but emphasized benchmarking and governance, thinking these are important for competitiveness and quality. With more well-trained graduates, Hong Kong's economic and social welfare would improve, according to the government, which seems to be looking through the lens of the theory of value-added. To address the decreased funding, a government report recommended that universities diversify their income sources and focus their resources on quality research and teaching. This recommendation in light of decreased resources places even more pressure on colleges in Hong Kong (Mok, 2005).

3.3.3 AUSTRALIA

Several new quality assurance policies in higher education went into effect in 2000. The policies' elements include the Australian Universities Quality Agency's yearly cyclical audits, state responsibility for nonuniversity higher education providers, commonwealth supervision of universities' work, universities' responsibility for attaining and enhancing quality, and compliance with guidelines and laws. This quality assurance framework is outcome based, not input based. Accreditation happens through external reviews, which have succeeded in promoting quality, establishing positions for staff to lead quality-enhancing initiatives, aligning operational units, enhancing performance reports, strengthening feedback and decision-making processes, and improving student retention and staff development. Shah and Grebennikov (2008, as cited in Shah, Nair, & Wilson, 2011) found external drivers prompted universities to improve their core services and assess themselves. Performance-based funding, with measures being retention and results of surveys, resulted from a government review in 2003/2004.

However, there is a possibility student survey data has been manipulated with funding on the line, and critics say loss of funding can demotivate institutions. Critics also point to the lack of penalty or reward for universities based on their external review results and the lack of supervision of academic outcomes and standards. Another limitation is the inconsistency of state-level performance reports, which complicates comparison of the retention and graduate outcomes of distant universities. As of 2011, universities were still acting on recommendations made after a government review of various groups' access to education, vocational colleges' collaboration with universities, research, and student experience that began in 2007. However, universities appear committed to creating rigorous processes in response to external audits and to attain their missions. Australian higher education faces the challenges of a 20-percent commonwealth funding decrease since the early 1990s and of mass access to universities (Shah et al., 2011).

3.3.4 UNITED KINGDOM

Traditionally, academic program reviews and external audits focusing on outcomes have ensured quality in higher education. Ranking institutions is familiar, and external reference points are the basis for assessment standards (Shah et al., 2011). Previously, the Quality Assurance Agency used inspections emphasizing processes and outcomes (Blackmore, 2004). Because of the high institutional cost of quality audits in the 1990s, the revised academic review combined what had been two processes and required institutions to publish their quality standards online for stakeholders' viewing. At least once every 6 years, institutions must now assess their departments, with summaries of the results and actions taken in response published online (Blackmore, 2004). The British Standards Institute auditing guidelines, originally intended for assessing corporations' quality, can also be used to assess institutions' quality, with the right training for auditors.

3.3.5 SPAIN

Quality assurance in higher education began in 1996 with the National Evaluation Plan for Quality in the Universities, so unlike in other European nations, universities' culture of quality is still developing (Esteve, Galán Palomares, & Pastor Valcárcel, 2010). The Plan ended in 2000, and Second Universities Quality Plan replaced it with the aim of helping establish regional accrediting agencies and developing institutional evaluation further. In 2003, the National Agency for Quality Assessment and Accreditation of Spain (ANECA) took over the Plan and along with regional agencies took responsibility for assessing and accrediting university services, university research and teaching management, and degree programs, with the goal of supervising objectively and transparently to ensure quality. ANECA's culture includes cooperation with regional agencies, collaboration in quality assurance procedures, and regard for institution autonomy, and its quality model recognizes the interworking of the organizational resources and structure, decision-making process, improvement, results reporting, and data collection and analysis. ANECA's guidelines instruct universities to have a culture of quality and put in place processes that enhance learning and resource usage. The Bologna Process also has influenced the quality assurance effort. This process, which began in 1999, mandated quality assurance and comparable degrees and credits across European higher education institutions (Edwards, Tovar Caro, & Sánchez-Ruiz, 2009). The Council of the European Union (2007, as cited in Edwards et al., 2009) built on the mandate in 2007 by encouraging peer review and independent evaluation in quality assurance.

Students participate in quality assurance, although this presents obstacles. ANECA formed a working group in 2006 to discuss potential ways for students to work with quality assurance agencies. Students ended up being observers of the external review process but practically performed the same work as the rest of the committee they were in. The experience was positive for these students and for ANECA because its quality assurance process was better for having a different perspective. In 2008, students also became members of committees tasked with evaluating and approving new degrees for Spanish colleges. These students were trained in quality assurance, which had the benefit of instilling a culture of quality in them. The first obstacle to student participation is that rather than desiring to participate, students have been required to according to the Bologna Process, which could be detrimental to their attitude and work ethic. Second, students and their representatives may be unfamiliar with quality assurance, which could lead to inaccurate assessments of universities and increased need to devote resources to training students and monitoring their work. However, colleges have embraced student participation because it widens the analysis and thus could enhance their ultimate quality (Esteve et al., 2010).

3.3.6 BRAZIL

McCowan (2004) writes, "Brazil's education system displays the extreme inequality that characterizes the country as a whole" (p. 456). Despite numerous acts by local governments and social movements "aiming to address these inequalities (Gandin & Apple, 2002; Gentili & McCowan, 2003; McCowan, 2003), educational opportunity on the national scale is deeply undemocratic" (McCowan, 2004, p. 456). These statements include higher education. "Students are almost exclusively from the upper socio-economic levels (71% of students are from the top quintile of family income)"; most colleges are in the wealthy southern areas, and few African Brazilian people enroll (McCowan, 2004, p. 456).

The *provão*, the nationwide, annual assessment introduced in 1995, is the main measure of higher education's quality. Undergraduates take it as an evaluation of their classes and colleges. The exam has problems as a quality indicator, however. McCowan (2004) explains, "There is no correction for differences in student intake: the assessment is measuring not the *value-added* of the institution but the academic level of the students, which is strongly influenced by their previous schooling" (p. 463). Public universities appear to outperform private ones because they typically receive secondary schools' best students.

3.4 COMPARISON OF DIFFERENT QUALITY MODELS

To ensure quality in higher education, Singapore enacted financial incentives for good teaching and research. Also, well-equipped teaching and research facilities and faculty training were ensured in higher education institutions, partly through importation of university education from foreign institutions.

Hong Kong, besides having most of the policies of Singapore, extended its quality assurance policy to include benchmarking and community service. Spain's more recent student-centered approach is showing promise, whereas historical inequity is detrimental to Brazil's quality assurance efforts.

Compared with systems in other countries, the higher education systems of Australia and the United Kingdom are more market oriented and research based. Quality assurance is one of the highest priorities there.

3.5 REFERENCES

Blackmore, J. A. (2004). A critical evaluation of academic internal audit. *Quality Assurance in Education, 12*(3), 128– 135.

Bogue, E. G. (1998). Quality assurance in higher education: The evolution of systems and design ideals. *New Directions for Institutional Research, 99*, 12–18. doi:10.1002/ir.9901

Edwards, M. E., Tovar Caro, E., & Sánchez-Ruiz, L. M. (2009). *Strengths and obstacles for quality assurance in the European Higher Education Area: The Spanish case.* Paper presented at International Conference on Engineering Education, Seoul, South Korea.

Deem, R., Mok, K. H., & Lucas, L. (2008). Transforming higher education in whose image? Exploring the concept of the 'world-class' university in Europe and Asia. *Higher Education Policy, 21*(1), 83-97.

Esteve, M. F., Galán Palomares, F. M., & Pastor Valcárcel, M. C. (2010). *2005-2010; 5 years of student participation on quality assurance in Spain.* Paper presented at 5th European Quality Assurance Forum, Villeurbanne, France.

Marginson, S. (2006). Dynamics of national and global competition in higher education. *Higher Education, 52*(1), 1–39.

McCowan, T. (2004). The growth of private higher education in Brazil: Implications for equity and quality. *Journal of Education Policy, 19*(4), 453–472.

Mok, K. H. (2005). Quest for world class university: Quality assurance and international benchmarking in Hong Kong. *Quality Assurance in Education, 13*(4), 277–304.

Mok, K. H. (2014). Enhancing quality of higher education for world-class status: Approaches, strategies, and challenges for Hong Kong. *Chinese Education and Society, 47*(1), 44–64.

Pusser, B., Ordorika, I., & Kempner, K. (Eds.). (2010). *Comparative education* (2nd ed.). In L. Foster & J. F. L. Jackson (Series eds.), ASHE Reader Series. New York, NY: Pearson Learning Solutions.

Olds, K. (2007). Global assemblage: Singapore, foreign universities, and the construction of a "global education hub". *World Development, 35*(6), 959–975.

Shah, M., Nair, S., & Wilson, M. (2011). Quality assurance in Australian higher education: Historical and future development. *Asia Pacific Education Review, 12*, 475–483.

Westerheijden, D. F. (2007). States and Europe and quality of higher education. In D. F. Westerheijden, B. Stensaker, & M. J. Rosa (Eds.), *Quality assurance in higher education: Trends in regulation, translation and transformation* (pp. 73–95). Dordrecht, the Netherlands: Springer.

CHAPTER 4:

European Standards in Higher Education

CHAPTER OBJECTIVE

This chapter provides a brief overview of the European quality assurance policy in higher education and helps identify standards of quality in higher education in Europe. It also discusses why standards vary and examines the weaknesses and strengths of European policy in higher education.

4.1 INTRODUCTION

Quality has become central to modernizing and converging European higher education. Convergence is necessary because the European Union has strengthened connections among its nations, and differing qualifications among graduates with the same degree but from different universities caused problems in the labor market (Westerheijden, 2007). The Bologna Process, which European ministers started in 1999, seeks to define methods and criteria for quality assessment in a way that is comparable across European universities and that enables staff and student mobility across institutions (Juradol et al., 2005, as cited in Edwards, Tovar Caro, & Sánchez-Ruiz, 2009). Agencies involved in carrying out the Bologna Process include the European University Association (EUA) and European Association for Quality Assurance in Higher Education (ENQA; ENQA, European Students' Union, EUA, & European Association of Institutions in Higher Education, 2015). Two main ways quality assurance is carried out in Europe are the *European Standards and Guidelines for Quality Assurance* and National Action Plans.

4.2 EUROPEAN STANDARDS AND GUIDELINES FOR QUALITY ASSURANCE

One achievement of the Bologna Process is the publication of the *Standards and Guidelines for Quality Assurance in the European Higher Education Area*, which are also called the European Standards and Guidelines (ESG). Their first publication and adoption by higher education ministers was in 2005, but to reflect the progress made in Process actions and quality assurance in 10 years, a revised version came out and was adopted in 2015 (ENQA et al., 2015).

4.2.1 CONTEXT AND TERMS

The ESG are a response to increasing diversity in, demand for, and access to higher education and add to the understanding of quality teaching and learning. *Quality assurance* describes any activity in continuous improvement, with accountability and enhancement at its core (ENQA et al., 2015). The ESG are not rigid quality requirements or recommendations for implementation. The purposes of the ESG are to support trust across territorial borders, create a unified framework for quality assurance of teaching and learning, facilitate quality assurance and enhancement in higher education, and inform about European quality assurance. The ESG are general to reflect the nations' diversity and suit their requirements. Four quality assurance principles are the foundation of the ESG. First, colleges are most responsible for their quality. Second, quality assurance considers institutional diversity. Third, it helps create a quality culture, and fourth, it considers stakeholders' expectations and needs (ENQA et al., 2015). The standards of the ESG lay out acceptable quality assurance in higher education, and their guidelines give suggestions for implementing and explain the importance of the standards. They acknowledge that differing contexts require differing implementation (ENQA et al., 2015).

4.2.2 WITHIN HIGHER EDUCATION INSTITUTIONS

There are 10 standards and associated guidelines for internal quality assurance. First, colleges need a quality assurance policy that forms part of their strategy, that is public, and that is enacted through internal stakeholders with external stakeholders' participation. This standard is first because processes and policies support sound quality assurance that builds accountability and continuous improvement and support taking responsibility for quality throughout institutions and fostering a culture of quality. The policy is implemented through various processes, with institution-wide participation. Second, academic programs must meet their set objectives and have a specific qualification that reflects the European Framework for Qualifications, which is important because programs of study are the heart of university teaching. Regarding implementation, programs should involve stakeholders and outside references in deciding the learning objectives and outcomes and how students will advance smoothly and should undergo institutional approval. The next standard is related in that it recommends program delivery that encourages active learning, with the following implementation suggestions:
- Consider learner diversity
- Encourage student autonomy
- Encourage respect between students and instructors
- Deal with student concerns appropriately

Student assessment guidelines include having well-trained evaluators, advance awareness of assessment method and grading criteria linked to desired learning outcomes, and fair application to students. Fourth, institutions' regulations concerning admission, progression, and certification must be published and consistent, which includes using tools and processes to collect and respond to data on student progress. Graduation documentation must clarify the learning outcomes achieved, qualification attained, and material and level of the completed studies. Fifth, institutions need competent staff. As Figure 4.1 summarizes, this is implemented through a supportive environment, meaning it uses understandable and transparent recruitment and employment practices that acknowledge teaching's significance and meaning it promotes staff's professional development, use of technology and new teaching methods, and research (ENQA et al., 2015).

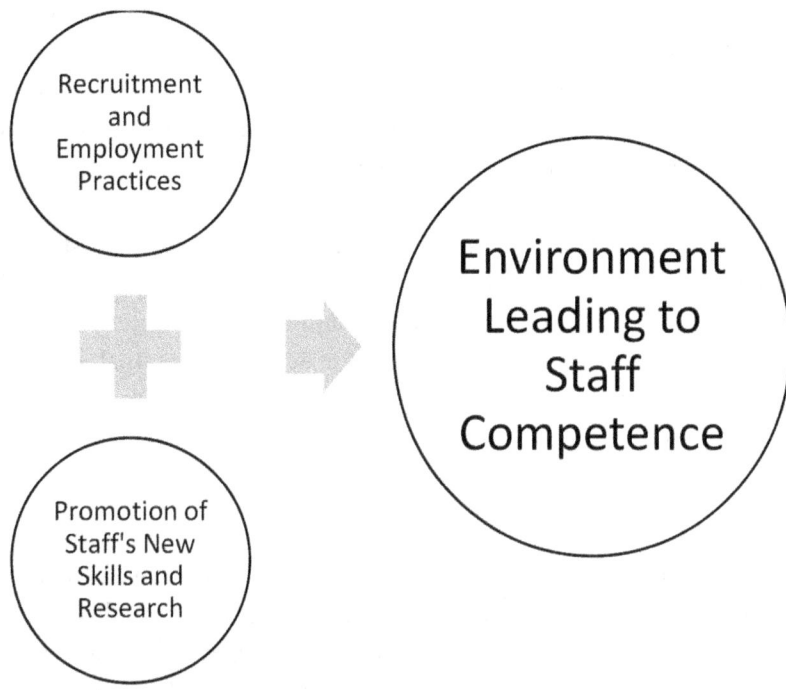

Figure 4.1: Implementation of Quality Staff Standard

Sixth, colleges must provide accessible student support, which includes staff (e.g., tutors and advisers) and tangible (e.g., computers and libraries) resources. Although its organization may vary, it must suit its purpose and be known on campus (ENQA et al., 2015). The next standards state institutions should gather and use information to manage their activities and to fuel internal quality assurance. Afterward, colleges should publish it to make stakeholders aware of programs offered, their learning outcomes and resulting qualifications, teaching and evaluation methods, and graduate employment data. Staff and students should participate in these information-related activities. Finally, colleges must ensure they meet their objectives and align with the ESG to ensure positive student outcomes and institutional learning and improvement (ENQA et al., 2015). These final standards align with the EUA's call to allow stakeholder participation and to have internal quality assurance that can itself be assessed (Edwards et al., 2009).

4.2.3 EXTERNAL QUALITY ASSURANCE

There are seven standards and guidelines for this process. First, external quality assurance procedures should consider the internal quality assurance processes' effectiveness. This is important to establish the connection between internal and external quality assurance because merely acknowledging colleges' quality assurance responsibility is not enough. Second, the aims of quality assurance processes should be determined before their processes' development, by all stakeholders. Aims and enactment must consider the student workload's cost and level and the need for institutional support in enhancing quality, enable universities to show increased quality, and generate information on results and follow-up. This is essential for objectivity and effectiveness. Third, the processes ought to be useful, be consistent, and be made public in a report that gives clear suggestions for institutional improvement that the agency will follow up on. Such implementation ensures processes' effects and acceptance. Fourth, experts and students should conduct external quality assurance to add a broader perspective. More specifically, the assessors must be chosen carefully, must possess the skills needed to assess quality, and must undergo training. Fifth, outcomes of quality assurance should rely on published and consistent criteria. The outcomes can be judgments, decisions, or recommendations, for example. The final standards address two specific outcomes: reports and appeals, which ensure universities can take action and that external quality assurance is accountable and open (ENQA et al., 2015).

4.2.4 QUALITY ASSURANCE AGENCIES

European ministers charged the ENQA in 2003 with creating a beneficial peer review of quality assurance agencies, for which the ENQA decided what quality standards the review should follow. The peer review is the way to attain comparability, awareness, and transparency of the agencies (ENQA, 2009). The European Register Committee determines which organizations are recognized as quality assurance agencies. This recognition clarifies which higher education providers are quality assured and therefore able to grant degrees recognized across borders (ENQA, 2009).

There are seven standards and associated guidelines for quality assurance agencies. First, agencies should conduct quality assurance regularly and with stakeholder participation so that the public and universities trust these organizations. Processes may include review, audit, or accreditation at the institutional or program level. Second, agencies ought to be legally established as quality assurance authorities, which is vital to provide assurance that their processes' outcomes are credible. Third, they should not have outside influence to ensure decisions rely on expertise alone. They must be independent in responsibility taken for outcomes and in operations. Fourth, they ought to publish descriptive reports of findings often, because analyzing the information will reveal trends, good practices, and challenges that apply not only to one institution but also to national and international higher education. Fifth, agencies ought to have the right resources, including funding, to perform their tasks as well as reflect on their work, improve it, and make people aware of it. The last two standards recommend that agencies conduct internal quality assurance and be subject to external review to be accountable, optimal, and trustworthy (ENQA et al., 2015).

4.3 NATIONAL ACTION PLANS

A process specifically for reconciling the difficulty in recognizing academic qualifications across European borders, also resulting from the Bologna Process and from the Lisbon Recognition Convention, is National Action Plans (Rauhvargers & Rusakova, 2008). The Lisbon Recognition Convention was an intergovernmental gathering in 1997 that introduced the idea of accepting, not just knowing about, foreign qualifications (Westerheijden, 2007).

4.3.1 CONTEXT AND TERMS

In 2005, European higher education ministers charged nations with solving foreign qualification recognition problems through National Action Plans. Mutual qualification recognition is a cornerstone of higher education that provides mobility for students, graduates, and staff and allows lifelong learning to be part of higher education (Rauvargers & Rusakova, 2008). In fact, program directors and deans ranked mobility as the top way to measure the Bologna Process's success (Adelman, 2009). The National Action Plans draw on standards from the Lisbon Recognition Convention and are showing evaluation of foreign qualifications differs greatly among countries, meaning evaluation outcomes may also differ among countries (Rauvargers & Rusakova, 2008). The standards are flexible and have been translated into nations' primary languages from European English, leaving the definition of terms such as *substantial differences* and *fair assessment* unclear (Adelman, 2009; Rauvargers & Rusakova, 2008). Therefore, what do the following requirements mean: recognizing qualifications when no substantial differences from the host country's qualification exist and granting fair assessment of previous qualifications? Rauhvargers and Rusakova (2008) call for clarification of such terms to ensure National Action Plans and thus quality assurance succeed.

4.3.2 BEST PRACTICES AND RECOMMENDATIONS

In some nations, Lisbon Recognition Convention principles are part of laws, so universities automatically follow the principles in National Action Plans. In addition, the principles are part of internal quality assurance because equitable qualification recognition links to it. However, these statements are not true for countries that have not updated education legislation to incorporate the Convention's results, preventing universities' effective implementation. Rauhvargers and Rusakova (2008) encourage governments and institutions to follow the Lisbon Recognition principles and recommend institutions work with one another to create cohesive nationwide recognition and implement the Convention at the department level. National Action Plans' intended outcome is consistent evaluation of qualifications in Europe.

4.4 STRENGTHS AND WEAKNESSES OF EUROPEAN QUALITY ASSURANCE

A major strength is Europe's vision of quality higher education and its willingness to execute it, as the numerous conventions and declarations since 1990 show. The number of agencies working to execute the vision is another strength. Four agencies alone wrote the ESG, and they and others have demonstrated the ability to work efficiently across national borders, which has the additional benefit of increasing trust in the higher education system. The frequent references to student outcomes show a third strength: focus on outcomes rather than inputs in higher education (ENQA et al., 2015). Fourth, Europe has a more sophisticated understanding of demographic trends' effects on higher education and a greater willingness to incorporate lifelong learning into it than the United States does. European higher education also has greater accountability than the U.S. system because despite the latter's focus on generating data, Adelman (2009) writes that accountability is more than publishing numbers. In Europe, there are more written statements of what competencies students gain through and what purpose is fulfilled by degree programs, which is one form of accountability not often used in the United States. In fact, the European model is worth implementing in the United States.

Even so, European higher education policy has room for improvement. Faculty approve of reformed qualification systems and degree plans, which eases reform, but must work to create quality assessments and criteria-based, written learning outcomes for the Bologna Process to succeed. A second weakness is that continent-wide quality assurance is underdeveloped without full national qualifications frameworks, whose establishment has been slow because of efforts to align them with the Lisbon Strategy and stakeholder negotiations (Adelman, 2009). Some countries have reformed education slower than others have. Also, there is inconsistency in the quantitative data collected related to student outcomes. Finally, mass access to higher education without increased funding for it has restricted quality, with Spain being an example of a country with this weakness (Edwards et al., 2009).

4.5 REFERENCES

Adelman, C. (2009). *The Bologna Process for U.S. eyes: Re-learning higher education in the age of convergence.* Washington, DC: Institute for Higher Education Policy.

Edwards, M. E., Tovar Caro, E., & Sánchez-Ruiz, L. M. (2009). *Strengths and obstacles for quality assurance in the European Higher Education Area: The Spanish case.* Paper presented at International Conference on Engineering Education, Seoul, South Korea.

European Association for Quality Assurance in Higher Education. (2009). *Standards and Guidelines for Quality Assurance in the European Higher Education Area* (3rd ed.). Helsinki, Finland: Author.

European Association for Quality Assurance in Higher Education, European Students' Union, European Universities Association, & European Association of Institutions in Higher Education. (2015). *Standards and Guidelines for Quality Assurance in the*

European Higher Education Area (ESG). Brussels, Belgium: European Association of Institutions in Higher Education.

Rauhvargers, A., & Rusakova, A. (2010). *Improving recognition in the European Higher Education Area: An analysis of National Action Plans*. Paper presented at Bologna Follow-up Group meeting, Paris, France.

Westerheijden, D. F. (2007). States and Europe and quality of higher education. In D. F. Westerheijden, B. Stensaker, & M. J. Rosa (Eds.), *Quality assurance in higher education: Trends in regulation, translation and transformation* (pp. 73–95). Dordrecht, the Netherlands: Springer.

CHAPTER 5:

Accreditation

CHAPTER OBJECTIVE

The main objective of this chapter is to discuss the importance of accreditation in higher education. This chapter also explains various accreditation standards of different programs and different universities. It also provides various accreditation models to analyze why accreditation is important for designing any program and its curriculum. The comparison of different accreditation agencies provides a clear understanding of how different universities or programs become accredited.

5.1 INTRODUCTION

To evaluate any academic program, accreditation is used. Accreditation can be considered the deliberate peer review process higher education institutions and industry experts use. It is a voluntary process anticipated to increase the quality of higher education and the academic outcomes of the students. A rudimentary level of quality in the education any institution provides is guaranteed by its accreditation. Accreditation also ensures that recognition of the degree attained is done for only genuine achievements of the students. Generally, accreditation can be defined as a process of evaluation through which colleges, universities, and other institutions of higher learning compare their standards with the conventional standards. The members of peer review boards set the standards. This peer review board helps in the creation and the evaluation of every possible new school accreditation and provides assistance in the renewals of previously accredited colleges and schools. Meeting the overall standards the peer review board sets is essential for each potential college to undergo the process of accreditation smoothly.

The evaluation of each educational program against the established standards is done through the process of accreditation, and after adherence to these standards, the educational program is recognized and certified by a third-party organization. Accreditation also provides an endorsement to the students that college and universities deliver valid education acknowledged by the U.S. Department of Education (USDE). Most of the accredited schools and colleges in the United States meet the standards the private agencies set. Not every country's government is as involved in accreditation. The main purpose of the process of accreditation is to ensure that each potential college program meets certain minimum standards and encourages higher education institutions to improve their quality of education (Eaton, 2012). It also aims to ensure the responsibility of these institutions to provide confidence in the students regarding higher education institutions. According to the perspective of various members of the educational field, the assurance of institution and program accreditation is also important to enhance the program curriculum and reputation.

5.2 WHY IS ACCREDITATION IMPORTANT?

To make a successful career, it is essential to choose a reputable college. Schools and colleges that are in compliance with recognized standards of the accreditation process offer degrees employers recognize. Accredited academic programs provide the assurance to employers that the candidates possess the education to be capable of joining their organization and make deciding whether to pay current employees' tuition easier (Eaton, 2012). Employers look for worthy candidates with the quality education accredited institutions offer. The accreditation process is important for the evaluation of any academic program with respect to certain components, such as the content and design of curriculum, institutional resources, requirements for admission and graduation, and the learning outcomes of the students (Eaton, 2012). The process of accreditation also provides a better chance for the students to transfer credits to other esteemed institutions easily when they progress in their education levels. If the students need to transfer their credits to any reputable accredited school, they should do so from accredited schools only. Furthermore, it is clear that if the students want financial aid, such as federal grants and loans, they should attend an accredited school or college (Eaton, 2012).

5.3 ACCREDITATION STANDARDS

In the United States the accreditation process is not mandatory for schools and colleges. Colleges and schools are accredited by national and regional agencies in which the peer review board sets the standards. Nationally accredited schools are more often for profit whereas regionally accredited schools are usually not for profit and emphasize academics. Both of these categories of schools differ in academic standards and courses offered, so credits transferred from nationally accredited schools may not be acceptable to the regionally accredited schools. In the United States there are three types of accreditation, namely institutional accreditation, which focuses on the quality of the institution; national accreditation for faith- or career-based institutions; and program accreditation, which focuses on academic programs. Generally, any school or college requests the independent, private agencies to evaluate the standards of their programs (Eaton, 2012). Every agency has its own set of standards, which must be met by the schools to earn the accreditation. Because the quality standards of the agencies differ from one another, some are considered more prestigious than others. The choice of the agencies entirely depends on the school and the standard of quality it wishes to achieve. The agency providing the accreditation reviews the school entirely based on different criteria, such as admission requirements, degree programs, and available services and resources. The accreditation of the school is periodically reviewed to ensure that the established standards are maintained (Council for Higher Education Accreditation, 2010). If any violation of standards is noticed, the accreditation of the school is delayed or canceled immediately. Schools pursue accreditation status to demonstrate their academic quality to students and the public and to become qualified for federal funds (Council for Higher Education Accreditation, 2010).

5.4 ACCREDITATION PROCESS

As Eaton (2012) states, accreditation is granted based on evidence, standards, trust, and judgment. Some programs and institutions get regional accreditation, and others get national agencies' accreditation. Also, specialized accrediting agencies focus on specific disciplines or types of educational programs. Each step of the accreditation process is in the list below.

During self-examination, the educational institutions prepare a written document highlighting their achievements and accomplishments based on the standards of the accreditation agency. Second is peer review, an intensive review of the self-examination document by administrative and faculty peers, who comprise the majority of those who make the accreditation decision, as discussed later in this paragraph. On-site examination takes place after the completion of the peer review. Most of the accreditation organizations send a team of professionals to visit the educational institution seeking accreditation status. The members of the team are often experts and public citizens with an interest in higher education who volunteer their time to assess and ensure high-quality education standards are being met. Once the peer review and verification of the institution seeking accreditation status is completed, the accreditation organization calls upon its decision makers to review the collected data. This commission accepts or rejects the application for accreditation status for the program or institution under scrutiny. Periodic review is the final step, meaning the institution has to undergo an accreditation renewal review periodically (Eaton, 2012). Thus, organizations seeking accreditation have an incentive to meet high-quality educational standards each year.

5.4.1 NATIONAL ACCREDITORS IN THE UNITED STATES

There are mainly six national accreditors that accredit high-quality higher education institutions (USDE, 2017).

Accrediting Bureau of Health Education Schools: The Accrediting Bureau of Health Education Schools is one of the healthcare education accrediting agencies recognized by the USDE, specifically for accrediting private and postsecondary institutions with health education programs. The Accrediting Bureau of Health Education Schools also accredits programs related to the fields of medical assistant, medical laboratory technician, and surgical technology (USDE, 2017).

Accrediting Commission of Career Schools and Colleges: The USDE recognized the Accrediting Commission of Career Schools and Colleges as a private nonprofit organization to accredit private secondary and postsecondary education institutions with programs for occupational, trade, and technical careers. This commission is also identified as an independent accreditation agency to offer the accreditation of nondegree programs, bachelor's and master's degree programs, and distance education programs (USDE, 2017).

Accrediting Council for Continuing Education and Training: The Accrediting Council for Continuing Education and Training (n.d.) has been recognized by the USDE as a national accrediting agency since 1978. Institutions such as noncollegiate education institutions and organizations that offer continuing education, corporate training, and vocational programs seek accreditation through the Council. The Accrediting Council for Continuing Education and Training also offers accreditation to institutions providing distance education.

Accrediting Council for Independent Colleges and Schools: The Accrediting Council for Independent Colleges and Schools is an autonomous national accrediting agency established in 1912. It offers accreditation for higher education institutions with bachelor's and master's programs in professional and occupational fields. This agency is recognized by the U.S. Secretary of Education and Council for Higher Education Accreditation (CHEA) and is one of two national accreditors with recognition by both (Accrediting Council for Independent Colleges and Schools, 2010).

Council on Occupational Education: The Council on Occupational Education (n.d.) is one of the national accreditation agencies recognized by the U.S. Secretary of Education. It is a nonprofit agency that accredits eligible educational institutions. Initially it was established as a regional accreditation agency and is now responsible for accrediting nondegree- and degree-awarding programs of technical schools after becoming independent from the Southern Association of Colleges and Schools.

Distance Education Accrediting Commission: The Distance Education Accrediting Commission is a nonprofit accreditation agency to accredit distance education institutions. Initially it was known as Distance Education and Training Council (USDE, 2017).

5.4.2 REGIONAL ACCREDITORS IN THE UNITED STATES

There are mainly six regional accreditors that accredit high-quality educational institutions (USDE, 2017).

The North Central Association of Colleges and Schools: The North Central Association of Colleges and Schools is one of the six regional accreditation agencies the USDE and the CHEA recognize. It consists of membership organizations offering accreditation to the schools, colleges, and universities in 19 states. The primary and secondary accreditation functions of this association are provided by the Higher Learning Commission (Higher Learning Commission, 2003).

Middle States Commission on Higher Education: The Middle States Commission on Higher Education is a voluntary accreditation agency that the U.S. Secretary of Education and CHEA recognize as an accreditor and pre-accreditor of schools in five states and the District of Columbia. It encourages excellence in education in institutions with diverse resources and students (Middle States Commission on Higher Education, 2017).

New England Association of Schools and Colleges: The New England Association of Schools and Colleges is the oldest regional accreditor in the United States, offering accreditation to more than 2,000 public and independent schools, colleges, and universities in the six-state New England region (New England Association of Schools and Colleges, n.d.). It offers accreditation for all levels of education from prekindergarten to the doctoral level. It also provides accreditation for some international schools (New England Association of Schools and Colleges, n.d.).

Northwest Commission on Colleges and Universities: The Northwest Commission on Colleges and Universities is an independent, authoritative regional accreditation association recognized by the USDE. It offers accreditation for effective, quality education institutions in the seven-state Northwest region of Alaska, Idaho, Montana, Nevada, Oregon, Utah, and Washington. This association makes decisions with 26 commissioners representing the diversity of public higher education institutions (Northwest Commission on Colleges and Universities, n.d.). It offers regional accreditation for 162 institutions (Northwest Commission on Colleges and Universities, n.d.).

Southern Association of Colleges and Schools: The Southern Association of Colleges and Schools and Commission on Colleges is one of the six regional accreditation associations, and it offers accreditation to universities and colleges in Florida, Georgia, Kentucky, Louisiana, Mississippi, North Carolina, South Carolina, Alabama, Tennessee, Texas, Virginia, Latin America, and other international sites. This agency has a vision of being the premier example for quality establishment and assurance in higher education worldwide (Southern Association of Colleges and Schools and Commission on Colleges, n.d.).

Western Association of Schools and Colleges: The Western Association of Schools and Colleges offers accreditation for the states of California and Hawaii in the United States, Guam, and areas of the Pacific and East Asia. It provides services to more than 4,600 elementary, secondary, and postsecondary institutions, and its commission has 32 members (Western Association of Schools and Colleges, 2016).

5.4.3 ACADEMIC PROGRAM ACCREDITORS IN THE UNITED STATES

The following is a selection of program accreditors to show their variety.

Accreditation Board for Engineering and Technology: The Accreditation Board for Engineering and Technology (more commonly called ABET) is a nongovernmental and nonprofit accrediting agency for certain programs in applied science, computing, engineering technology, and engineering. It is a voluntary agency that accredits about 3,700 programs at more than 750 colleges and universities in 30 countries and is recognized as an accreditor by the CHEA (ABET, n.d.). ABET ensures that the quality standards of the profession are met by related programs. It was founded in 1932 (ABET, n.d.).

Association for the Accreditation of Human Research Protection Programs: The Association for the Accreditation of Human Research Protection Programs (2012) accredits the human research protection program of an organization through peer review of procedures and policies to determine willingness to conduct ethical human research. Many organizations perform human research. These programs fulfill critical functions, such as contractual arrangement of ethics review of the research program with respect to other organizations and human subjects (Michigan State University Human Research Protection Program, n.d.).

Association to Advance Collegiate Schools of Business International: The Association to Advance Collegiate Schools of Business International accredits business and management education. It was established in 1916 as a nonprofit organization. The Association provides services to accelerate business and management education and its impact. It believes business schools transform societies (Association to Advance Collegiate Schools of Business International, n.d.).

Commission of Collegiate Nursing Education: The Commission on Collegiate Nursing Education is a national accreditation agency, recognized by the U.S. Secretary of Education, for the programs of nursing for improvement in the public's health. It ensures the quality of undergraduate, graduate, and residency nursing programs. It identifies the programs that have effective education practices and serves the public through assessment. The Commission encourages a self-regulatory process to assess the nursing programs and support their continuous growth and improvement as well as improvement of professional education (Commission on Collegiate Nursing Education, n.d.).

Commission on Accreditation in Physical Therapy Education: The Commission on Accreditation in Physical Therapy Education (2016) is the only accreditation agency that accredits the qualified programs of physical therapists and physical therapist assistants at the beginners' level. It was officially recognized by the USDE and the CHEA as a specialized and independent agency in 1977.

Council on Social Work Education: The Council on Social Work Education is a nonprofit accreditation agency with 730 members and accredited master's and baccalaureate programs in and educators and practitioners of professional social work. It was established in 1952 and was recognized as the only accrediting agency for social work education in this country by the CHEA (Council on Social Work Education, n.d.-a). The Council on Social Work Education's commission ensures the accreditation standards enable the improvement of social work programs. Its Office of Social Work Accreditation uses a multistep accreditation process including its reviews and site visits and self-studies (Council on Social Work Education, n.d.-b).

Joint Review Committee on Education in Radiologic Technology: The Joint Review Committee on Education in Radiologic Technology (n.d.) is the only accreditation agency for educational programs for radiography, radiation therapy, magnetic resonance, and medical dosimetry for both traditional and distance learners. It is recognized by the USDE and the CHEA. It supports safe patient care and excellent education.

National Association of Schools of Music: The National Association of Schools of Music (n.d.-b) is an accreditation organization with approximately 650 accredited institutional members, such as schools, universities, and conservatories. It was founded in 1924 and establishes national degree and credential standards. The comprehensive review process of the accreditation has five steps (National Association of Schools of Music, n.d.-a).

5.5 ACCREDITATION AGENCIES IN DIFFERENT COUNTRIES

One accreditor from the following countries is described to show their similarities to U.S. higher education accreditors: Canada, India, China, the United Kingdom, Germany, Australia, New Zealand, South Africa, and Kenya.

5.5.1 CANADA

The Association of Accrediting Agencies of Canada was established as an organization of accrediting agencies for professional education nationwide in 1994. This association has a collaborative forum to review the institutions of higher education and assess the quality of education programs. The Association promotes the importance of accreditation in improving education quality and promotes advancement in the knowledge and practices of accreditors (Association of Accrediting Agencies of Canada, 2010).

5.5.2 INDIA

The University Grants Commission is the accreditation organization set up by the Ministry of Human Resource Development under the union government of India and is headquartered in New Delhi, according to the University Grants Commission Act of 1956 (University Grants Commission, 2002). The primary objectives of this statutory body are to design and maintain the standards of higher education, promote education, and supervise university education developments (University Grants Commission, 2015).

5.5.3 CHINA

The China National Accreditation Service for Conformity Assessment is a national accreditation agency of China. It accredits organizations such as certification bodies, laboratories, and inspection bodies. It is approved by the Certification and Accreditation Administration of the People's Republic of China. Its members are from 65 organizations representing conformity assessment bodies, clients and users of conformity assessment, technical experts, and government employees (China National Accreditation Service for Conformity Assessment, 2016).

5.5.4 UNITED KINGDOM

The British Accreditation Council is an independent accreditation agency established in 1984 for the improvement of higher education. It provides a thorough quality assurance system. The Council is identified as the clearest private-sector sign of educational quality by students, government officials, and agents. The British Accreditation Council (2017) is not only committed to encouraging the best standards of education given by independent colleges but also committed to nurturing colleges to raise and maintain their standards.

5.5.5 GERMANY

The Accreditation Agency in Health and Social Sciences was established to pursue an increase in quality of higher education teaching and learning. Through the approval of accreditation procedures, its goal is transparency and equity in institutions and study programs, nationally and internationally. The Agency accredits study programs and establishments in varied instructional fields, along with a specific concentration on health and social sciences. "Its work focuses on guaranteeing uniform, internationally-competitive standards for a wide range of degrees by supporting quality assurance and development" (European Consortium for Accreditation, 2014, para. 1).

5.5.6 AUSTRALIA

"In Australia, professional certification of entry to practice engineering programs is the responsibility of Engineers Australia" and is generally carried out on a 5-year cycle (Engineers Australia, n.d., para. 1). Accreditation makes sure educational establishments regularly meet benchmarks. This organization is also a professional organization for engineers.

5.5.7 NEW ZEALAND

The New Zealand Qualifications Authority (n.d.) is the premier accreditation body for secondary and nonuniversity education institutions. This organization gives assurance of program relevance and quality to its customers and clients and acts as a liaison for foreign certifying bodies to ensure New Zealand qualifications are recognized worldwide.

5.5.8 SOUTH AFRICA

The South African National Accreditation System (2015) is the only national accreditor that assesses conformity with the Conformity Assessment, Calibration and Good Laboratory Practice Act of 2006. The System communicates the conformity competence of laboratories, publishers, inspection bodies, and certification bodies.

5.5.9 KENYA

Kenya Accreditation Service (2016) confirms conformity assessment bodies' competence. Those bodies evaluate products, suppliers, and services for compliance with specifications. This accreditor focuses on medical laboratories and business certifications.

5.6 CONCLUSION

Accrediting organizations are reviewed to make sure that they have processes and outcomes in place to protect students and the public. An accrediting organization that has been reviewed and determined to meet the standards of an external body, such as the USDE or CHEA, is considered a recognized organization (Eaton, 2012). Accrediting organizations require institutions and programs to set standards for student learning outcomes and provide evidence that the learning outcomes are achieved. The expected outcomes and the evidence vary, depending on the level of education provided and the different skills or competencies required of graduates in different fields. All accredited institutions and programs must provide resources to assist students toward successful completion of their courses of study. Although similar resources may be available in institutions or programs that are not accredited, accreditation provides external assurance that those resources are in place. All accrediting organizations provide information to the public about the institutions and programs they accredit, about when they are reviewed, and about the general results of the most recent accreditation review.

5.7 REFERENCES

Accreditation Board for Engineering and Technology. (n.d.). *History*. Retrieved from http://www.abet.org/about-abet/history/

Accrediting Council for Continuing Education and Training. (n.d.). *Mission, scope, overview*. Retrieved from https://accet.org/about-us/mission-scope-overview

Accrediting Council for Independent Colleges and Schools. (2010). *Accrediting Council for Independent Colleges and Schools*. Retrieved from http://www.acics.org/

Association for the Accreditation of Human Research Protection Programs. (2012). *Our mission, vision, and values*. Retrieved from http://www.aahrpp.org/learn/about-aahrpp/our-mission

Association of Accrediting Agencies of Canada. (2010). *Association of Accrediting Agencies of Canada*. Retrieved from http://aaac.ca/english/index.php

Association to Advance Collegiate Schools of Business International. (n.d.). *About us*. Retrieved from http://www.aacsb.edu/about

British Accreditation Council. (2017). *The British Accreditation Council*. Retrieved from http://www.the-bac.org/about/

China National Accreditation Service for Conformity Assessment. (2016). *CNAS introduction*. Retrieved from https://www.cnas.org.cn/english/introduction/12/718683.shtml

Commission on Accreditation in Physical Therapy Education. (2016). *What we do*. Retrieved from https://www.capteonline.org/WhatWeDo/

Commission on Collegiate Nursing Education. (n.d.) *CCNE accreditation*. Retrieved from http://www.aacn.nche.edu/ccne-accreditation

Council for Higher Education Accreditation. (2010). *The value of accreditation*. Retrieved from http://archive.org/details/ERIC_ED514889

Council on Occupational Education. (n.d.). *History, mission, core values*. Retrieved from http://www.council.org/history-mission-core-values/

Council on Social Work Education. (n.d.-a). *About CSWE*. Retrieved from http://www.cswe.org/About-CSWE.aspx

Council on Social Work Education. (n.d.-b). *About CSWE accreditation*. Retrieved from http://www.cswe.org/Accreditation

Eaton, J. S. (2011). *An overview of U.S. Accreditation*. Washington DC: Council for Higher Education Accreditation.

Engineers Australia. (n.d.). *Program accreditation overview*. Retrieved from https://www.engineersaustralia.org.au/About-Us/Accreditation/Accreditation-Overview

European Consortium for Accreditation. (2014). *AHPGS - Accreditation Agency in Health and Social Sciences*. Retrieved from http://ecahe.eu/w/index.php/AHPGS_-_Accreditation_Agency_in_Health_and_Social_Sciences

Higher Learning Commission. (2003). *Handbook of accreditation* (3rd ed.). Chicago, IL: Author.

Joint Review Committee on Education in Radiologic Technology. (n.d.). *Joint Review Committee on Education in Radiologic Technology*. Retrieved from http://www.jtcert.org

Kenya Accreditation Service. (2016). *What is accreditation*. Retrieved from http://kenas.go.ke/what-is-accreditation-3/

Michigan State University Human Research Protection Program. (n.d.). *About the Human Research Protection Program*. Retrieved from https://hrpp.msu.edu/about

Middle States Commission on Higher Education. (2017). *Dedicated to educational excellence & improvement since 1919*. Retrieved from http://www.msche.org/

National Association of Schools of Music. (n.d.-a). *Comprehensive review process*. Retrieved from https://nasm.arts-accredit.org/accreditation/comprehensive-review-process/

National Association of Schools of Music. (n.d.-b). *Welcome to NASM*. Retrieved from https://nasm.arts-accredit.org/

New England Association of Schools and Colleges. (n.d.). *Improving education through accreditation*. Retrieved from https://www.neasc.org/

New Zealand Qualifications Authority. (n.d.). *What we do*. Retrieved from http://www.nzqa.govt.nz/about-us/our-role/what-we-do/

Northwest Commission on Colleges and Universities. (n.d.). *Northwest Commission on Colleges and Universities*. Retrieved from http://www.nwccu.org/index.htm

South African National Accreditation System. (2015). *South African National Accreditation System*. Retrieved from http://home.sanas.co.za/

Southern Association of Colleges and Schools and Commission on Colleges. (n.d.). *Southern Association of Colleges and Schools and Commission on Colleges*. Retrieved from http://www.sacscoc.org/index.asp

U.S. Department of Education. (2017). *Accreditation in the United States*. Retrieved from https://www2.ed.gov/print/admins/finaid/accred/accreditation.html#Overview

University Grants Commission. (2002). *The University Grants Commission Act, 1956 (as modified up to the 20th December, 1985) and rules & regulations under the act*. New Delhi, India: Secretary, University Grants Commission.

University Grants Commission. (2015). *Mandate*. Retrieved from http://www.ugc.ac.in/page/Mandate.aspx

Western Association of Schools and Colleges. (2016). *ACS WASC overview*. Retrieved from http://www.acswasc.org/wasc/acs-wasc-overview/

CHAPTER 6:

Metacognition

CHAPTER OBJECTIVE

This chapter defines metacognition and the components of metacognition. It also expands upon metacognitive learning strategies and describes the relationship between metacognition and student learning.

6.1 INTRODUCTION

A student can become a better learner by developing learning strategies and using them in the appropriate context. Metacognition skills include planning, selecting learning strategies, monitoring progress of learning, and changing strategies as needed to achieve desired objectives. Metacognition is an important concept that students can use to become better learners, which increases the quality of their education.

6.2 METACOGNITION DEFINITION

John Flavell (1979, p. 906, as cited in Lai, 2011) created the term *metacognition*, meaning "cognition about cognitive phenomena" or "thinking about thinking." Metacognition's two parts are knowledge and regulation. Lai (2011) explains, "Metacognitive knowledge includes knowledge about oneself as a learner and the factors that might impact performance, knowledge about strategies, and knowledge about when and why to use strategies" (p. 2). Metacognitive regulation is essentially monitoring cognition and comprises planning and mindfulness of understanding and performance, including of the monitoring process itself (Ku & Ho, 2010).

Flavell (1979, as cited in Lai, 2011) "defines cognitive knowledge as knowledge about one's own cognitive strengths and limitations, including the factors (both internal and external) that may interact to affect cognition" (p. 5). He (as cited in Lai, 2011) made three divisions of this knowledge:
- Person knowledge, anything believed about the qualities of humans as cognitive processors
- Task knowledge, the requirements of tasks
- Strategy knowledge, sorts of strategies that ought to benefit most

6.3 COMPONENTS OF METACOGNITION

Metacognition connects to other cognitive psychology concepts (Lai, 2011), so understanding the following four concepts and their components is useful in understanding metacognition.

6.3.1 METAMEMORY

Lai (2011) writes, "Metamemory is closely related to metacognition, particularly cognitive knowledge" (p. 10). Metamemory means awareness and knowledge of planned behaviors and memory frameworks. "This type of knowledge includes, but is not limited to, awareness of different memory strategies, knowledge of which strategy to use for particular memory tasks, and knowledge of how to use given strategies" (Osman & Hannafin, 1992, p. 84). Teaching of metamemory methods should emphasize person variables, along with task and strategy variables. Other individual factors include perceptions of ongoing comprehension. "A learner's feeling (or illusion) of knowing, as well as judgment of recall readiness, often influences en route metacognitive decisions" (Osman & Hannafin, 1992, p. 85).

Successful learning maintenance is typical for students who have superior task-related metamemory skills. "Task-related metamemory skills are maintained most successfully when accompanied by information regarding their values, range of applications, and mode of execution" (Osman & Hannafin, 1992, p. 85). In short, research findings indicate that knowledge and awareness of personal strategies and memory cues relate proportionally to successful metamemory. "Good performance is more highly related to procedural knowledge and metamemory monitoring strategies than to simple metamemory knowledge. Moreover, specific strategy knowledge generally is more effective than general strategy knowledge in directing strategy use" (Osman & Hannafin, 1992, p. 85).

6.3.2 CRITICAL THINKING

Common elements of most definitions of critical thinking include the following component skills (Lai, 2011), as shown in Figure 6.1:
- Analyzing the credibility of arguments
- Evaluating or judging
- Inferring through deductive or inductive reasoning
- Deciding or resolving issues based on reasoning

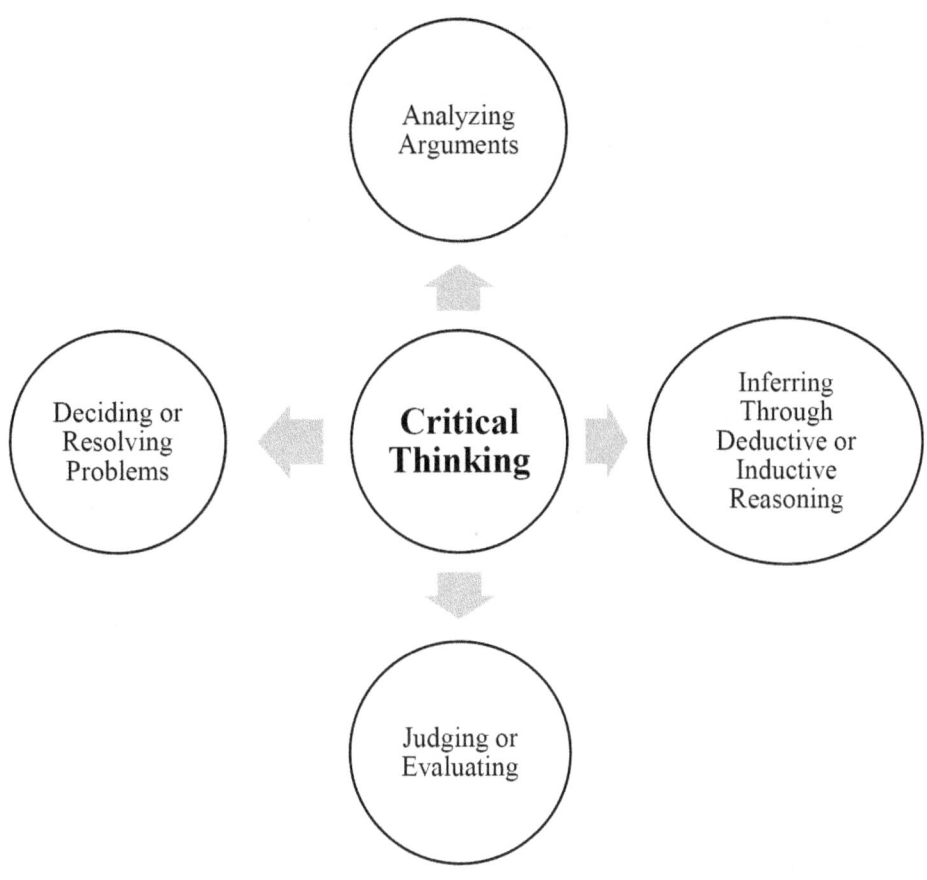

Figure 6.1: Component Skills of Critical Thinking

"Flavell (1979) and Martinez (2006) maintain that critical thinking is subsumed under metacognition" (Lai, 2011, p. 11). Hennessey (1999) lists metacognitive skills with similarities to skills typically part of definitions of critical thinking, as shown in Figure 6.2:

- Understanding causes for one's beliefs
- Ignoring personal beliefs temporarily to evaluate those of others
- Seeing the role of supporting or refuting evidence in personal understanding
- Seeing clearly the status of personal beliefs
- Assessing how generalizable and constant personal understanding is

Schraw, Crippen, and Hartley (2006) report metacognition and critical thinking, as a component of cognition, are part of self-regulated learning. Lai (2011) concludes, "At the very least, metacognition can be seen as a supporting condition for critical thinking, to the extent that monitoring the quality of one's thought makes it more likely that one will engage in high-quality (critical) thinking" (p. 12).

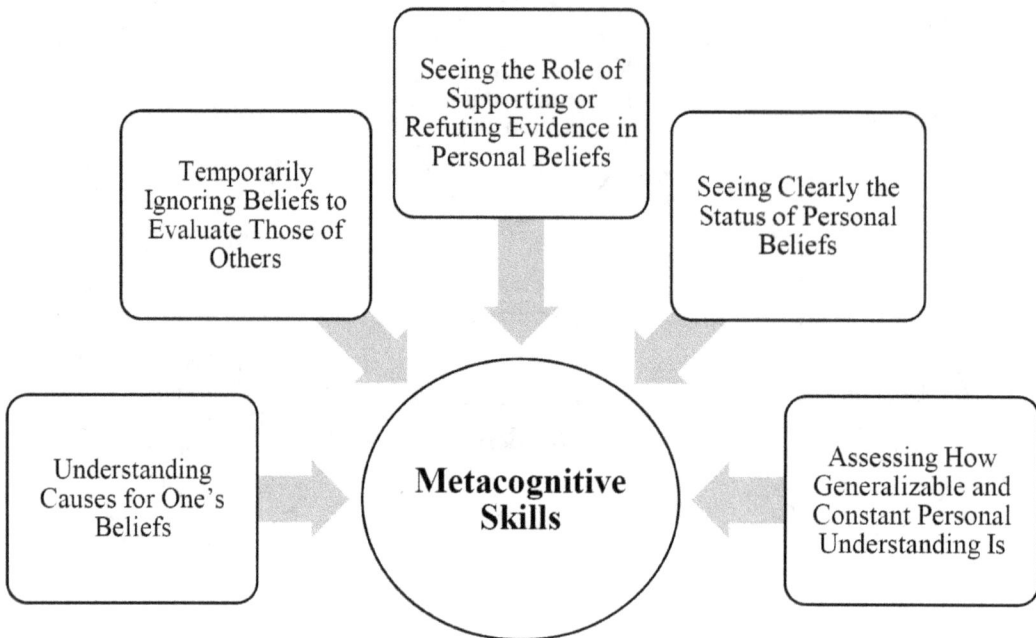

Figure 6.2: Metacognitive Skills

6.3.3 MOTIVATION

Metacognitive motivation is "beliefs and attitudes that affect the use and development of cognitive and metacognitive skills" (Schraw et al., 2006, p. 112). Motivation has two primary subcomponents, as depicted in Figure 6.3: self-efficacy and epistemological beliefs (Schraw et al., 2006). Martinez (2006) points out management of affective states is part of metacognition, and metacognitive strategies can make students more motivated to persist when facing challenges.

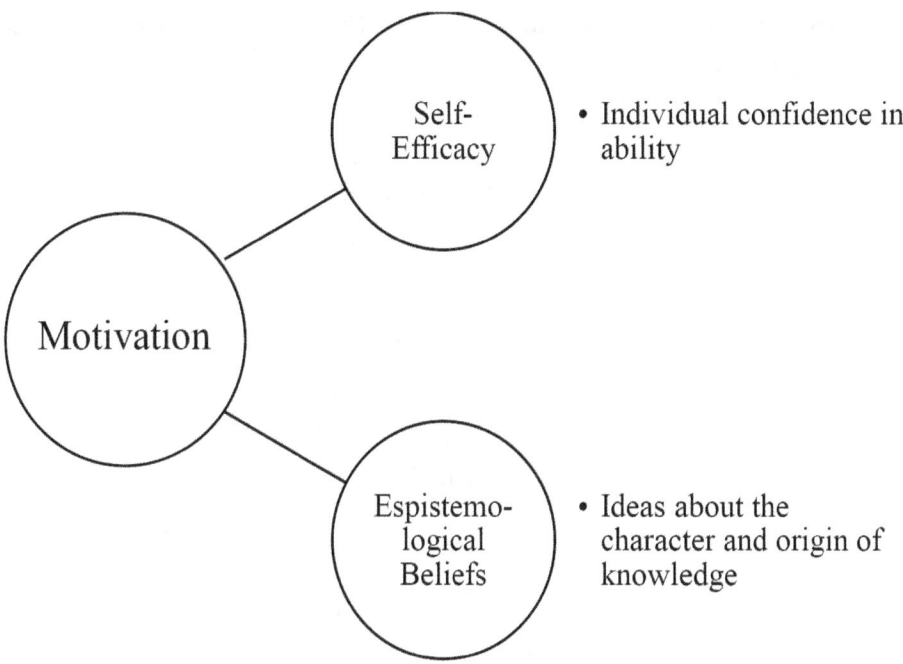

Figure 6.3: Subcomponents of Motivation

6.3.4 METACOMPREHENSION

Metacomprehension, or comprehension monitoring, consists of understanding what comprehension is and how to do it (Brown, 1975, as cited in Osman & Hannafin, 1992). "This process involves both recognizing the failure to comprehend and employing repair strategies once a failure has been recognized" (Flavell, 1981; Wagoner, 1983; as cited in Osman & Hannafin, 1992, p. 85).

6.4 METACOGNITIVE PROCESSES

Metacognition affects behavior and not only in learning environments. Here, however, the emphasis is on metacognitive processes that affect learning.

6.4.1 SELF-REGULATION

Self-regulation is the minor metacognitive refinements students make in answer to feedback or lack thereof on errors (Brown, Bransford, Ferrara, & Campione, 1983, as cited in Osman & Hannafin, 1992). There are three types of self-regulation: autonomous, active, and conscious, as shown in Figure 6.4 (Piaget, 1976, as cited in Osman & Hannafin, 1992). "Autonomous regulation refers to an inherent part of any knowing act....Active regulation is analogous to trial and error" (Osman & Hannafin, 1992, p. 88). Conscious regulation creates testable hypotheses.

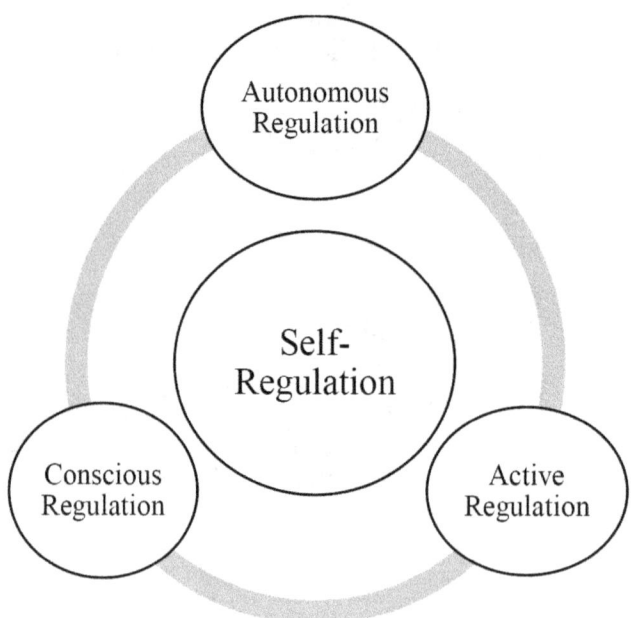

Figure 6.4: Types of Self-Regulation

Self-regulation functions, including error detection and correction, play a central role in successful learning (Osman & Hannafin, 1992, p. 88). These functions may be taught through or separately from feedback. "A complementary relationship between external and internal regulation mechanisms, whereby the learners acquire and use metacomprehension strategies," may give the best mix of alternatives (Osman & Hannafin, 1992, p. 89).

6.4.2 SCHEMA TRAINING

Schema training has at its foundation a belief that students learn new material by incorporating it into an existing cognitive category. The incorporation enables them to give characteristics to and make inferences about the new material. The assignment and inferences will be accurate only if students have accurate cognitive frameworks that can accommodate challenging material, such as heat transfer and diffusion. Instructors and students can use accurate assessment instruments to correct inaccurate cognitive frameworks. Schema training assists in applying new information (Miller, Streveler, Yang, & Santiago Roman, 2009).

6.4.3 MONITORING AND CONTROL

Monitoring and control are two metacognitive processes. Metacognitive monitoring includes processes that enable individual reflection on or observation of personal cognitive processes. Metacognitive control includes the decisions, conscious and unconscious, made depending on metacognitive monitoring processes. "Control processes are revealed by the behaviors a person engages in as a function of monitoring....The idea of control processes is key to the development of applied metacognition" (Schwartz & Perfect, 2002, pp. 4–5).

6.4.4 TRANSFER

Students must be able to transfer their learning to contexts besides the classroom. Halpern (1998) created a four-part model to improve learning transfer, especially transfer of critical thinking. First, students must be prepared for the mental exertion critical thinking requires and know which contexts require the effort of using critical thinking. Second, students must know the five categories of critical thinking: verbal reasoning, argumentative analysis, determining likelihood, thinking as testing theories, and solving problems and making choices (Halpern, 1998). Third, the structure of issues and concepts must be made useful so that students remember them, for example by frequently using real-world materials (Derry, Levin, & Schauble, 1995, as cited in Halpern, 1998). Finally, instructors should elicit metacomprehension by asking guiding questions and giving feedback during class time (Halpern, 1998).

6.5 STUDY SKILLS AND METACOGNITIVE LEARNING STRATEGIES

Metacognition strategies help students become better learners. Among various strategies, the following were found to be effective and useful to students. Teachers can also teach these strategies to their students so that appropriate strategies can be used based on the content and context of the learning environment.

    a) Organize/Plan

        i. Set specific, measurable, attainable, realistic, and timely (SMART) goals.

        ii. Develop a plan to perform the activities needed to accomplish the goals.

    b) Manage Learning

        i. Determine how you learn most effectively.

        ii. Create environments that help you learn.

        iii. Focus attention on topics to be learned and practice learning topics.

    c) Monitor Progress

        i. Check your understanding of the subject.

        ii. Check your progress on your level of understanding and comprehension of the material.

iii. Continue your study until you achieve a higher level of understanding of the subject.

d) Evaluate

i. Self-assess your level of accomplishment of your learning goals.

ii. Assess how effective the learning strategies were in accomplishing your goals.

e) Use Prior Knowledge

i. Explore what you already know that is related to the subject or topic.

ii. Relate your prior knowledge to the new topic by its relevance and making associations.

f) Make Inferences

i. Develop strategies to infer from the materials to enrich learning.

ii. Understand the underlying meaning by reading between the lines.

g) Make Predictions

i. Predict new information that may appear.

ii. Make assumptions about what may happen.

h) Apply Knowledge

i. Apply what you have learned to new situations.

i) Organize Knowledge

i. Develop metaphors or create an image to understand or represent information.

ii. Develop mental rules and patterns to remember the material learned.

j) Take Notes

i. Write down important information.

ii. Highlight information in the book.

iii. Paraphrase information in your own words in writing that helps you understand the subject.

k) Use Graphic Organizers

    i. Develop a visual representation of the subject or topic using concept maps, flowcharts, Venn diagrams, charts, and so on.

    ii. Understand the relationship between multiple concepts and topics in graphic form.

l) Summarize

    i. Summarize what you have learned in mental, oral, and written forms using keywords.

    ii. Rank your level of understanding of different topics as low, medium, or high.

    iii. Identify topics on which you have a low level of understanding.

m) Improve

    i. Focus on topics with low levels of understanding and high levels of importance.

    ii. Repeat learning of topics until higher levels of understanding develop.

    iii. Assess level of learning and continue the process when learning the next topics.

6.6 METACOGNITION AND ENGINEERING DESIGN

Engineering design problems are complex, requiring much self-regulation and commitment, which makes metacognition an asset for engineers and engineering students in particular. Lawanto (2009) investigated engineering students' metacognition during design tasks. A major metacognitive change occurred in mechanical engineering students and was speculated to be the result of a change in learning approach.

Because students rarely realize how complex a project will become, they may fail to prepare themselves to fill in the future knowledge gaps. It is better for teachers to allocate time early in the project to emphasize the importance of exercising metacognitive skills. Some of the self-appraisal and self-management issues may be discussed more openly at the early stage of the project to lay the foundation for the design process at later stages. The use of students' metacognition in an engineering design project is important and useful.

6.7 ASSESSMENT OF STUDENT LEARNING

A number of investigations have evaluated the effect of metacognition on student learning. However, assessing metacognition poses a challenge because (Lai, 2011):

- Metacognition includes various sorts of knowledge and skills, making it an intricate concept.
- In practice, metacognition can be difficult to distinguish from memory capacity and verbal skills.
- Direct observation of metacognition is impossible.
- Current metacognitive assessments are usually administered outside of school and focused too narrowly.

Methods using teacher observation of student learning in natural settings may be more valid because they (Whitebread et al., 2009):

- Do not rely on memory, which can be inaccurate
- Include indicative nonverbal communication
- Include insightful social processes

Metacognitive processes are internal and thus difficult to evaluate, but there are a few evaluation instruments. The Executive Process Questionnaire and Behavior Rating Inventory of Executive Function assess executive control and metacognitive behaviors, and the Metacognitive Awareness Inventory assesses both components of metacognition and their subprocesses (Mytkowicz, Goss, & Steinberg, 2014). These authors also examined students' grade point averages to determine that a learning strategies course improved their metacognition. Having students create electronic portfolios can promote metacognition, too (Mytkowicz et al., 2014).

Young and Fry (2008) write, "Schraw and Dennison (1994) developed the Metacognitive Awareness Inventory (MAI) to assess metacognitive knowledge and metacognitive regulation" (p. 3). By measuring metacognition through multiple performance assessments, evidence supporting a link between metacognition and high grades is generated. Therefore, comprehensive metacognitive assessments are necessary. Young and Fry (2008) found that the correlation between the Metacognitive Awareness Inventory and academic achievement scores was strong.

6.8 SUMMARY OF METACOGNITION

Lai (2011) writes, "Metacognition is a complex construct, involving cognitive knowledge and cognitive regulation. Moreover, there are multiple types of cognitive knowledge (declarative, procedural, conditional) as well as different types of cognitive regulation (planning, monitoring or regulating, and evaluating)" (p. 27). Affect and motivation are also part of metacognition. Although this construct is useful in creating learning strategies, assessing its results on learning remains a challenge. Details are shown in Figure 6.5 (Lai, 2011).

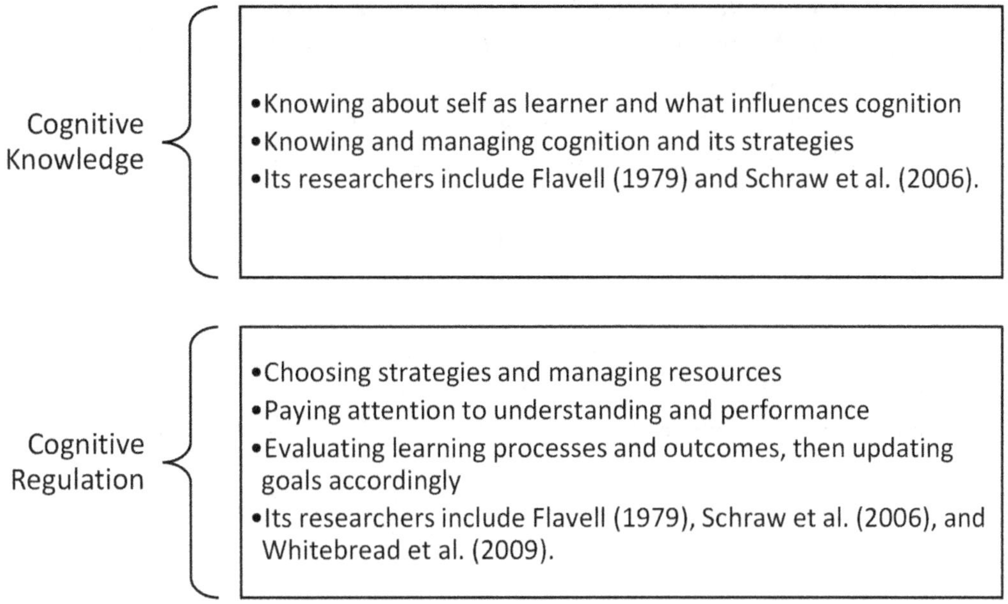

Cognitive Knowledge
- Knowing about self as learner and what influences cognition
- Knowing and managing cognition and its strategies
- Its researchers include Flavell (1979) and Schraw et al. (2006).

Cognitive Regulation
- Choosing strategies and managing resources
- Paying attention to understanding and performance
- Evaluating learning processes and outcomes, then updating goals accordingly
- Its researchers include Flavell (1979), Schraw et al. (2006), and Whitebread et al. (2009).

Figure 6.5: Metacognitive Components Summary

6.9 REFERENCES

Halpern, D. F. (1998). Teaching critical thinking for transfer across domains: Dispositions, skills, structure training, and metacognitive monitoring. *American Psychologist, 53*(4), 449–455.

Hennessey, M. G. (1999). *Probing the dimensions of metacognition: Implications for conceptual change teaching-learning.* Paper presented at the annual meeting of the National Association for Research in Science Teaching, Boston, MA.

Ku, K. Y. L., & Ho, I. T. (2010). Metacognitive strategies that enhance critical thinking. *Metacognition Learning, 5*(3), 251–267.

Lai, E. R. (2011). *Metacognition: A literature review.* Boston, MA: Pearson.

Lawanto, O. (2009). Students' metacognition during an engineering design project. *Performance Improvement Quarterly, 23*(2), 117–136.

Martinez, M. E. (2006). What is metacognition? *Phi Delta Kappan, 87*(9), 696–699.

Miller, R. L., Streveler, R. A., Yang, D., & Santiago Roman, A. Y. (2009). *Identifying and repairing students' misconceptions in thermal and transport science.* Proceedings of American Institute of Chemical Engineers annual conference, Nashville, TN.

Mytkowicz, P., Goss, D., & Steinberg, B. (2014). Assessing metacognition as a learning outcome in a postsecondary strategic learning course. *Journal of Postsecondary Education and Disability, 27*(1), 51–62.

Osman, M. E., & Hannafin, M. J. (1992). Metacognition research and theory: Analysis and implications for instructional design. *Educational Technology Research & Development, 40*(2), 83–99.

Schraw, G., Crippen, K. J., & Hartley, K. (2006). Promoting self-regulation in science education: Metacognition as part of a broader perspective on learning. *Research in Science Education, 36*(1–2), 111–139.

Schwartz, B. L., & Perfect, T. J. (2002). Toward an applied metacognition. In T. J. Perfect & B. L. Schwartz (Eds.), *Applied metacognition* (pp. 2–11). Cambridge, United Kingdom: Cambridge University Press.

Whitebread, D., Coltman, P., Pasternak, D. P., Sangster, C., Grau, V., Bingham, S., ... Demetriou, D. (2009). The development of two observational tools for assessing metacognition and self-regulated learning in young children. *Metacognition Learning, 4*(1), 63–85.

Young, A., & Fry, J. D. (2012). Metacognitive awareness and academic achievement in college students. *Journal of the Scholarship of Teaching and Learning, 8*(2), 1–10.

CHAPTER 7:

Motivation in Higher Education

CHAPTER OBJECTIVE

The objective of this chapter is to provide a brief overview of student motivation in higher education. It describes why motivational learning is important to students. It also provides adequate details of some relevant motivational theories that are currently in practice. This chapter also determines how different theories could improve student motivation.

7.1 INTRODUCTION

Motivation for conceptual change determines how the student will approach the task of learning a subject. One of the critical challenges of higher education is to develop students' skills with the extensive technical expertise needed to lead innovation. This challenge demands a robust understanding of how students learn in order to create environments that best support technical mastery through deep conceptual understanding of core concepts. During the transition to higher education, most students experience social displacement because they are entering a new environment including social contexts with new peers, lecturers, and staff. The change that occurs through introducing new learning and teaching methods while being in a new environment prompts students to create a new identity in terms of learning and self-sufficiency. Students' motivation for learning plays a key role in the quality of learning in higher education and different educational outcomes within the different educational levels. However, students' motivation is not a stable characteristic, because it can vary across various contexts. Changes in students' motivation can occur due to the context of higher education, which provides challenges and opportunities according to conceptual characteristics. The increasing flexibility within higher education allows students to shape their own educational program in addition to choosing their own area of study. This flexibility will result in better motivation.

7.2 THE CHALLENGE AND IMPORTANCE OF MOTIVATION

The most difficult challenge for many instructors is to motivate students. Even though students are enthusiastic to learn, sometimes they expect the instructors to inspire and stimulate them to improve their learning. Motivation is an essential factor to become a better learner. Students must see a purpose and value to develop motivation for their academic success.

A goal of any effective instructor is to make the students interested in learning the topics. Student motivation plays a vital role in the development of metacognitive skills, as well as vital problem-solving skills. The perceptions that students hold about their future linked to motivational attributes, such as expectations and values, will help them face the rapid changes in technology and globalization that will take place in the near future. Self-directed learning is enhanced by primary factors that include motivation to learn and metacognitive strategies. Self-directed learning can be defined as the process that initiates and monitors students' learning and enables them to evaluate themselves on their own in terms of the effectiveness of their learning strategies and motivation (Loyens, Magda, & Rikers, 2008).

Motivational learning is the key factor to improving students' tendency to understand the importance of learning activities. Motivation is also a key factor in academic performance because it stresses the idea of active learning (Loyens et al., 2008). It is particularly necessary to encourage student motivation because of the difficulty of the higher education curriculum, which can affect the success of a student negatively. Besides technical competencies, it is important for students to develop motivational frameworks to evaluate and enhance their motivation. These frameworks also allow the educators and academic institutions to enhance the motivation of their students.

7.3 WHAT IS MOTIVATION?

Motivation includes affect, attitude, and interest as a need to prevail that urges or drives a person to action. Affect and attitude describe a student's emotions and thoughts about a fact or state, and interest describes special attention paid to something. Generally, motivation is influenced by both intrinsic and extrinsic factors. Intrinsic factors refer to an individual's desire to feel satisfaction that motivates him or her. Extrinsic factors refer to external forces that motivate an individual to accomplish a task (Deci & Ryan, 1985, as cited in Guay, Vallerand, & Blanchard, 2000). With respect to motivation, students who have learning goals and higher self-efficacy have enhanced motivation (Issacson & Fujita, 2006). Self-efficacy means one's belief that he or she can do a given task. Correll (2004) showed this construct is a predictor of career aspirations.

7.4 THEORIES OF MOTIVATION FOR HIGHER EDUCATION

To evaluate students' motivation in higher education and the relationship of motivation with quality of education, many scholars have proposed different theories of motivation. Some of the motivation theories are explained briefly here to help analyze the quality of higher education in terms of motivation.

7.4.1 EXPECTANCY THEORY

This is one of the major process theories of motivation, published by Victor Vroom in 1964. This theory suggests that an individual's success can be affected by expectations about the outcome of a task. Betz (2010) explains, "Therefore, this theory is based on cognition and thought processes. It is part of a broad set of cognitive process theories on motivation" (p. 15.888.3). Process theories use deliberate decision-making to explain motivation. In particular, expectancy theory emphasizes how people select certain behaviors and how they decide whether these behaviors fulfill their requirements. Learning outcomes and performance are additional areas of focus (Betz, 2010).

This theory suggests that the amount of motivation a student will have for and effort a student will put into learning depends on three perceptual relationships, as shown in Figure 7.1. Expectancy is a student's estimated chance of success on a particular assignment. Faculty can influence this by knowing and providing what information students require to succeed (Betz, 2010). Instrumentality is a student's estimated chance that his or her work will lead to positive results. Faculty ought to reward all student effort to improve instrumentality (Betz, 2010). Valence is the value each outcome holds for students. Faculty should find out what outcomes feel rewarding to students and make those outcomes a reality (Betz, 2010). The combination of all three influences motivation. Therefore, faculty should have thorough understanding of students with respect to the three, possibly through advance surveys to define the factors. All three need to be high to cause high student motivation, and if one is missing, the student will lack motivation. "Thus, the faculty should attempt to ensure that their students believe that increased effort will improve performance and that performance will lead to valued rewards" (Betz, 2010, p. 15.888.3). In education, the theory explains grade motivation and college student retention.

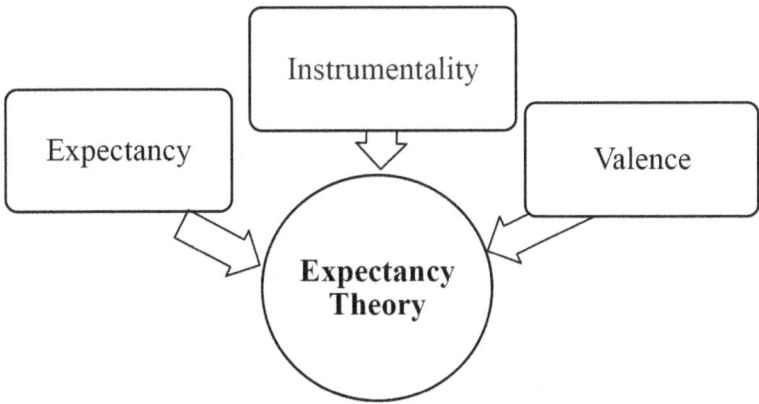

Figure 7.1: Expectancy Theory

As part of a large group of process theories, expectancy theory forces learners to determine their perception of how useful their efforts are in attaining positive outcomes. A student survey can determine these perceptions. Expectancy theory can be both practical and theoretical. Expectancy theory is supposed to be a practical teaching tool to boost student effort and learning (Betz, 2010). Vroom's expectancy theory on motivation can be applied to a group of students to discover what motivates better academic performance. Using the theory's concepts, it is possible to discern the relevant ways for faculty to motivate students beyond their existing self-motivation to learn and perform (Betz, 2010).

Vroom's theory has become well known and has shed light on organizational behavior, leadership, training motivation, and goal setting. However, it is not always practical. Betz's (2010) study found that expectancy theory was an ineffective motivational model for architectural engineering technology students because they were already motivated and the theory was too complicated. Another criticism is that taking time to figure out what motivates students may take away from time spent addressing learning outcomes.

7.4.2 SELF-DETERMINATION THEORY

Motivation can enhance learning, making it significant to educators (Pintrich, 2003, as cited in Nitrou & Economides, 2014). Self-determination theory describes motivation as a multidimensional concept, where different categories of motivation can be placed on a scale in terms of more or less self-determination. Per the theory, to begin behavior, basic psychological needs, such as autonomy (independence), competence (capability), and relatedness (understanding), must be satisfied (Guay et al., 2010). According to the theory, when people are engaged in an activity, there exist four types of motivation, as shown in Figure 7.2 (Guay et al., 2010). Intrinsic motivation is acting because of the task's pleasure. Identified regulation is doing an activity one chooses. External regulation is acting in response to external demands. Finally, amotivation is a disconnect between behavior and result (Guay et al., 2010).

Figure 7.2: Self-Determination Theory

This theory refers to self-determined types of motivation, such as intrinsic motivation and identified regulation, which lead to greater satisfaction and better performance by students in higher education. The Situational Motivational Scale is a self-reported scale Guay et al. (2010) developed to measure the four types of motivation: intrinsic motivation, identified regulation, external regulation, and amotivation.

This theory helps examine the nature of students' motivation during the Hour of Code activities. Using a 7-point Likert scale during the Hour of Code activity, in which high school and first-year college students spent 1 hour writing computer code, Nikou and Economides (2014) asked students perform a self-report on their motivation with respect to the four factors mentioned. Intrinsic motivation and identified regulation were high in both high school and college students, although amotivation and external motivation were also present. This theory shows that designing educational activities to improve intrinsic motivation is helpful for better learning outcomes. The Hour of Code activity "is a good example and may provide inspiring directions in designing" large-scale motivating teaching methods (Nikou & Economides, 2014, p. 744).

7.4.3 EXPECTANCY-VALUE THEORY

This theory interacts with student persistence and achievement. Expectancy-value theory focuses on social and psychological reasons for choices (Wigfield & Eccles, 1992, as cited in Jones, Paretti, Hein, & Knott, 2010). This model suggests that academic motivation is affected by perceived competence beliefs, as well as beliefs about the worth, utility, and intrigue of the task. The model predicts that student motivation to study engineering is influenced by both students' expectancy of success and their belief in the utility of the field. Researchers of this model have suggested that all the constructs regarding expectancy and value are significantly and distinctly correlated. The importance of both the expectancy-related perspectives and the value-related perspectives in academic motivation and decision-making is extremely evident.

Expectancy-value theory suggests that in fields related to math and physical sciences (e.g., engineering), women are unlikely to enter and persist because they lack confidence in their abilities in these fields and place less value on these fields in comparison with other fields. An analysis based on expectancy-value theory found the expectancy to be different for male and female engineering students: Male students reported higher expectancies for success, though their grade point averages were statistically similar to female students' grade point averages (Jones et al., 2010).

7.4.4 ATTRIBUTION THEORY

"Attribution theory emphasizes that a person's motivation increases or decreases proportionally to his or her expectation of achieving a goal" (Weiner, 2004, as cited in Torres-Ayala & Herman, 2012, Attribution Theory). According to this theory, current and future motivation is influenced by one's beliefs about why things happen. Three dimensions make up these causes, as shown in Figure 7.3: locus of control, stability, and controllability (Torres-Ayala & Herman, 2012):

- **Locus of control:** People think that failure or success results from internal or environmental factors. Previous research suggests this dimension can pose a problem for engineering students in that female students tend to incorrectly believe luck causes success whereas male students tend to believe their abilities cause success (Berndt, Berndt, & Kaiser, 1982; Boggiano & Barrett, 1991; Felder, Felder, Mauney, Hamrin, & Dietz, 1995; as cited in Torres-Ayala & Herman, 2012).
- **Stability:** People think that failure or success results from stable or changing factors. Thinking that success is more likely with more effort may be motivational, for instance. Unstable factors can also boost motivation when change is possible and helpful.

- **Controllability:** People think that failure or success results from controllable or uncontrollable causes. Thinking that one will fail a class because the instructor dislikes him or her is demotivating, for instance.

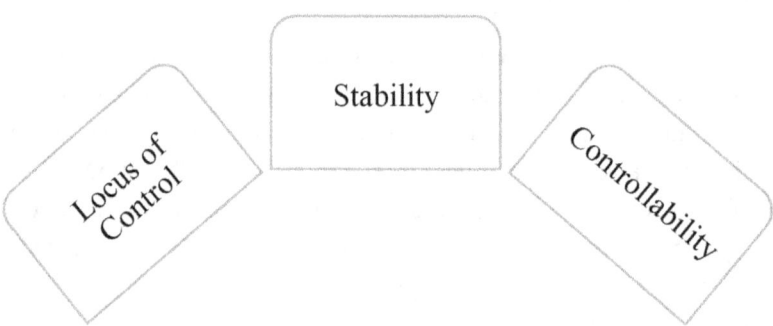

Figure 7.3: Causes of Success and Failure Characterized by Three Dimensions

"Students commonly attribute success or failure to luck, task difficulty, ability, or effort" (Weiner, 2004, as cited in Torres-Ayala & Herman, Attribution Theory). Here is how to understand those four in the context of attribution theory (Torres-Ayala & Herman, 2012):

- Luck is an environmental, changing, and uncontrollable cause. Because this seems out of students' control, students who blame bad luck for failure usually will not attempt to improve.
- Task difficulty is also environmental and uncontrollable but is stable. Students who blame failure on the assignment being too challenging could feel unable to succeed.
- Ability usually is an internal, unchanging, and uncontrollable cause. Therefore, students blaming failure on poor ability may believe increased effort cannot change future results.
- Effort is also internal but is an unstable and controllable cause. Students can adjust their effort to perform better if they think their failure results from poor effort.

Dweck (2006, as cited in Torres-Ayala & Henson, 2012) expanded upon the third cause by explaining two mind-sets about it: fixed and growth mind-set. Learners with the former think that one's intelligence level is predetermined, but learners with the latter think that one's intelligence level can increase. Previous research suggests that teachers and students with a growth mind-set do better, even in the face of challenges (Dweck, 2010, as cited in Torres-Ayala & Henson, 2012). This mind-set makes ability controllable, similar to effort, which boosts motivation. Therefore, teachers can make students more motivated by developing growth mind-sets and positive perceptions of ability and task difficulty, and students' success is more common when they believe their effort leads to success (Torres-Ayala & Henson, 2012).

7.4.5 GOAL THEORY

Goal theory explains "why students engage in their academic tasks by describing the types of goals that students set and how they pursue those goals" (Torres-Ayala & Henson, 2012, Goal Theory). As shown in Figure 7.4, "orientation (mastery versus performance) and state (approach versus avoidance)" characterize goals (Pintrich, 2000, as cited in Torres-Ayala & Henson, 2012, Goal Theory). Mastery orientation goals make people focus on mastering the steps in performing tasks. Performance orientation goals make people compare their performance ability to others' (Pintrich, 2000, as cited in Torres-Ayala & Henson, 2012). Mastery orientation goals promote more in-depth learning than performance goals do (Ambrose, Bridges, DiPietro, Lovett, & Norman, 2010, as cited in Torres-Ayala & Henson, 2012).

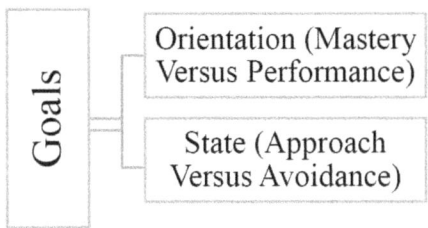

Figure 7.4: Goals' Attributes

It is also important to understand with what state students will work toward goals (Elliot & Covington, 2001, as cited in Torres-Ayala & Henson, 2012). The approach state directs action toward a desirable result. The avoidance state directs action to avoid an undesirable result.

Combining the two states with the two orientations results in four compounded orientations: approach-performance, approach-mastery, avoidance-performance, and avoidance-mastery (Weiner, 2004, as cited in Torres-Ayala & Henson, 2012). Approaching, not avoiding, and striving for mastery, not comparing, are best when working toward goals.

7.5 SUMMARY OF MOTIVATION THEORIES

Five leading motivation theories are attribution theory, expectancy theory, self-determination theory, expectancy-value theory, and goal theory (see Table 7.1). Each provides understanding of what holds back or improves student motivation, and some work together or overlap. Teachers ought to think about self-efficacy, autonomy, control, and goal types, among other motivation-related concepts (Torres-Ayala & Henson, 2012).

Table 7.1 Overview of the Theories

Name of the Theory	Researchers	Concepts
Expectancy theory	Vroom, 1964	Expectancy, instrumentality, and valence
Self-determination theory	Ryan and Deci, 2000; Guay et al., 2010	Intrinsic motivation, identified regulation, external regulation, and amotivation
Expectance-value theory	Wigfield and Eccles, 1992	Expectancy, value, utility, interest
Attribution theory	Weiner, 2004	Locus of control, stability, and controllability
Goal theory	Pintrich, 2000; Weiner, 2004	Orientation and state

7.6 REFERENCES

Betz, J. (2010). *Motivating students to learn more: A case study in architectural education.* Paper presented at American Society for Engineering Education Annual Conference and Exposition, Louisville, KY.

Correll, S. J. (2004). Constraints into preferences: Gender, status, and emerging career aspirations. *American Sociological Review, 69*(1), 93–113.

Guay, F., Vallerand, R. J., & Blanchard, C. (2000). On the assessment of situational intrinsic and extrinsic motivation: The Situational Motivation Scale. *Motivation and Emotion, 24*(3), 175–213.

Issacson, R. M., & Fujita, F. (2006). Metacognitive knowledge monitoring and self-regulated learning: Academic success and reflections on learning. *Journal of the Scholarship of Teaching and Learning, 6*(1), 39–55.

Jones, B. D., Paretti, M. C., Hein, S. F., & Knott, T. W. (2010). An analysis of motivation constructs with first-year engineering students: Relationships among expectancies, values, achievement, and career plans. *Journal of Engineering Education, 99*(4), 319–335.

Kermally, S. (2005). Victor Vroom (1932-). In *Gurus on people management* (pp. 51–55). London, United Kingdom: Thorogood Publishing.

Loyens, S. M. M., Magda, J., & Rikers, R. M. J. P. (2008). Self-directed learning in problem-based learning and its relationships with self-regulated learning. *Educational Psychology Review, 20*(4), 411–427.

Nikou, S. A., & Economides, A. A. (2014). *Measuring student motivation during the "Hour of Code" activities.* Paper presented at International Conference of Advanced Learning Technologies, Athens, Greece.

Torres-Ayala, A. T., & Herman, G. L. (2012). *Motivating learners: A primer for engineering teaching assistants.* Paper presented at American Society for Engineering Education Annual Conference and Exposition, San Antonio, TX.

CHAPTER 8:

Learning Styles

CHAPTER OBJECTIVE

This chapter describes different learning styles and compares different models and assessments of them. It also explains learning style preferences by students in different disciplines to show how the models can be applied to improve the quality of education.

8.1 INTRODUCTION

Learning styles describe the methods individuals prefer to use in acquiring and understanding new information and skills. "A multitude of models and instruments have been reported in literature with variable effectiveness claimed for each model. Although these models differ in some aspects, they all concur that everyone should not be taught in the same manner" (Mazumder & Karim, 2012, p. 1). Higher education administrators and professors should work with the learning style differences among the students in mind.

The following is a list of widely used learning style models:
1. Felder and Soloman's Index of Learning Styles (1997)
2. Honey and Mumford's learning styles (2004)
3. Kolb and Kolb's experiential learning theory (2013)
4. Fleming and Mills's Visual, Aural, Read/Write, and Kinesthetic (VARK) model (1992)
5. Malcolm Knowles's assumptions (updated in 2014)
6. Dunn and Dunn's learning style (1978)
7. Vermunt Inventory of Learning Styles (1992)
8. Towler Dipboye's Learning Style Orientation Inventory (2003)

8.2 THE INDEX OF LEARNING STYLES

The Index of Learning Styles is a self-scoring, web-based instrument that assesses preferences. Richard Felder and Barbara Soloman (1997, as cited in Felder & Brent, 2005) created the index to classify students as having preferences for one category or the other in each of the following four dimensions, as shown in Figure 8.1:
- Sensing or intuitive
- Visual or auditory
- Active or reflective
- Sequential or global

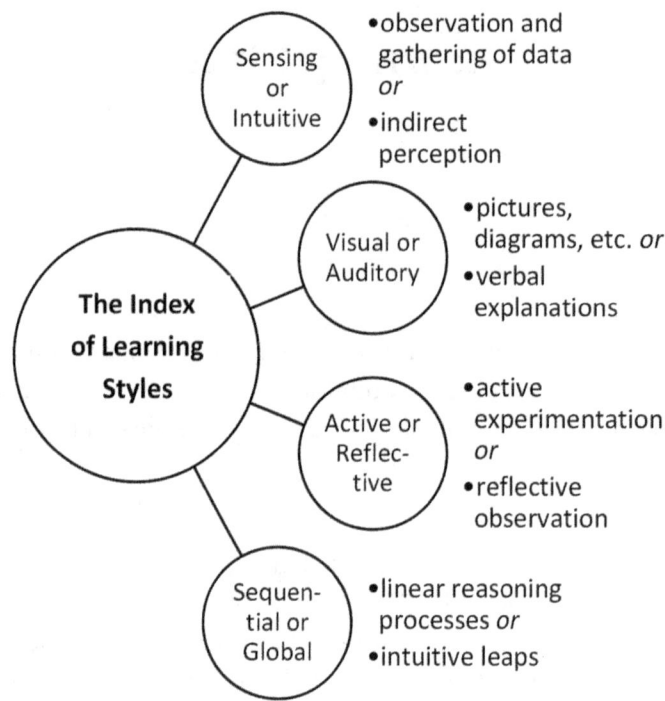

Figure 8.1: The Index of Learning Styles

Intuition uses indirect perception in unconscious hunches, speculation, and imagination. Sensing uses the senses to observe and obtain data. A distinguishing characteristic is intuitors more readily use symbols than sensors do. Neither learner type is superior because both sensors and intuitors are essential to engineering practice, for instance. Felder and Silverman (1988) explain, "Many engineering tasks require the awareness of surroundings, attentiveness to details, experimental thoroughness, and practicality that are the hallmarks of sensors" (p. 676).

Sights such as diagrams, pictures, movies, and demonstrations are most memorable for visual learners. Pure lectures are often forgotten. However, auditory learners are the opposite and learn much from discussion and describing concepts to others (Felder & Silverman, 1988).

The conversion of perceived data into knowledge has two methods: active experimentation and reflective observation (Kolb, 1984, as cited in Felder & Silverman, 1988). "Active experimentation involves doing something in the external world with the information… reflective observation involves examining and manipulating the information introspectively" (Felder & Silverman, 1988, p. 678).

Much formal education relies on the calendar and logic to structure information, which sequential learners are comfortable with because they attain mastery as teachers present concepts. A partial understanding of concepts is enough for sequential learners to work with them. They use linear reasoning to solve problems, but global learners use intuition to make breakthroughs that have difficult-to-explain steps (Felder & Silverman, 1988). When they make the leap that shows how parts of a problem come together, their ability to apply information may surpass that of sequential learners (Silverman, 1987, as cited in Felder & Silverman, 1988). "Sequential learners may be strong in convergent thinking and analysis; global learners may be better at divergent thinking and synthesis" (Felder & Silverman, 1988, p. 679). Sequential learners thrive with an incremental progression in complexity of material whereas global learners often prefer going straight to challenging concepts. School is not structured in this way, making it frequently difficult for global learners (Felder & Silverman, 1988, p. 679).

8.3 THE HONEY AND MUMFORD MODEL

The Honey and Mumford model has some parallels with the Index of Learning Styles and has four learner types of which learners may demonstrate one primary type: activist, theorist, pragmatist, or reflector (see Figure 8.2; Graduate School, University of Leicester, n.d.). For activist learning, learners need:
- Open-mindedness
- Self-paced learning
- Experiences with other students (Graduate School, University of Leicester, n.d.)

For theorist learning, learners need:
- Objective concepts
- Recognition of their clear synthesis of information (Graduate School, University of Leicester, n.d.)

For pragmatist learning, learners need:
- Contextual learning
- Case studies, examples, or overviews of how each element has real-world applications (Graduate School, University of Leicester, n.d.)

For reflector learning, learners need:
- Case studies and past experiences
- Resources to see problems from different perspectives (Graduate School, University of Leicester, n.d.)
- Incentives for beginning work (Huang & Busby, 2007)

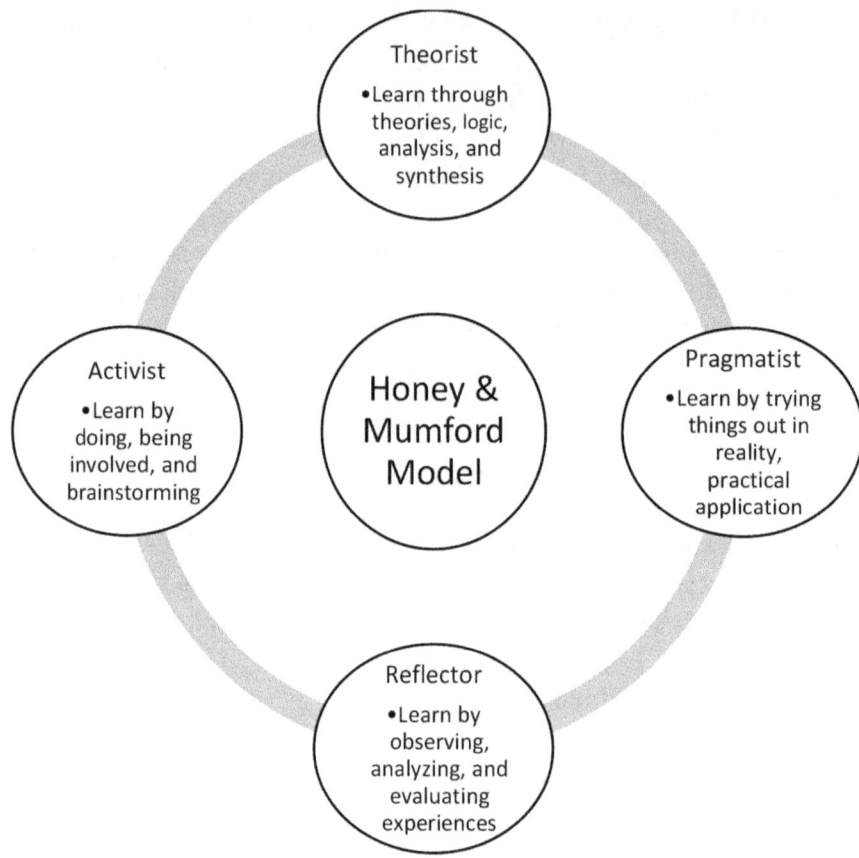

Figure 8.2: Honey and Mumford Model

8.4 KOLB AND KOLB'S FOUR LEARNING STYLES

Kolb and Kolb's (2013) experiential learning theory has a four-stage process:
1. Concrete experience
2. Observation and reflection
3. Formation of abstract concepts
4. Generalizations resulting in testing of the implication of these concepts in new situations

The Kolb Learning Style Inventory was created for analyzing students' preferences, as detailed in Figure 8.3 (Kolb & Kolb, 2013):

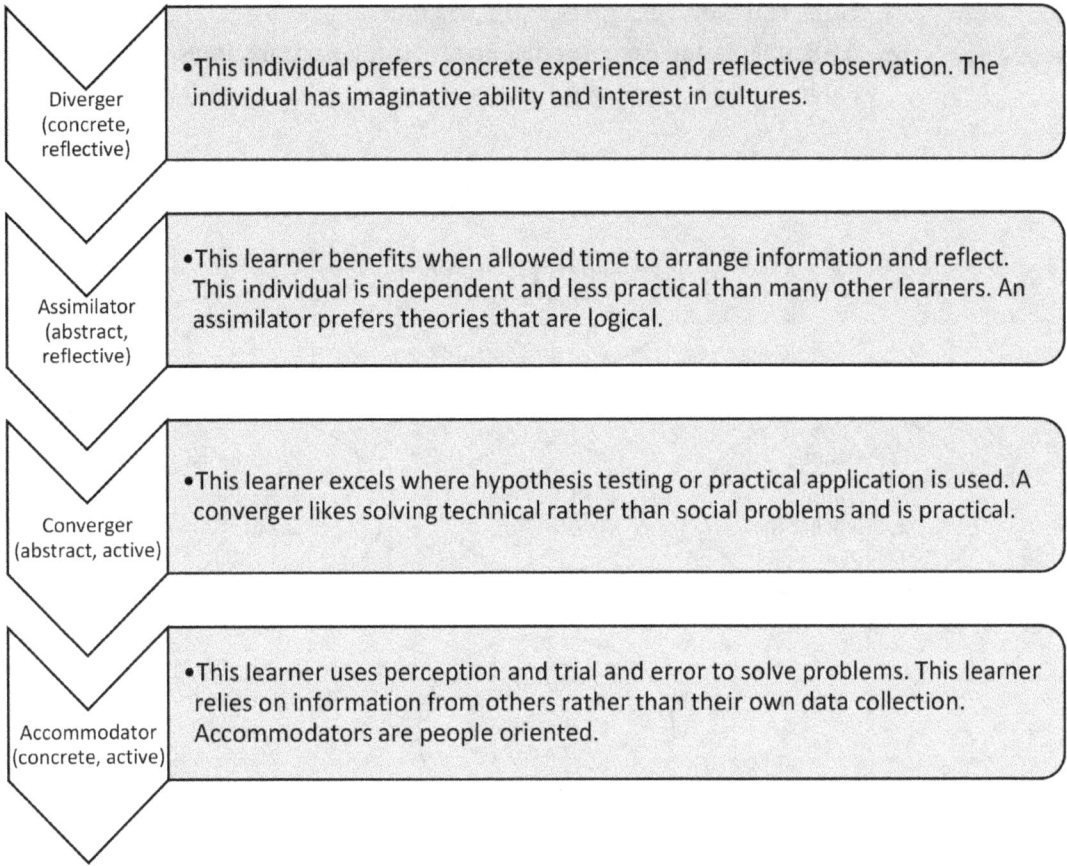

Figure 8.3: Kolb and Kolb's Four Learner Profiles

8.5 VISUAL, AURAL, READ/WRITE, AND KINESTHETIC

The model many educators use is Neil D. Fleming and Colleen Mills's (1992) four VARK modalities, as shown in Figure 8.4. Visual learners prefer:
- Labeled illustrations, charts and diagrams, infographics, and so on
- Videos that place the concept into a visual representation (VARK Learn, n.d.)

Auditory, or aural, learners prefer:
- Class discussions
- Listening to lectures and podcasts (VARK Learn, n.d.)

Read/write learners prefer:
- Using manuals
- Using lists
- Reading blogs and forums (VARK Learn, n.d.)

Kinesthetic learners prefer:

- Using real-world examples and case studies
- Assignments and exercises that involve using software, tools, or tangible models (VARK Learn, n.d.)

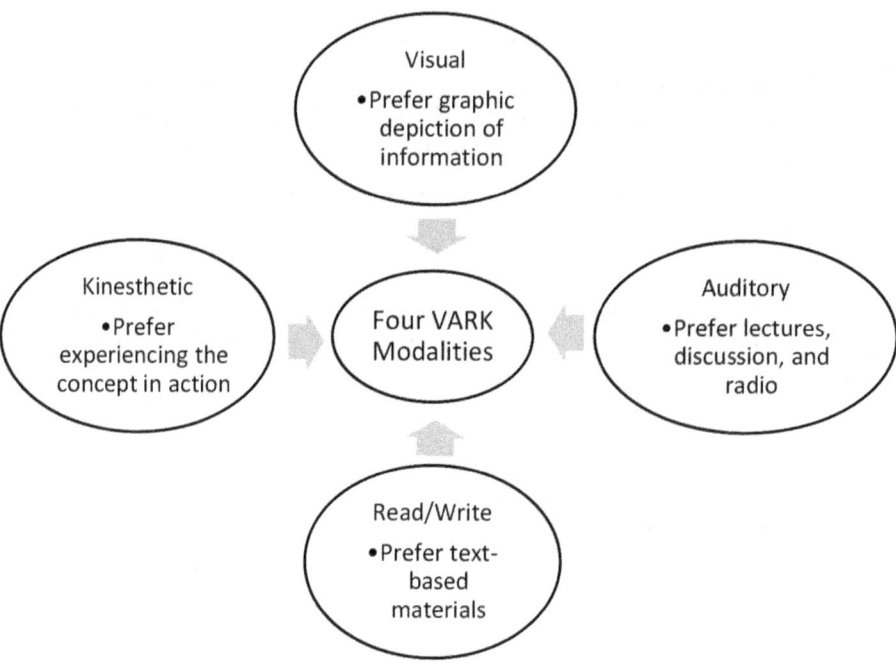

Figure 8.4: VARK Modalities

Effective visual teaching aids are not photographs of reality or PowerPoint presentations. Simply putting words in boxes is more useful for read/write learners. "The auditory preference includes talking out loud as well as talking to oneself. Often people with this preference want to sort things out by speaking first, rather than sorting out their ideas and then speaking" (VARK Learn, n.d., para. 4). Also, they sometimes repeat what they have heard or ask a question for which the answer has already been given.

Many teachers and high-performing students strongly prefer reading/writing. Employers demand effective reading and writing skills. This learning preference focuses on text-based learning processes and outcomes (VARK Learn, n.d.). Kinesthetic refers to the "perceptual preference related to the use of experience and practice" (Fleming & Mills, 1992, The Catalyst). Concrete examples are the focus (VARK Learn, n.d.).

8.6 MALCOLM KNOWLES'S ASSUMPTIONS

Some learning style models are based on preferences, but others are based on assumptions common to learners. Malcolm Knowles identified the following six assumptions specific to adult learners (see Figure 8.5). Learners' need to know means:

- They should be involved in planning training programs
- They should know why they are learning the material (Knowles, Holton, & Swanson, 2014)

Learners' life experience suggests they need:
- Opportunities to make connections between their past and the present content
- Rewards for sharing their life experience (Knowles et al., 2014)

Learners' need for self-direction requires:
- Courses that can be undertaken in a flexible structure that best suits their need
- Collaboration tools, such as wikis (Knowles et al., 2014)

Learners' readiness to learn in response to need suggests they require:
- Flexible structure that allows them to complete the most relevant modules at the most relevant time
- Software plugins that allow them to seek learning when and where they need it (Knowles et al., 2014)

Learners' life orientation suggests their need for:
- Participation in activities that allow identification of problems and their solutions
- Collaboration tools, communities, and forums that bring real-world problems into the learning environment (Knowles et al., 2014)

Learners' intrinsic motivation suggests the need for:
- Combining self-paced and structured learning to both respond to motivation and foster it
- Having learning available anytime, anywhere, and on any device to allow them to learn when and where they are most motivated (Knowles et al., 2014)

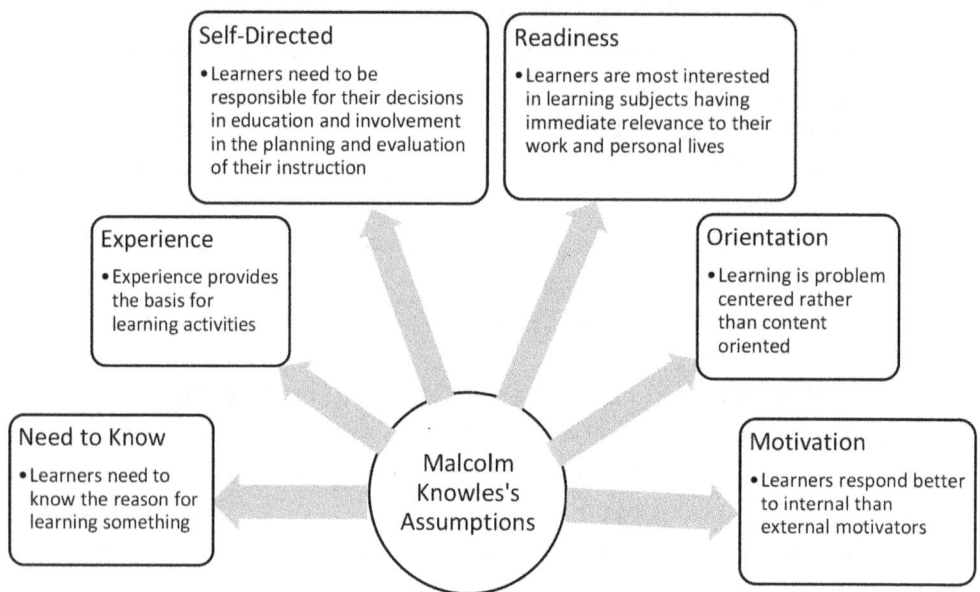

Figure 8.5: Malcolm Knowles's Learning Assumptions

8.7 DUNN AND DUNN'S LEARNING STYLE

Rita and Kenneth Dunn proposed a widely used learning style model (Dunn & Griggs, 2000). They identified five key dimensions on which student learning styles differed (Dunn & Griggs, 2000):

- Environment
- Emotional support
- Sociological composition
- Physiological element
- Psychological element

Figure 8.6 shows the details of each dimension.

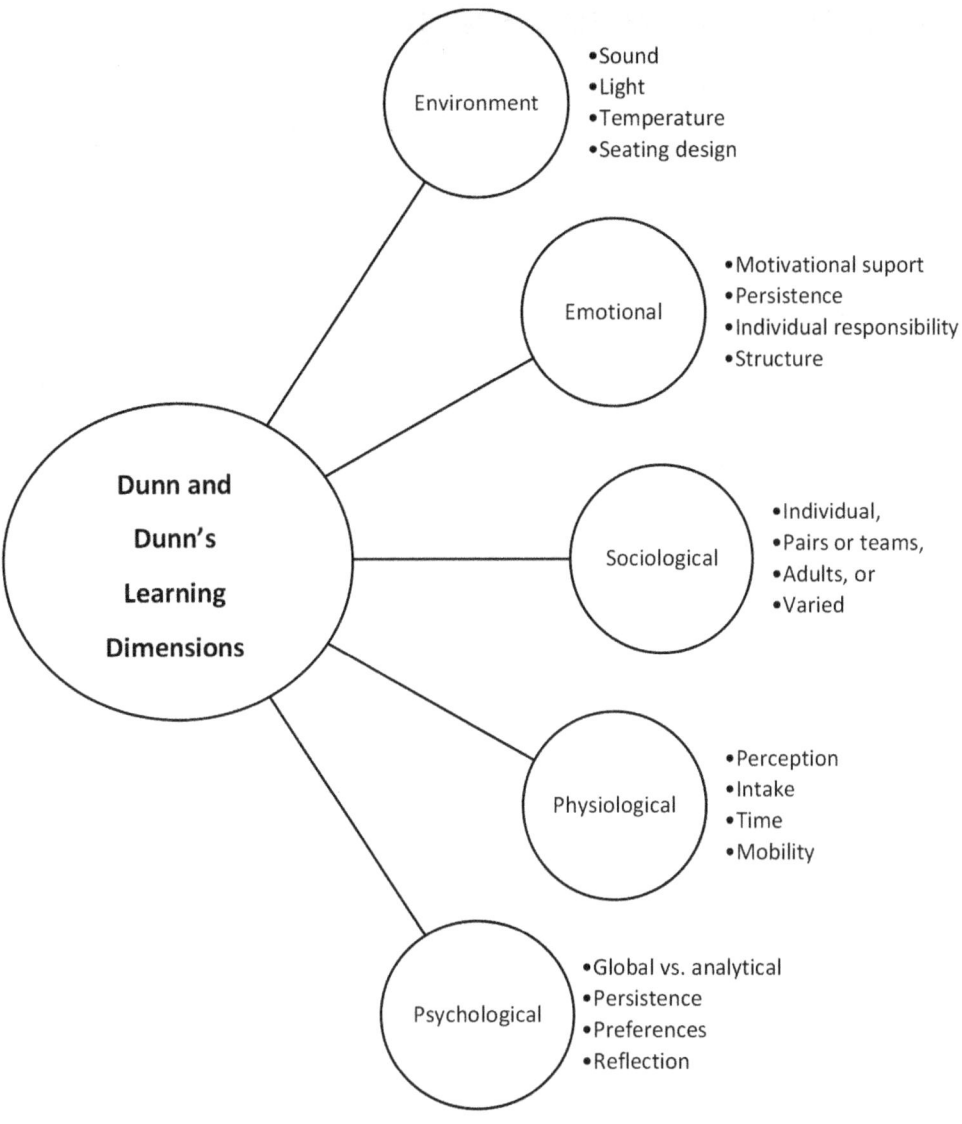

Figure 8.6: Dunn and Dunn's Learning Dimensions

Some students learn better in a quiet, brightly lit classroom with desks in rows, but others prefer a noisy, dim place, such as a busy coffee shop. Teachers should be motivating and reward individual initiative and persistence to address emotional traits. To consider sociological preferences, instructors should give students freedom to study with partners, with groups, or by themselves. Giving freedom to move around the room or eat or chew gum while working accommodates physiological traits, and allowing time for reflection and synthesis and encouraging persistence accommodate psychological traits (Dunn & Griggs, 2000).

8.8 VERMUNT INVENTORY OF LEARNING STYLES

Vermunt's model resulted from studying college students' self-regulation. It includes undirected, application-directed, reproduction-directed, and meaning-directed learning styles. Undirected learning involves learning more from peers than from instructors and an ambivalent attitude toward content and outcomes. Application-directed students seek skills useful in careers and view learning as both teachers' and their own responsibility whereas reproduction-directed students focus on remembering what exams cover and proving their knowledge to others. Meaning-directed learners create their own understanding based on prior knowledge and their studies with interest in the material (Vermunt & Vermetten, 2004).

8.9 LEARNING STYLE ORIENTATION INVENTORY

The Learning Style Orientation Inventory has five learning styles, namely discovery based learning, group based learning, experiential learning, structured learning, and observational learning. Table 8.1 provides a sample of the inventory (Towler & Dipboye, 2003, p. 227).

Table 8.1: Learning Style Orientation Inventory

Discovery Based Learning	I like instructors who make me think about abstract ideas
	I like classes where there is no one correct answer but a matter of opinion
	I am a reflective person when learning
	I learn a lot from instructors who stray from the main topic
Group Based Learning	I enjoy studying in a group
	When learning, I like to go through the process with others
	I like group discussions
Experiential Learning	I like to put my ideas straight into practice when learning
	I learn best when given the opportunity to obtain practical experience
	I don't like to sit and listen
Structured Learning	I enjoy work schedules
	I enjoy making outlines of text and lecture material
	I like to break a task into simpler terms
	I like the instructor to give me many practical examples
Observational Learning	I like to see actual demonstrations of what I am learning
	I prefer things that I can actually see or touch

8.10 LEARNING STYLES USED IN DIFFERENT DISCIPLINES

The learning styles tend to be different when students are in different majors. Instructors should be aware of this when determining how to ensure students understand the concepts taught in their classes.

8.10.1 BUSINESS

Naik (2003, as cited in Wu & Fazarro, 2013) had about 150 business students complete the Index of Learning Styles and found most preferred sequential and visual learning. Loo (2002, as cited in Wu & Fazarro, 2013) used the Kolb Learning Style Inventory to determine finance, accounting, management information systems, and marketing students tended to be assimilators. Rupasinghe (2008, as cited in Wu & Fazarro, 2013) "discovered significant differences in learning even among students majoring in marketing and entrepreneurship" (p. 3) through the Learning Style Orientation Inventory Towler and Dipboye developed. James J. Buckley (2007) showed that business majors were less likely to be field-independent learners than mechanical engineering majors.

8.10.2 NURSING

Aina-Popoola and Hendricks (2014) write that more than other models, Kolb's experiential learning theory has been studied in relation to nursing students. Nursing education research has also focused on the VARK and on Knowles's learning assumptions. Nursing students who prefer active types of learning benefit from hands-on simulations, and by helping plan learning activities, they can obtain evidence that can improve nursing practice and education (Aina-Popoola & Hendricks, 2014). However, it is possible that students' learning styles switch during course progression (Alkhasawneh, 2013, as cited in Aina-Popoola & Hendricks, 2014).

8.10.3 ENGINEERING

For engineering students, two main learning style assessments are widely used: the Kolb Learning Style Inventory and Felder-Soloman Index of Learning Styles. Their associated learning styles are described in detail in previous sections. Studies of engineering students have found the assimilator and converger types of Kolb and Kolb's model are most common and most likely to have high academic performance, but the common teaching method of lecturing benefits assimilators only. Studies following Felder and Soloman's theory found most engineering students were visual learners, but instruction is typically verbal and emphasizes theory (Felder & Brent, 2005). Table 8.2 summarizes the learning styles applied to the three disciplines.

Table 8.2 Summary of Applied Learning Styles

Discipline	Main Learning Styles
Business	Felder and Soloman's learning styles, Kolb and Kolb's learning styles, and Towler and Dipboye's learning dimensions
Nursing	Kolb and Kolb, VARK, and Knowles's learning assumptions
Engineering	Felder and Soloman and Kolb and Kolb

8.11 REFERENCES

Aina-Popoola, S., & Hendricks, C. S. (2014). Learning styles of first-semester baccalaureate nursing students: A literature review. *Institute for Learning Styles Journal, 1*(1), 1–10.

Buckley, J. J. (2007). *Learning styles: Are there differences between academic majors?* Vallejo: California Maritime Academy.

Dunn, R. S., & Dunn, K. J. (1978). *Teaching students through their individual learning styles: A practical approach.* Reston, VA: Reston.

Dunn, R. S., & Griggs, S. A. (Eds.) (2000). *Practical approaches to using learning styles in higher education.* Westport, CT: Bergin & Garvey.

Felder, R. M., & Brent, R. (2005). Understanding student differences. *Journal of Engineering Education, 94*(1), 57–72.

Felder, R. M., & Silverman, L. K. (1988). Learning and teaching styles in engineering education. *Engineering Education, 78*(7), 674–681.

Fleming, N. D., & Mills, C. (1992). Not another inventory, rather a catalyst for reflection. *To Improve the Academy, 11.* Retrieved from http://vark-learn.com/wp-content/uploads/2014/08/not_another_inventory.pdf

Graduate School, University of Leicester. (n.d.). *Honey and Mumford.* Retrieved from http://www2.le.ac.uk/departments/gradschool/training/eresources/teaching/theories/honey-mumford

Huang, R., & Busby, G. (2007). Activist, pragmatist, reflector or theorist?: In search of postgraduate learning styles in tourism and hospitality education. *Journal of Hospitality, Leisure, Sport & Tourism Education, 6*(2), 92–99.

Knowles, M. S., Holton, E. F., III, & Swanson, R. A. (2014). *The adult learner: The definitive classic in adult education and human resource development.* New York, NY: Routledge.

Kolb, A. Y., & Kolb, D. A. (2013). *The Kolb Learning Style Inventory 4.0: A comprehensive guide to the theory, psychometrics, research on validity and educational applications.* Retrieved from https://www.researchgate.net/profile/David_Kolb/publication/303446688_The_Kolb_Learning_Style_Inventory_40_Guide_to_Theory_Psychometrics_Research_Applications/links/57437c4c08ae9f741b3a1a58/The-Kolb-Learning-Style-Inventory-40-Guide-to-Theory-Psychometrics-Research-Applications.pdf

Mazumder, Q. H., & Karim, M. R. (2012). *Comparative analysis of learning styles of students of USA and Bangladesh.* Paper presented at American Society for Engineering Education Annual Conference & Exposition, San Antonio, TX.

Towler, A. J., & Dipboye, R. L. (2003). Development of a learning style orientation measure. *Organizational Research, 6*(2), 216–235.

VARK Learn. (n.d.) *The VARK modalities.* Retrieved from http://vark-learn.com/introduction-to-vark/the-vark-modalities/

Vermunt, J. (1992). *Leerstijlen en sturen van leerprocessen in het hoger onderwijs—naar procesgerichte instructie in zelfstandig denken* [Learning styles and regulation of learning processes in higher education—towards process-oriented instruction in autonomous thinking]. Amsterdam, the Netherlands: Swets & Zeitlinger.

Vermunt, J. D., & Vermetten, Y. J. (2004). Patterns in student learning: Relationships between learning strategies, conceptions of learning, and learning orientations. *Educational Psychology Review, 16*(4), 359–384.

Wu, C. Y., & Fazarro, D. E. (2013). Investigation of learning style preferences of business students. *Online Journal for Workforce Education and Development, 6*(2), 1–20.

CASE STUDY: COMPARATIVE ANALYSIS OF LEARNING STYLES OF STUDENTS OF USA AND BANGLADESH

Quamrul H. Mazumder, University of Michigan–Flint, and Md. Rezaul Karim, Khulna University, Bangladesh

© 2012 American Society for Engineering Education

San Antonio, TX

ABSTRACT

A study was conducted to compare and evaluate the learning styles of students in Bangladesh and the United States. The objective was to identify the similarities and differences among student learning styles using the Fielder-Silverman model and an index of learning styles, which was compiled using student response data from two universities in Bangladesh and one American university. Statistical analysis was performed to identify the factors affecting learning style, such as the number of years spent in school, cultural background, and academic major. Altogether, eight dimensions were used to study the students' learning preferences. The analysis concluded there was no difference between the learning styles of American and Bangladeshi engineering students. However, the results discovered a difference between first year (freshmen) and final year (senior) engineering students on the sensing/intuitive dimension. Differences in learning style were also observed between students from different academic majors on the sensing/intuitive and visual/verbal dimensions.

LITERATURE SURVEY

To study the learning styles in an international business management class, Glauco de Vita used the index of learning styles. The results demonstrated large variations in learning preferences in multi-cultural classrooms since international students preferred to learn differently than the typical methods of instruction in an American school[1]. In contrast, Monika and Edward Lumsdaine used the four quadrants of the Herrmann Brain Dominance Instrument (HBID) to evaluate the thinking preferences of students. They reported that the students' thinking preferences underwent an enormous change as they advanced from freshmen to seniors[2]. In addition, most of the students cloned the thinking preferences of the faculty. A male-female difference also existed with females scoring significantly higher on the C quadrant of the HBID instrument. While studying female student's poor academic performance in Chemical Engineering, Felder identified that one of the causes of such performance may be the misalignment between the learning styles of the female students and the characteristic instructional styles of the engineering professors[3]. Another study by the same author showed that students from urban and suburban backgrounds outperformed students from rural and small town backgrounds. Rosati reported that seniors were more inclined toward group studies (active learning preference) compared to first year students, and first year students were more sequential[4]. Felder and Spurlin reported validity of the ILS (Index of Learning Styles) instruments using results from engineering students' style preferences5. The current study uses ILS due to its higher reliability and relevance to the group of students used in this study. A search of literature did not reveal any previous study comparing the learning styles of students from different academic majors.

STATISTICAL ANALYSIS

The Chi Square test is one of the most common methods to determine correlation between two or more categorical variables. When hypothesis testing involves categorical variables, the Chi Square test can evaluate the significance of the results. The Chi Square distribution is a continuous theoretical probability distribution that is widely used in significance testing because many test statistics follow this distribution when the null hypothesis is true6. The Chi Square test of equality of proportions was used as the data was collected from multiple independent populations and the hypothesis to be tested was that the distribution of some variable is the same in all populations. Students were categorized into the dimensions of active/reflective, sensing/intuitive, visual/verbal, and sequential/global. Therefore, a 2x2 contingency table Chi Square test was preferred since it would provide meaningful results for the current data set. Statistical analysis was performed for each dimension of learning style to test the following three hypotheses:

1. Students from the University of Michigan-Flint (UM-F) and Khulna University, Bangladesh have different learning styles due to their cultural backgrounds.
2. The learning styles of first year students are different from those of final year students regardless of their cultural background.
3. The learning styles of students majoring in business are different from those majoring in engineering.

The above hypotheses were tested to determine whether the distribution of some variable in one particular learning style dimension was similar. The Chi Square test and p-value were used to determine whether there is a significant preference for the active learning style or the reflective learning style. If both groups showed a preference for active over reflective, the null hypothesis could not be rejected, concluding that there is no significant difference in the active/reflective dimension. The Chi Square test of independence was not used since there was no concern with the dependency of variables. In addition, the Chi Square test of goodness of fit was not considered appropriate since there was no concern about whether the categorical variable followed a specific pattern. Pearson's Chi Square tests were used since the current data was collected in independent observations with categories that are mutually exclusive and exhaustive. A small number of the data sets contained sparse data (with expected value less than one and with more than 20% of the cells having an expected value less than five) that was analyzed using Fisher's exact test.

ANALYSIS OF LEARNING STYLES

A number of previous studies showed that engineering students from different geographical backgrounds exhibit similar learning styles[8-21] although culture plays an important role. The first hypothesis test involved engineering students from significantly different cultural backgrounds. A total of sixty-eight students, of which twenty-five were from the University of Michigan-Flint (UM-F) and forty-three were from Khulna University, Bangladesh, were used in the analysis. To compare students within the discipline, the null hypothesis was tested for each learning style dimension to determine whether there is a significant difference in learning styles between these two groups. From the Chi Square and p-values reported in row 1–6 of Table 1, no significant difference in learning style preference exists between these two groups in any dimension. The null hypothesis cannot be rejected, stating that both groups prefer active to reflective, sensing to intuitive, and sequential to global learning styles.

Table 1: Comparison of Learning Style Preferences of Students

	UMF	Khulna		UMF	Khulna		UMF	Khulna		UMF	Khulna
ACT	29	19	SEN	29	22	VIS	39	23	SEQ	24	15
REF	14	6	INT	14	3	VER	4	2	GLO	19	10
Total	43	25	Total	43	25	Total	43	25	Total	43	25
Chi-Square: 0.558			Chi-Square: 3.563			Chi sq.: 0.033			Chi-Square: 0.113		
P-Value: 0.455			P-Value: 0.059			P-Value: 0.855			P-Value: 0.736		

	First Year	Fourth Year		First Year	Fourth Year		First Year	Fourth Year		First Year	Fourth Year
ACT	17	10	SEN	19	11	VIS	20	18	SEQ	13	9
REF	5	10	INT	3	9	VER	2	2	GLO	9	11
Total	22	20	Total	22	20	Total	22	20	Total	22	20
Chi-Square: 3.394			Chi-Square: 5.05			Chi-Square: 0.01			Chi-Square: 0.834		
P-Value: 0.065			P-Value: 0.025			P-Value: 0.92			P-Value: 0.361		

	Eng	Bus		Eng	Bus.		Eng	Bus		Eng	Bus
ACT	48	57	SEN	51	49	VIS	62	69	SEQ	39	60
REF	20	33	INT	17	41	VER	6	21	GLO	29	30
Total	68	90	Total	68	90	Total	68	90	Total	68	90
Chi-Square: 0.915			Chi-Square: 7.044			Chi-Square: 5.756			Chi-Square: 1.436		
P-Value: 0.339			P-Value: 0.008			P-Value: 0.016			P-Value: 0.231		

An analysis was also performed to explore the learning preference differences of freshman engineering students and senior engineering students. Since the influence of culture on learning styles was eliminated in the previous analysis, the Bangladeshi and American engineering students were considered to be a homogenous group in this section of the study. Therefore, this section of the study included twenty-two freshman students and twenty senior students from both universities. The second hypothesis test involved students from the same discipline but with different years of college experience. This analysis involved forty-two students, of which twenty-two were freshman and twenty were seniors from UM-F and Khulna University. The null hypothesis was tested for each of the four dimensions of learning style to determine whether there was a significant difference in the learning preferences of freshman compared to that of seniors. From the Chi Square and p-values in rows 7–12 of Table 1, there was not sufficient evidence to prove a significant difference in the learning style preference (active/reflective) of freshman compared to that of seniors. Therefore, the null hypothesis could not be rejected since both groups preferred active to reflective. Similarly, p-values also showed that both groups preferred visual to verbal and sequential to global learning styles. However, the p-value for the sensing/intuition dimension showed the preference to be different for the two groups. The third and final hypothesis was tested to determine the learning style preferences of students with different majors. This analysis involved sixty-eight engineering students from both the University of Michigan-Flint and Khulna University and ninety business students from Eastern University, Bangladesh. The null hypothesis was tested for each dimension of learning style to determine if there was a significant difference in the learning preferences of engineering and business students. From the Chi Square and p-values in rows 13–18 of Table 1, there was not sufficient evidence to show a significant difference in the learning style preference of engineering students compared to that of business students. Therefore, the null hypothesis could not be rejected since both groups preferred active to reflective and sequential to global learning styles. The p-values for sensing/intuitive and visual/verbal showed both groups to have different learning styles preferences. The distribution of the four dimensions of learning style preferences of the students from the University of Michigan-Flint and Khulna University is presented in Figures 1 and 2 below. It appears that engineering students from both groups prefer active, sensing, visual, and sequential learning styles. The statistical analysis presented in Table 1 confirmed that despite cultural differences both groups exhibit similar learning preferences due to similar academic disciplines.

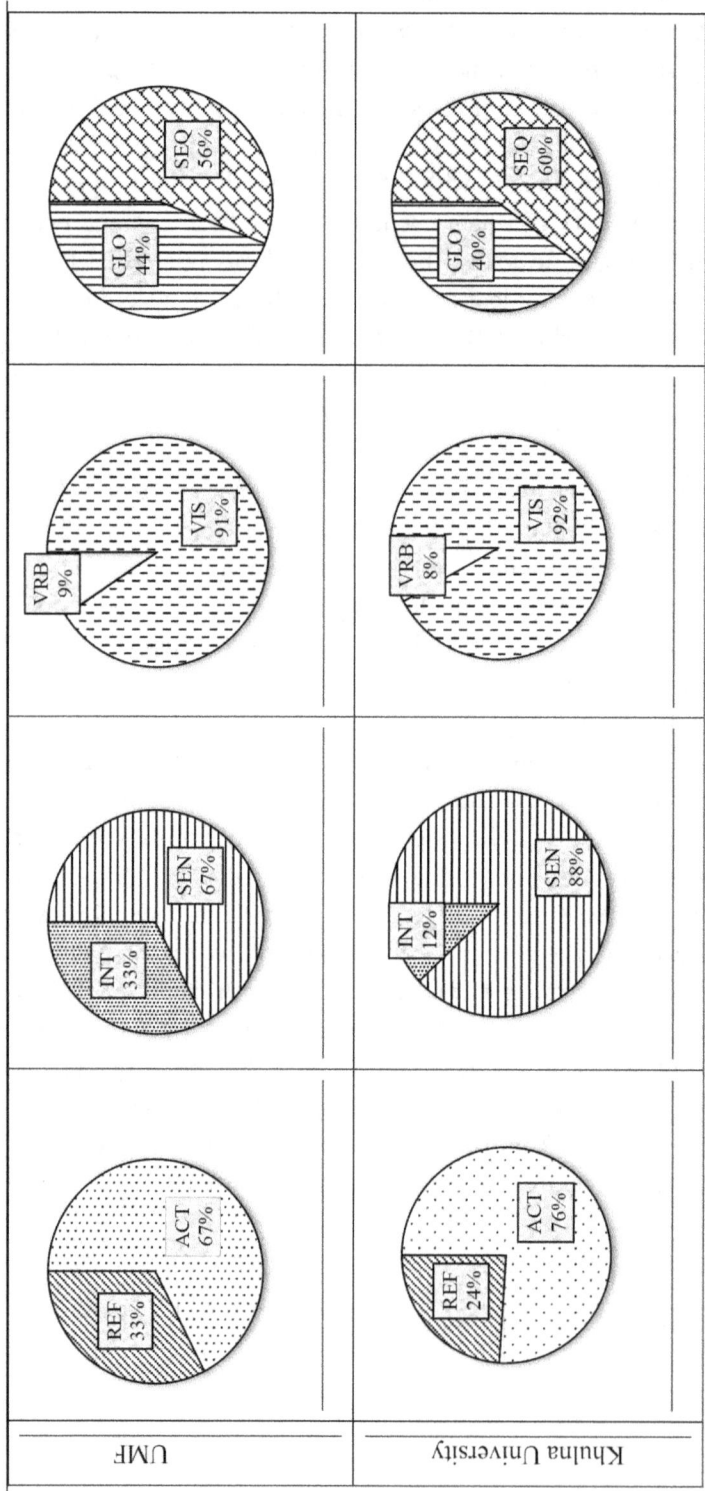

Figure 1: Distribution of Learning Style Preferences of UM-F and Khulna University Students

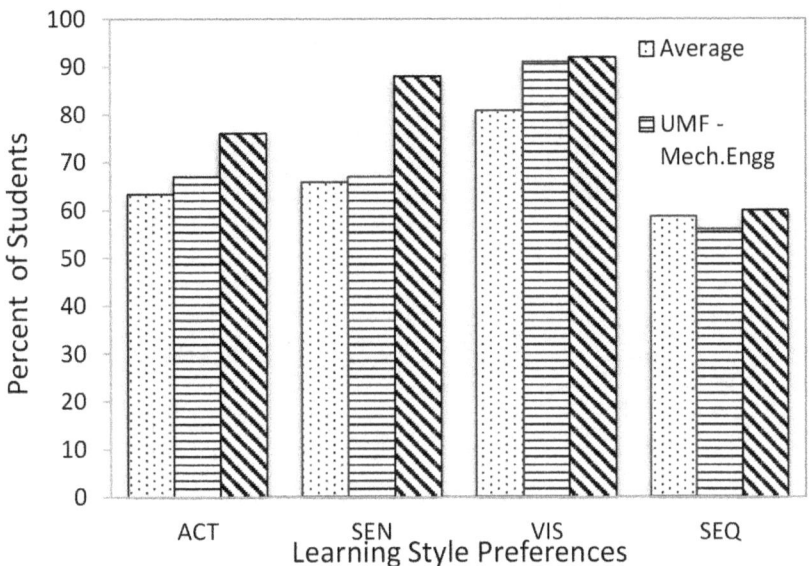

Figure 2: Comparison of Learning Style Preferences of Engineering Students

The distribution of the four dimensions of learning style preferences of freshman students and senior students from the three universities is presented in Figure 3. This confirms senior students prefer intuitive learning. In contrast, freshman students prefer sensing learning by a large margin. Both groups reported that they do not prefer the verbal learning style, which poses a challenge to the traditional lecture-based engineering courses.

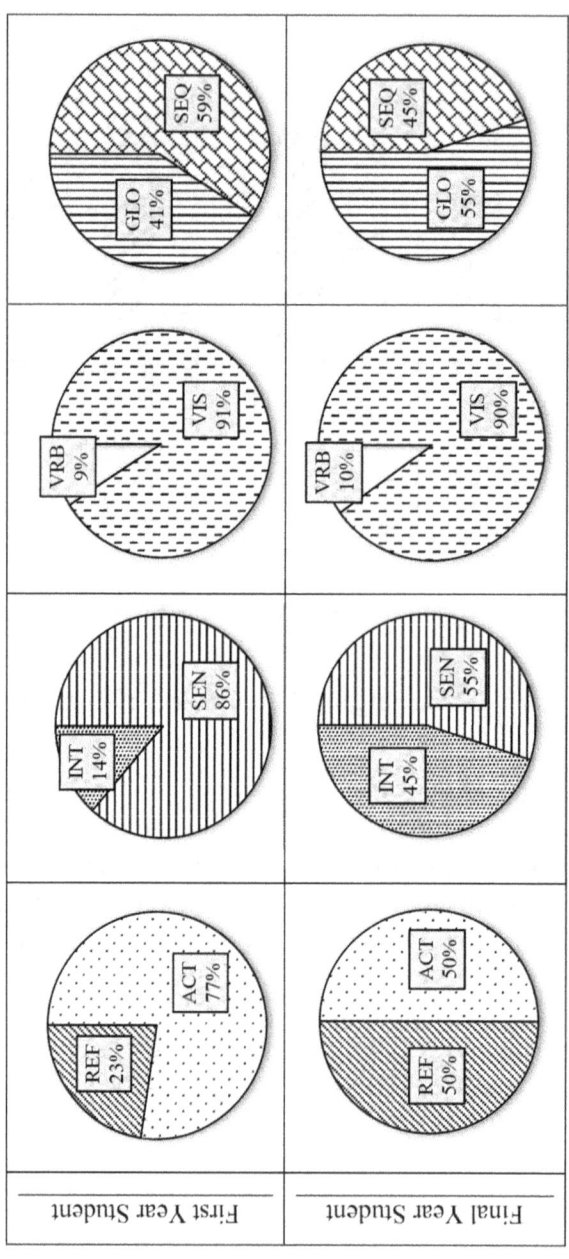

Figure 3: Distribution of Learning Style Preferences of Freshmen and Senior Students

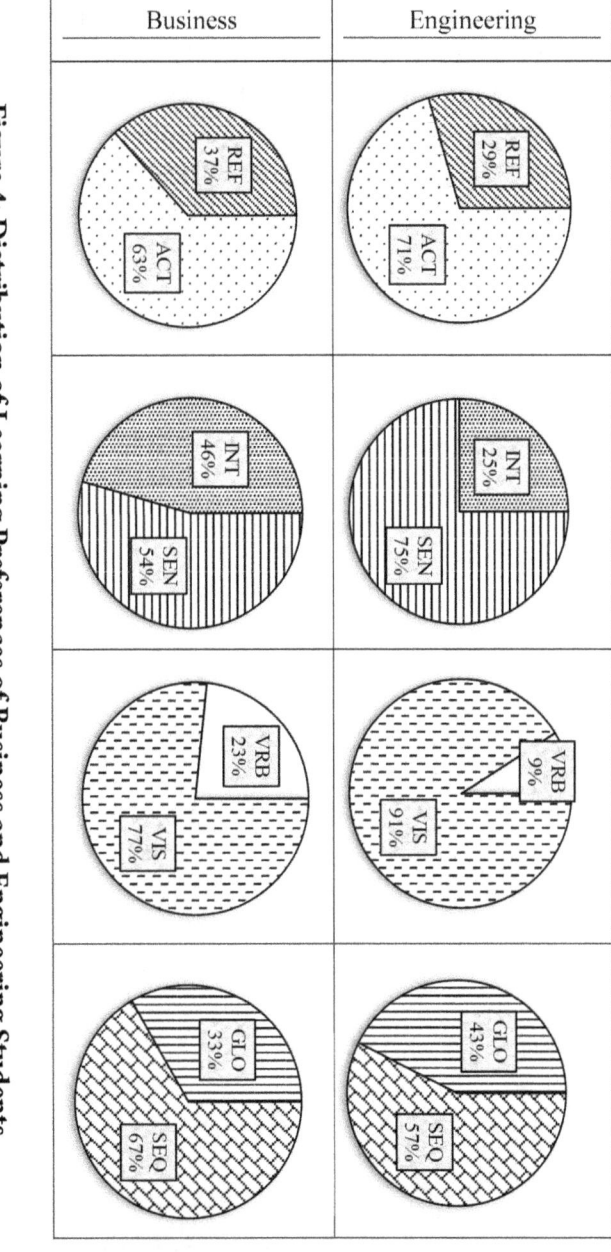

Figure 4: Distribution of Learning Preferences of Business and Engineering Students

The distribution of the four dimensions of learning style preferences of students with engineering majors was compared with that of students with business majors from all three universities and is presented in Figure 4. Students from both majors preferred active to reflective and sequential to global learning styles. Business majors are more intuitive and verbal compared to engineering students as substantiated by the statistical analysis. This is an area that requires attention from engineering educators to improve the verbal communication skills of engineering students. The data collected from the students from the three different universities was compared with previous data reported in the literature[7] and is presented in Table 2. It can be observed that the current data shows similar learning preferences with the previous data, validating the integrity and reliability of the data.

Table 2: Comparison of Current Data with Previous Results

Population	ACT	SEN	VIS	SEQ	Total	Reference
		Percentages				
Iowa State, Materials Eng.	63	67	85	58	129	(Constant, 1997)
Michigan Tech, Environmental, Eng.	56	63	74	53	83	(Patterson, 1999)
Ryerson University, Electrical Eng.						
Students 2000	53	66	86	72	87	(Zywno and Waalen, 2001)
Students 2001	60	66	89	59	119	(Zywno, 2002)
Students 2002	63	63	89	58	132	(Zywno, 2003)
Tulane University, Engr.						
Students Second Year	62	60	88	48	245	(Livesay et al., 2002)
Students First Year	56	46	83	56	192	(Dee et al., 2003)
University of Limerick Mfg., Eng.	70	78	91	58	167	(Seery et al., 2003)
University Of Michigan, Chemical Eng.,	67	57	69	71	143	(Montgomery, 1995)
Electrical and Comp Eng.	47	61	82	67	?	(Baxeda et al., 2001)
University of Sao Paolo, Eng.						
Civil	69	86	76	54	110	(Kuri and Truzzi, 2002)
Electrical	57	68	80	51	91	(Kuri and Truzzi, 2002)
Mechanical	53	67	84	45	94	(Kuri and Truzzi, 2002)
Industrial	66	70	73	50	56	(Kuri and Truzzi, 2002)
University Of Technology Kingston Jamaica	55	60	70	55	?	(Smith et al., 2002)
University of Western Ontario, Engr.	69	59	80	67	858	(Rosati, 1999)
First	66	59	78	69	499	(Rosati, 1996)
Fourth	72	58	81	63	359	(Rosati, 1996)
Eng. Student Average	61.3	64.1	81	58.6	3364	Current Data-Mazumder
UM-Flint Mechanical Engineering	67	67	91	56	43	Current Data-Mazumder
Khulna University URP. - Bangladesh	76	88	92	60	25	Current Data-Mazumder
Current Eng. Student Average	62.4	65.5	82	58.5	3432	Current Data-Mazumder

123

SUMMARY AND CONCLUSION

A study was conducted to evaluate the similarities and differences of the learning style preferences of students using the Fielder-Silverman index of learning styles (ILS) using student response data from two different universities in Bangladesh and from an American university. Statistical analysis of the data concluded that engineering students from different cultural backgrounds show similar learning style preferences. The current results were consistent with previous studies conducted on the engineering students in different countries and universities as reported in the literature. Additionally, engineering students prefer sensing, active, visual, and sequential styles of learning. The study also showed a difference between freshman and senior engineering students, especially on the sensing/intuitive dimension. Freshman students appear to be more sensing than senior students, and vice versa. This finding validates previously reported data on the difference in the learning style preferences of freshman students compared to those of senior students. Finally, the study also revealed the difference between engineering students and business students: business students prefer visual and sensing learning styles.

REFERENCES

1. Glauco De Vita, "Leaning Styles, culture and inclusive instruction in multi-cultural classroom: A Business and Management Perspective," Innovations in education and Teaching International; May 2001; 38, 2; Research Library pg.165.
2. Monika Lumsdaine and Edward Lumsdaine, "Thinking Preferences of Engineering Students: Implications for Curriculum Restructuring," Journal of engineering education; April 1995, pp. 193-204.
3. Richard M. Felder., Gary N. Felder., Meredith Mauney, Charles E. Hamrin, JR., E. Jacquelin Dietz, " A Longitudinal Study of Engineering Student Performance and Retention.III. Gender Differences in Student Performance and Attitudes," Journal of engineering education; April 1995, pp. 151-163.
4. P.A Rosati, "Comparison of learning preferences in and Engineering Program," Frontiers in education conference, 1996, vol, pp.1441-1444.
5. R. Felder and J. Spurlin, "Applications, Reliability, and Validity of Index of Learning Styles," International Journal of Engineering education, 2005, pp. 103-111.
6. Paul Andrew Watters and Sarah Boslaugh, "Statistics in a Nutshell: A Desktop Quick Reference,"O'Reilly 2008.07.25.
7. Richard M Felder; Rebecca Brent, "Understanding Student Differences", Journal of engineering education; Jan 2005; Vol 94, No 1; pg.57.
8. Constant K.P, " Using Multi Media techniques to address diverse learning styles in materials education,"
9. Patterson K.G., "Students Perception of Internet Based Learning Tools in Environmental Engineering Education," Journal of Engineering Education, Vol 88, No. 3, 1999, pp. 295-304.

10. M.S. Zywno, J.K. Waalen, "The effect of Hypermedia Instruction and Achievement and Attitudes of Students with Different Learning Styles," 2001 ASEE Annual Conference and exposition proceedings, Session 1330.
11. M.S Zywno, " Instructional Technology, Learning Styles, and Academic Achievement, 2002 ASEE Annual Conference and exposition proceedings Montreal, Quebec; June 2002, Session 2422.
12. M.S. Zywno, "A Contribution of Validation of Score Meaning for Felder-Soloman's Index of Learning Styles," proceedings, 2003 ASEE conference and exposition, Washington, D.C.: American Society for Engineering Education
13. Livesay, G.A., Dee, K.C., Nauman, E.A., and Hites, Jr., L.S., "Engineering Student Learning Styles: A Statistical Analysis Using Felder's Index of Learning Styles," Presented at 2002 ASEE Conference and Exposition, Montreal, Quebec, June 2002.
14. Dee, K.C., Livesay, G.A., and Nauman, E.A., "Learning Styles of First- and Second – Year Engineering Students," Proceedings, 2003 ASEE/WFEO International Colloquium, and Washington, D.C.: American Society for Engineering Education.
15. Seery, N., Gaughran, W.F., and Waldmann, T., "Multi-Modal Learning in Engineering Education," Proceedings 2003 ASEE conference and exposition, Washington, D.C.: American Society for Engineering Education.
16. S. Montgomery, "Addressing Diverse Student Learning Styles Through the use of Multimedia," 1995 Frontiers of Education Conference Washington, D.C: ASEE/IEEE, 1995, vol, pp.3a2.13-3a2.21.
17. Baxeda, R., Jimenez, L., and Morell, L. "Transforming Engineering Course to Enhance Student Learning," Proceedings 2001, International Conference on Engineering Education, Arlington, Va.: International Network of Engineering Education and Research.
18. Kuri, N.P., and Truzzi, O.M.S., "Learning Styles of Freshman Engineering Students," Proceedings 2002, International Conference on Engineering Education, Arlington, Va.: International Network of Engineering Education and Research.
19. N.G.Smith, J. Bridge and E. Clarke, "An evaluation of students' performance based on their preferred learning styles,"3rd Global Congress on engineering Education Glasgow, Scotland, UK; June 2002, vol, pp.284-287.
20. P.A Rosati, "Specific Differences and Similarities in the Learning Preferences of Engineering Students," Frontiers in education conference Washington D.C, Nov 1999, vol, pp.12c1-17- 12c1-22.

CHAPTER 9:

Learning Strategies

CHAPTER OBJECTIVE

This chapter describes the importance of learning strategies and how they improve the academic performance of students. In fact, it describes different theories of learning strategies by drawing from research on metacognition and motivation.

9.1 INTRODUCTION

The contributing factors to successful learning have become interesting field research topics because many outcomes of academic success are based on learning. One active and constructive learning strategy is self-regulated learning. This allows the learners to set the goals and helps them control their cognition to motivate their behavior toward the achievement of goals. Contextual factors such as task value, authority, evaluation, and classroom teaching define the learning environment. Here, task value refers to the degree of challenge and meaning in tasks given to the students in the classroom. Authority refers to addressing the issues of students in the classroom optimally. Evaluation refers to assessing student work and guiding for improvement. Other important factors, such as classroom management, teacher scaffolding, and teacher modeling, also contribute to the active learning of the students. Teacher scaffolding deals with the issues related to motivation and cognition. Teacher modeling is related to engaging students and guiding their interest toward the desired type of thinking. Classroom management is about how efficiently a teacher makes use of class time and engages students in different activities. All of these factors aid students in improving their cognitive skills and motivating them to become active learners.

The classroom contextual factors constructively build the learning environment by incorporating learning practices in both cognitive and perceptual positions. Individual active learning helps the students use their potential knowledge, conceptual skills, and transformational experiences in learning new aspects of their desired field. Learning discipline is defined by strategies such as memorizing the content repeatedly and creating timetables. Learning discipline can also be characterized by learning content using previous knowledge and critical examination. Students need to do more than just rely on listening to learn. They should advocate active and cooperative learning as a pedagogical approach to be used by the instructors in conjunction with lectures. The ideal method to promote higher-level thinking skills is active learning.

9.2 WHAT ARE LEARNING STRATEGIES?

The University of Kansas Center for Research on Learning (2005) defines learning strategies as the "person's approach to learning and using information" (p. 1). The purpose of learning strategies is to help learners understand concepts and solve problems. Students who do not use effective learning strategies are often passive and prone to eventual failure. The instruction of learning strategies emphasizes making students more active learners and teaches them how to learn and use knowledge for success. Many studies showed that the vital ingredients for success in instruction are intensive, clear, and consistent support and teaching (University of Kansas Center for Research on Learning, 2005).

Analyzing and reflecting on material makes learning more effective by allowing students to recall and apply concepts. Using learning strategies incorrectly or inconsistently can cause dissatisfaction with studying. Learning strategy instruction for foreign languages, specifically, provides vocabulary for discussing learning activities and shows when and how to use one's skill set. Matching appropriate tasks to strategies is likely to increase language-learning success. However, learning requires direction and guidance from the teacher, who helps students understand when and in what contexts to use particular strategies or groups of strategies (Chamot, Meloni, Bartoshesky, & Kadah, 2004).

9.3 MOTIVATED STRATEGIES FOR LEARNING

Pintrich, Smith, Garcia, and McKeachie (1993) created their Motivated Strategies for Learning Questionnaire using a cognitive view of learning strategies and motivation and a view of students as active information processors influenced by thoughts and beliefs. The importance of and variations between cognitive strategies and metacognitive strategies are mentioned in this framework. Rehearsal, elaboration, and organization strategies are cognitive strategies whereas planning, monitoring, and regulating are metacognitive strategies (see Figure 9.1), which are characterized as comprehension-monitoring strategies. Metacognitive strategies are relevant as well as different cognitive strategies for dealing with complex content (Pintrich et al., 1993).

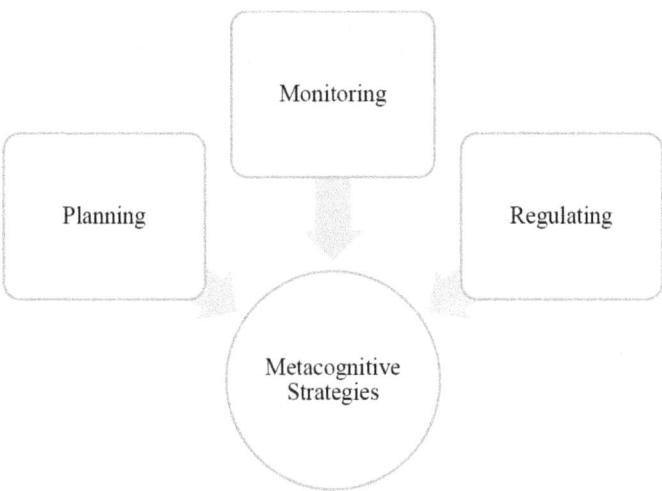

Figure 9.1: Metacognitive Strategies

The Motivated Strategies for Learning Questionnaire includes two main sections, namely learning and motivation strategies. The learning strategies' scales are divided into three categories: use of metacognitive strategies, use of cognitive strategies, and management of different learning resources. The metacognitive strategies' subscales measure resource management, time management, study environment, effort management, peer learning, and help seeking. Cognitive strategies are separated into rehearsal, elaboration, critical thinking, and organization (see Figure 9.2). This framework assumes that motivation and learning strategies are dynamic and contextually bound and that learning strategies can be learned and brought under the control of the course rather than dynamic traits of the learner (Pintrich et al., 1993). The questionnaire uses an 81-item self-report Likert-type scale on which students rate statements about their motivational orientation and use of different learning strategies. The study clearly shows the six factors for cognitive learning strategies and the nine subscales in the learning strategy section. Each of them separately was found to represent a coherent conceptual and empirically validated framework to assess the students (Pintrich et al., 1993).

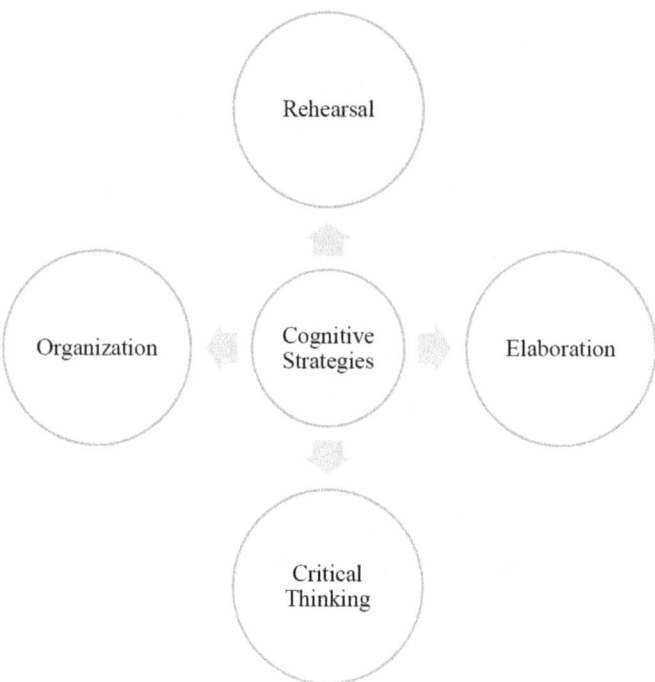

Figure 9.2: Types of Cognitive Strategies

A 2011 analysis of studies that used the Motivated Strategies for Learning Questionnaire found that the instrument remains valid and has shed light on students' academic performance. Credé and Phillips (2011) write that studies have supported the idea that motivation and cognition affect learning strategies. When students use appropriate strategies, such as asking questions to guide readings and making an outline afterward, they achieve better grades. Use of learning strategies also varies depending on what classes students take. Finally, the questionnaire is useful for determining and improving individuals' approach to learning (Credé & Phillips, 2011).

9.4 THEORY OF SELF-REGULATED LEARNING

Self-regulated learning includes metacognition, motivation, and behavior processes that acquire knowledge and build skills for setting goals, planning, and learning strategies. This perspective moves focus from students' abilities and environments to students' ways of improving both. Learning is proactive, not a reaction to teaching. Self-regulated learning involves not only discovery learning, self-learning, and computer-assisted instruction but also modeling, feedback, and guidance. Even if the student is isolated, if he or she takes initiative and persists in learning, that is self-regulated (Zimmerman, 2015).

Studying human self-control led to research of students' self-regulated learning. Investigations on use of self-regulatory processes, such as goal setting, self-reinforcement, and self-instruction, made educational researchers think about these processes in higher education. Limitations of previous attempts to enhance achievement by emphasizing social background, mental capacity, and qualitative school standards also stimulated research in self-regulated learning. Most of the self-regulation theorists refuse to point out the differences in internal and external learning control and discuss self-regulation in more interactive and broader language. Self-regulation is a variable process, not a personal characteristic. Novice learners depend on naive forms, such as nonstrategic methods and inaccurate forms of self-monitoring, whereas expert learners depend on powerful self-regulation (Zimmerman, 2015).

Pintrich's (2000, as cited in Montalvo & Torres, 2004) model of the process of self-regulated learning describes four phases, which include task analysis involving strategic planning in phase one and monitoring of the learning process in the second phase. Self-control (volitional control) and task-related strategies, self-reflection, and adjustment make up phase three. The fourth phase is called reaction and reflection and consists of all evaluations, judgments, and attributions that one makes subsequent to a learning episode. Each of these phases represents a time-ordered sequence with different metacognitive processes and relevant strategies to apply when planning, controlling, and evaluating the learning process. However, all four phases do not always take place consecutively in every learning process. The four phases of self-regulated learning can occur in four different areas: context, motivation, behavior, and cognition. The phases and areas of regulation are not always representative of chronological phases of learning (Montalvo & González Torres, 2004).

Self-regulated learning is based on different concepts, such as (Zimmerman, 2015):
- Self-regulation processes that are self-initiated with positive or negative effects on learning
- Self-regulation strategies that enhance problem-solving skills and overall learning
- Self-regulation phases that are processes used before, during, and after learning
- Self-monitoring that monitors self-regulatory learning processes or outcomes
- Self-efficacy that involves beliefs in performance ability
- Self-regulation of performance that controls adverse behaviors during learning
- Self-regulation events that measure self-regulation, such as thinking aloud

9.5 SOCIAL-COGNITIVE THEORY

Albert Bandura drew from theories of behavioral learning and cognition to generate social-cognitive theory. The underlying premise is that when people watch modeled behavior and its consequences, they learn skills and abilities. Social-cognitive theory attempts to describe human behavior and learning by exploring how cognition, behavior, and environment interact (Hartman & Branoff, 2005).

Weaknesses in earlier theories are the focus of many social-cognitive assumptions. Bandura's studies centered on the inefficient way previous theories examined relationships between children and adults and on children's imitation of others. Previous theories also dismissed the effect of personal decisions, especially when exploring antisocial and prosocial behavior. Theories are unable to explain complicated learning through basic interactions of the person and environment. Another difference in Bandura's ideas is his belief that performance was not needed to show someone had learned (Hartman & Branoff, 2005).

According to social-cognitive theory, people gain internal behavior codes that they could act on later, and learning and performance are distinct because learning involves gaining symbolic representations that prompt future behavior. The major parts of learning in social-cognitive theory are the model of behavior, the modeled behaviors' consequences, internal processes, and perceived self-efficacy (see Figure 9.3). The behavioral model passes key data to the learner, increases or decreases the chance of certain behaviors, and demonstrates new behavioral tendencies. The results of modeled behaviors include vicarious consequences (pertaining to observed behaviors) and voluntary consequences (self-reinforcement in perceived behavioral standards or outside reinforcing events). Cognition also has a role in social-cognitive theory and includes attention (correct perception of behaviors), retention (symbolizing and storing perceived behaviors), production (responses based on the symbolized behaviors), and motivation (doing activities that have positive outcomes; Bandura, 1977, as cited in Hartman & Branoff, 2005). The ultimate element of learning in this theory is self-efficacy, which motivates learners. Self-efficacy is belief in one's capability to succeed, especially on tasks that are new or ambiguous. It develops through "mastery experiences, vicarious experiences, social persuasion, and physiological and emotional states" (Gredler, 2001, p. 327, as cited in Hartman & Branoff, 2005, p. 10).

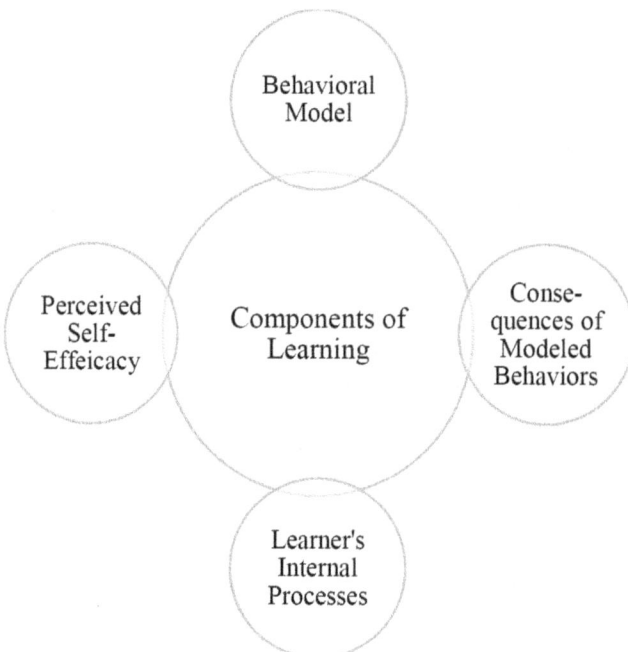

Figure 9.3: Components of Learning in Social-Cognitive Theory

Advanced learning requires instructors to concentrate on the learner's self-regulatory system. Learners who are ready to perform advanced tasks in a certain subject not only exhibit strategy and metacognitive information, but also they are ready to set personal goals, self-monitor their learning, and choose acceptable learning methods. The learner's self-efficacy is essential to determine whether learning goals are realistic. In social-cognitive theory, the instructor's role is to spot acceptable models for college students in the room, establish the practical worth of behavior, and lead students' internal processes. Engineering graphics educators who follow social-cognitive theory would recommend that students have some sort of sketchbook. Students would keep sketches, notes, and other representations of concepts there. Finally, students have a greater chance of behaving according to models if the behavior has practical worth, the model is admirable, and the behavior has desirable outcomes (Hartman & Branoff, 2005).

9.6 INFORMATION PROCESSING THEORY

Information processing theory makes up the foundation of the cognitive learning perspective, and it focuses on how people get, encode, and recall information (Gredler, 2001, as cited in Hartman & Branoff, 2005). Developed after studying computing systems during the 1960s and 1970s, this theory explains the order of mental processes and information received during cognitive task performance (Anderson, 1990, as cited in Hartman & Branoff, 2005). Information processing theory's assumptions are that previous knowledge affects learning and that the memory system arranges and processes information (Hartman & Branoff, 2005).

Information processing leading to knowledge creation is not independent because experiences, current knowledge, and learning context have influences on information perception, coding, and storage. The interaction between activities during learning and learning environment causes learning (Gredler, 2001, as cited in Hartman & Branoff, 2005). Prior knowledge and experience filter the coding process. Therefore, learning strategies should emphasize effective information coding by maintaining attention and linking previous and new information. Instructors should make students separate relevant and irrelevant information as an organization method and make students create ways to monitor performance and learn in every context (Hartman & Branoff, 2005). Application of current knowledge also reflects the information processing approach (Gredler, 2001, as cited in Hartman & Branoff, 2005).

9.7 MODEL OF PERSONALIZED LEARNING STRATEGIES

Personalized learning strategies use personal learning environments, which enhance self-organized and networked learning while translating connectivism and constructivism into real-life contexts. Students create these environments based on their needs (Chatti, Jarke, & Specht, 2010, as cited in Keppell, 2014). This approach can combine informal and formal learning and enable self-regulated learning in higher education (Dabbagh & Kitsantas, 2011, as cited in Keppell, 2014). In next-generation learning environments, personalized learning strategies incorporate a range of knowledge and attitudes to enable the learner to have control. The interaction of next-generation learners is done through the technology of the digital age in which all the learners can adapt and customize their learning through personalizing their interactions. Next-generation learners have six personalized learning strategies: digital citizenship, seamless education, engagement, learning-oriented evaluation, life-wide (learning from life experience) and lifelong learning, and desire paths (Keppell, 2014).

Regarding the first factor, all digital-age learners need abundant knowledge and skill sets concerning digital citizenship. For instance, digital literacy is the ability to use digital tools to access, assess, and communicate new knowledge (Martin, 2005, as cited in Keppell, 2014). Similarly, being digitally literate is possessing the skills required to adopt technologies for personal and professional life confidently and quickly (Beetham, 2010, as cited in Keppell, 2014).

Seamless learning refers to "connecting learning across settings, technologies and activities" (Sharples et al., 2012, as cited in Keppell, 2014, p. 5). Continuity and fluidity across physical and virtual spaces are key to it. Boundaries vanish between physical and virtual spaces and between informal and formal learning (Keppell, 2014). Seamless learning has the challenge of connecting learning activities, seeing misunderstandings, and experiencing new ideas (Sharples et al., 2012, as cited in Keppell, 2014). Kuh (1996, as cited in Keppell, 2014) writes six guiding principles for universities forming seamless learning spaces:

1. Create enthusiasm for change in the institution.
2. Develop a united learning vision.
3. Create a united language.
4. Enable cross-functional discussion and teamwork.
5. Assess how student culture affects learning.
6. Emphasize system-wide change.

The understanding of the influence of student culture on student learning associated with use of social media, smartphones, and other electronic devices is essential.

The third factor, learner engagement, means "active and collaborative learning, participation in challenging academic activities, formative communication with academic staff, involvement in enriching educational experiences, and feeling legitimated and supported by university learning communities" (Coates, 2007, as cited in Keppell, 2014, p. 7). Unifying pedagogical, technical, and administrative aspects is additionally a required condition of success in making an interesting learning setting. Learner engagement measures students' intrinsic involvement, academic outcomes, and interactions with their colleges (Coates, 2007, as cited in Keppell, 2014, p. 7). Student engagement can also reflect the energy, time, and resources students use to enhance their college education. To make meaningful engagement, students need empowerment and support. Understanding the effect of the learning environment on engagement is a necessary skill for students (Keppell, 2014).

Learning-oriented assessments address a pitfall of traditional assessments: their inadequate measurement of outcomes associated with self-regulated and team learning. The most powerful means of adjusting instructional practices is to alter assessment because assessment practices have a robust influence on education (Hakkinen & Hamalainen, 2012, as cited in Keppell, 2014). The alternative approach, a learning-oriented assessment, has three fundamental traits: evaluation used to teach, assessment with student participation, and forward-looking responses (Carless, Joughin, Liu, & Associates, 2006, as cited in Keppell, 2014). Assessment as a learning activity makes assessments that encompass the training outcomes. Students involved in evaluation are aware of its features. With actionable feedback given to learners, they can be prepared for the future. Assessments typically determine student effort, so it is vital that learners find them relevant, genuine, and interesting. Active learning assists learners in grasping the importance of assessment in education and of assessment itself, and these learners can assess their work quality by self-regulating and reflecting. Two important strategies are responding to feedback to enhance later performance (Keppell & Carless, 2006, as cited in Keppell, 2014) and gaining an attitude of learning being continuous (Keppell, 2014).

Desire paths are the simplest navigated routes between the origin and destination, which are typically seen as walking or biking shortcuts that diverge from the prescribed path created by those who design walking or biking paths. Learners typically want the shortest path to attain their certification or qualification. They additionally want to tailor education to best work for their circumstances, desires, and work aspirations. Personalized learners ought to frequently refine their learning by contemplating their desire paths at different parts of their learning journey (Keppell, 2014). Finally, to be lifelong learners, people must have high motivation and the ability to create a desire path appropriate for their circumstances (Keppell, 2014). Regardless of the instructional method used, students can take responsibility for their learning or any material in any context by selecting appropriate learning strategies.

9.8 REFERENCES

Chamot, A. U., Meloni, C. F., Bartoshesky, A., & Kadah, R. (2004). Defining and organizing language learning strategies. In *Sailing the 5 Cs with learning strategies*. Retrieved from http://www.nclrc.org/sailing/chapter2.html

Credé, M., & Phillips, L. A. (2011). A meta-analytic review of the Motivated Strategies for Learning Questionnaire. *Learning and Individual Differences, 21*(4), 337–346.

Hartman, N. W., & Branoff, T. J. (2005). Learning theories: Applications for instruction in constraint based solid modeling and other engineering graphics topics. *Engineering Design Graphics Journal, 69*(2), 6–15.

Keppell, M. (2014). Personalized learning strategies for higher education. In *The future of learning and teaching in next generation learning spaces* (pp. 3–21). Bingley, United Kingdom: Emerald Group.

Montalvo, F. T., & González Torres, M. C. (2004). Self-Regulated learning. *Electronic Journal of Research in Educational Psychology, 2*(1), 1–34.

Pintrich, P. R., Smith, D. A. F., Garcia, T., & McKeachie, W. J. (1993). Reliability and predictive validity of the Motivated Strategies for Learning Questionnaire (MSLQ). *Educational and Psychological Measurement, 53*(3), 801–813.

University of Kansas Center for Research on Learning. (2005). *Learning strategies*. Retrieved from https://www.scribd.com/document/183995070/LSoverview-pdf

Zimmerman, B. J. (2015) Self-Regulated learning: Theories, measures, and outcomes. In J. D. Wright (Ed.), *International encyclopedia of the social & behavioral sciences* (2nd ed., pp. 541–546). Oxford, United Kingdom: Elsevier.

CASE STUDY: A COMPARATIVE STUDY OF MOTIVATION AND LEARNING STRATEGIES BETWEEN HIGH SCHOOL AND UNIVERSITY STUDENTS

Quamrul H. Mazumder, University of Michigan–Flint, and Ulan Dakeev, University of Michigan–Flint
© American Society for Engineering Education, 2015
Seattle, WA

ABSTRACT

To compare the level of motivation and strategies used by high school and university students, a study was conducted between two groups of students. One group was high school students who were dual enrolled in university courses and the other group was first year university students. Both groups were enrolled in similar courses with instructors using similar teaching methods and materials. The study used a Motivated Strategy Learning Questionnaire (MSLQ) that consisted of 18 categories, of which 6 related to motivation and 9 related to learning strategies. The participants included fifty two high school students and forty five university students. An independent sample t-test and variance analysis were performed to compare the responses of these two groups of students. The analysis results showed college student with higher levels of motivation and better learning strategies that high school students. Additionally, gender comparison showed Female students are more motivated with better learning strategies than male students.

INTRODUCTION:

Previous investigators[1, 2] reported that academic motivation is a powerful factor for students in terms of completing their academic work and making them more interested toward learning. High school and university students, based on their[3] theory of learning styles, map the differences in how they learn. Furthermore, there is a relationship between high academic success and self-regulated learning strategies[4] and it is possible that high school students may be more self-regulated with respect to their learning strategies[5]. Several studies have been conducted on learning strategies and motivation using specific populations like high school and university students. Studies on motivational and learning strategies amongst diverse populations can help to develop an improved perception of how different campus communities, societies and experiences shape students' learning and also aid in the development of effective curriculum.

This will enable students to receive better education and take full advantage of learning outcomes at various institutions. Hence, the MSLQ (Motivational Strategy for Learning Questionnaire), a self-report instrument to measure motivational orientation and self-regulated learning strategies[6], is used in the study reported in this paper. The motivation and learning strategy scales are listed below. The MSLQ reliability coefficients, alphas were between 0.52 and 0.93 for different scales validating the instruments higher level of reliability.

Table 1: Motivation and Learning Strategy Scales

Categories	MSLQ Scales
Motivation	Rehearsal
	Elaboration
	Organization
	Critical Thinking
	Metacognitive Self-regulation
Learning Strategies	Intrinsic Goal Orientation
	Extrinsic Goal Orientation
	Task Value
	Control of Learning
	Self-efficacy
	Test Anxiety
Motivation	Time/Study Management
	Effort Regulation
	Peer Learning
	Help Seeking
Other	Theory of Intelligence
	Achievement Goal Questionnaire
	Percentage of Instrumentality

HYPOTHESIS

To evaluate motivation and learning strategies of high school students and university students, two hypotheses were examined in the current work.

1. There is no significant difference between high school and college/university level students
2. There is no significant difference between males and females in both college/university and high school level students.

LITERATURE REVIEW

The MSLQ is more narrowly focused and oriented similarly; it encompasses students' motivation and their learning strategies, thereby providing different information. It is based on important theoretical insights into the nature of learning and the determinants of academic performance7 which have been used by several studies. Self-regulated learning is an integrated learning process, which consists of behavior growth that affects students' learning. Moreover, the learning process is planned and adjusted according to the student's objective, so that changes will be made in the learning situation8. It is dimensionally constructed and includes at least three aspects which include but are not limited to cognition, individual motivation and goal directed behavior9.

Academic performance has been widely reported to correlate significantly and positively with the choice and application of self-regulated learning strategies10. However, learning strategies involve students who engage in self-regulated learning and can be defined as learners who effectively control their own learning experiences in many different ways including organizing information to be learned, holding positive beliefs about their own capabilities, and valuing learning. Motivational strategies are closely related to the grades of university students. However, the most robust factors for motivation and learning strategies could be self-efficacy and effort regulation.

RESEARCH METHODOLOGY:

QUESTIONNAIRE:

Data was collected using the Motivated Strategies Learning Questionnaire, developed originally by Pintrich, Smith, Gracia & Mckeavhie[11]. The questionnaire is an 81-item, self-reported, Likert-scaled instrument which students use to rate statements about their motivational orientation and use the different learning strategies for a specific course from "1" (not at all true for me) to "7" (very true for me).

PARTICIPANTS:

The questionnaire was distributed to High school (52) and College Level (45) students as illustrated in Figure 1 below. A total number of 97 students participated in the current study. Forty seven male and five female students from university and thirty one male and thirteen female high school students participated in the study. The overall response rate was 96 out of 129 (74%) as the responses were voluntary with no incentive to the students. The percentage of male and female participants were 80% and 19% as shown in figure 2 [omitted]. This closely represents the distribution of male and female students in undergraduate engineering classes. One of the hypotheses of this study was to investigate differences between male and female students; therefore one undefined student was omitted from the statistical analysis as the student did not want to disclose the information.

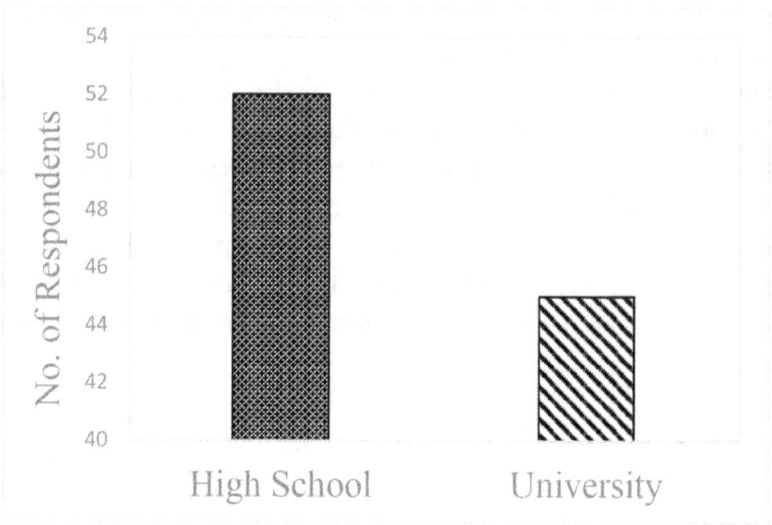

Figure 1: Number of Respondents by Institution

DATA ANALYSIS/PROCEDURE:

Statistical analyses were performed using independent sample t-test and F-test to determine the mean values of 18 categories among students. SPPS22 statistical analysis software was used for the analysis. The purposes of this test were to determine if there is any significant difference between:
- High school and college/university students
- Male & Female student

RESULTS:

Statistical analyses were performed using independent sample t-test, variance (F), and descriptive statistics to compare high school and college/university students (hypothesis one) as well as male and female students (hypothesis two). Tables 2 and 3 summarize the analyses results related to hypothesis one and tables 3 and 4 summarize the results related to hypothesis two.

Table 2: Descriptive Statistics of High School and College/University Students

Category		N	Mean	Std. Deviation	Std. Error Mean
Task Value	High School	52	5.01	1.89	0.26
	College	45	5.53	1.43	0.21
Peer Learning	High School	52	4.12	1.95	0.27
	College	45	4.52	1.54	0.23
Percent Instrumentality	High School	52	4.31	1.75	0.24
	College	45	4.67	1.19	0.18

Statistical analysis results are presented on the categories that showed significant differences between high school and college/university students. Three different categories are presented, one from motivation (Task Value), one from learning strategy (Peer Learning) and one from others (Percent Instrumentality). Task Value measures students' perception of the course materials in terms of interest, importance and utility in the future. Peer learning refers to the extent of dialogue students have with peers to clarify course materials and reach insights that may not have been attained on their own. Percent Instrumentality refers to students' perception of the importance and usefulness of information learned in math classes in future classes, education, academic and occupational success. The mean values in all three categories were higher for college/university students (4.52 to 5.53) when compared with high school students (4.12 to 5.01) showing that the college students have better study skills, more effective peer learning and higher scores in percent instrumentality. This may be attributed to students' level of maturity and exposure to different learning environments between high school and colleges.

Table 3: Sample t-test and variance (F) for High School and College/University Students

		Levene's Test for Equality of Variances		t-test for Equality of Means						
		F	Sig.	t	df	Sig. (2-tailed)	Mean Difference	Std. Error Difference	95% Confidence Interval of the Difference	
									Lower	Upper
Task Value	Equal variances assumed	3.56	.06	-1.50	95.00	.14	-.52	.35	-1.20	.17
	Equal variances not assumed			-1.53	93.38	.13	-.52	.34	-1.19	.16
Peer Learning	Equal variances assumed	3.58	.06	-1.10	95.00	.27	-.40	.36	-1.11	.32
	Equal variances not assumed			-1.12	94.26	.27	-.40	.36	-1.10	.31
Percent Instrumentality	Equal variances assumed	4.23	.04	-1.18	95.00	.24	-.36	.31	-.98	.25
	Equal variances not assumed			-1.21	90.14	.23	-.36	.30	-.96	.23

The independent sample t-test and F-test results for high school and college/university students are presented in Table 3. Analyses were performed assuming both equal and not equal variances to evaluate any significant differences. No significant difference was observed in the results of t-test for equality of means. However, significant differences were observed in Levene's F-test for equality in the category of percent instrumentality (p = 0.04 ≤ 0.05). This refers to the fact that more college students believe that the information learned in math classes is important and useful in future classes, education, academic and occupational success compared to high school students.

Table 4: Descriptive Statistics of Male and Female Students

Category	Gender	N	Mean	Std. Deviation	Std. Error Mean
Extrinsic	Female	18	5.97	0.80	0.19
	Male	79	5.17	1.87	0.21
Task Value	Female	18	5.81	0.78	0.18
	Male	79	5.12	1.83	0.21
Time Study Mgt.	Female	18	4.97	0.49	0.12
	Male	79	4.63	1.52	0.17
Help Seeking	Female	18	3.66	0.80	0.19
	Male	79	3.68	1.61	0.18
Percentage of Instrumentality	Female	18	4.88	0.50	0.12
	Male	79	4.38	1.66	0.19

Statistical analysis results are presented on the categories that showed significant differences between male and female students in five different categories. Two of these categories are in motivation (extrinsic goal orientation and task value), two are in learning strategy (time/study environment management and help seeking), and one is from others (percentage of instrumentality). Extrinsic goal orientation concerns the degree to which a student perceives himself or herself to be participating in a task for reasons such as grades, rewards, performance, evaluation by others and competitions. Time and study environment management involves scheduling, planning and managing one's study time. Study environment refers to the setting where the student studies or does the class work. Help seeking includes seeking help from both peers, tutors, instructors and others to comprehend course materials and academic success. The mean values in four of the five categories were higher for female students (4.88 to 5.97) compared to male students (4.12 to 5.01). Male students scored 3.68 compared to 3.66 of female students in help seeking showing that male students are more active in seeking help from peers and instructors.

Table 5: Sample t-test and variance (F) for Male and Female Students

		Equality of Variances		t-test for Equality of Means					95% Confidence Interval of the Difference	
		F	Sig.	t	df	Sig. (2-tailed)	Mean Difference	Std. Error Difference	Lower	Upper
Extrinsic	Equal variances assumed	7.12	0.01	1.78	95.00	0.08	0.80	0.45	-0.09	1.70
	Equal variances not assumed			2.84	64.32	0.01	0.80	0.28	0.24	1.37
Task Value	Equal variances assumed	5.91	0.02	1.57	95.00	0.12	0.69	0.44	-0.18	1.57
	Equal variances not assumed			2.51	64.11	0.01	0.69	0.28	0.14	1.25
Time Study Mgt	Equal variances assumed	4.20	0.04	0.94	95.00	0.35	0.34	0.36	-0.38	1.06
	Equal variances not assumed			1.66	84.62	0.10	0.34	0.21	-0.07	0.75
Help Seeking	Equal variances assumed	3.97	0.05	-0.03	95.00	0.97	-0.01	0.39	-0.79	0.76
	Equal variances not assumed			-0.05	53.03	0.96	-0.01	0.26	-0.54	0.51
Percentage of Instrumentality	Equal variances assumed	4.47	0.04	1.26	95.00	0.21	0.50	0.40	-0.29	1.28
	Equal variances not assumed			2.25	87.95	0.03	0.50	0.22	0.06	0.94

The independent sample t-test and F-test results for male and female students are presented in Table 5. Analyses were performed assuming both equal and not equal variances to evaluate any significant differences. Significant differences were observed in the results of ttest for extrinsic (p = 0.01 ≤ 0.05), task value (p = 0.01 ≤ 0.05) and percentage of instrumentality (p = 0.03 ≤ 0.05). Significant differences were observed in Levene's F-test in all five categories listed in Table 5 (p = 0.01, 0.02, 0.04, 0.05, 0.04 ≤0.05).

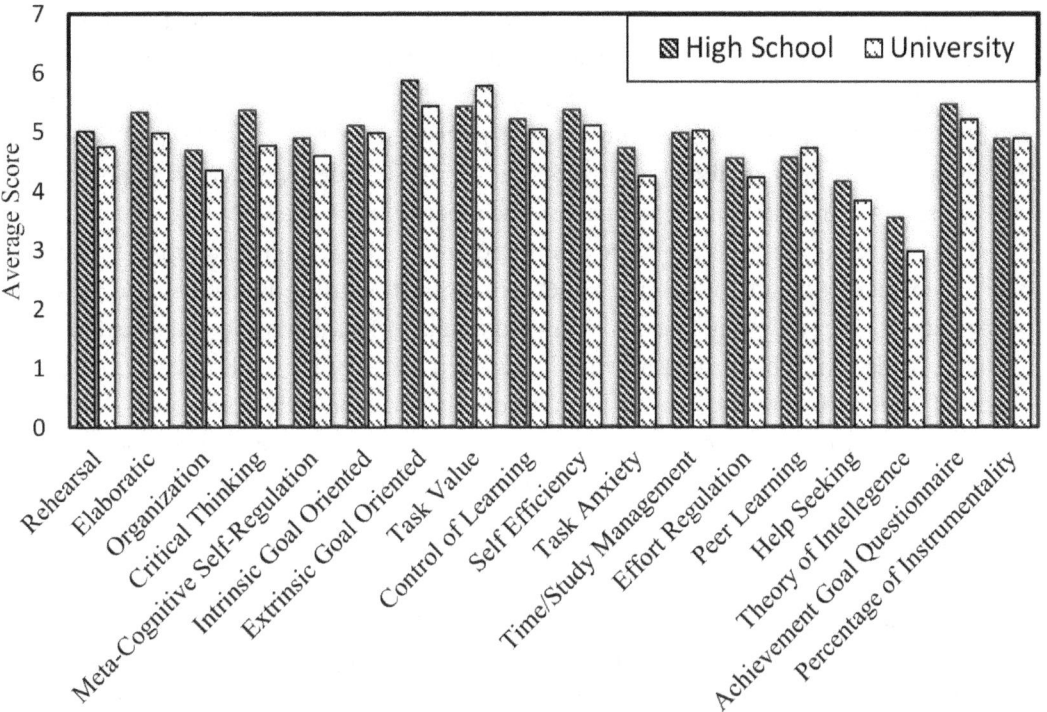

Figure 3: Comparison of Mean Scores of High School & University Students

The mean MSLQ scores of high school students and college/university students for all eighteen categories are presented in Figure 3. Higher scores were observed in extrinsic goal orientation, task value and achievement goal questionnaires. The lowest scores were in theory of intelligence and help seeking categories.

SUMMARY AND CONCLUSION:

The study revealed an important distinction between dual enrolled high school students and college students as well as male and female students in first year engineering classes. The study used the MSLQ questionnaire, a widely used instrument with high reliabilities. The study measured to what extent students will use the material learned in a specific class in other classes. It also measured whether the grade received in the class was relevant and important to their learning process. The results indicated college students believe the material to be more relevant and useful to other classes compared to high school students. College students showed higher level of recognition of grades as related to their learning and academic success. High school students dual enrolled in college courses are among the high achieving students in their class and supposedly have better academic preparation than first year college students. However, the current study results showed higher levels of motivation and better learning strategies among college/university students.

Significant differences were observed between male and female students in both high schools and universities in extrinsic goal orientation, task value, time/study management, help seeking and percentage of instrumentality ($p < 0.05$). Female students showed higher extrinsic goal orientation, higher task value, better time/study management skills and higher percentage of instrumentality compared to male students, whereas, male students were more active in help seeking to improve their learning process.

Overall, college students are more motivated and better learners than high school students and female students showed higher level of motivation towards academic success than male students. The study was based on a limited number of students and will be extended to a larger population to better understand the characteristics of high school and college students. Although these results may not lead to conclusions about the motivation and learning strategies of these two groups of students, they shed some light on an extremely important topic about how to motivate students towards success in engineering.

ACKNOWLEDGEMENT:

The authors would like to thank University of Michigan Flint dual enrollment extended partnership (DEEP) program for their support in collecting data from high school students, institutional review board of office of research, mechanical engineering program and undergraduate research opportunity programs (UROP).

REFERENCES

[1] Lavasani, M. G., Mirhosseini, F. S., Hejazi, E., & Davoodi, M. (2011). *The effect of self-regulation learning strategies training on the academic motivation and self-efficacy*. Procedia - Social and Behavioral Sciences; 29 (2011), 627 – 632.

[2] Artino, R. A., & Stephens, M. J. (2008). *Promoting Academic Motivation and Self-Regulation: Practical Guidelines for Online Instructors*. Society for Information Technology & Teacher Education International Conference. ISBN 978-1-880094-64-8

[3] Zajacova, B. (2013). *Learning styles in physics education: introduction of our research tools and design*. Procedia-Social and Behavioral Sciences; 106 (2013), 1786-1795.

[4] Salamonson, Y., Everett, B., Koch, J., Wilson, I., Davidson, M. P. (2009). *Learning strategies of first year nursing and medical students: A comparative study*. International Journal of Nursing Studies; 46 (2009), 1541–1547.

[5] Mazumder, Q. H., Karim, R. M. (2012). *Comparative Analysis of Learning Styles of*

Students of USA and Bangladesh, Paper no: AC2012-5075, 119th ASEE Annual Conference, June 10-13, 2012, San Antonio, TX, USA

[6] Sadi, O. & Uyar, M. (2013). *The relationship between cognitive self-regulated learning strategies and biology achievement: A path model*. Procedia-Social and Behavioral Sciences; 93 (2013), 847-852.

[7] Crede, M., & Philips, A. L. (2011). *A meta-analytic review of the motivated strategies for learning questionnaire*. Learning and Individual Differences; 21 (2011), 337-346.

[8] Puteha, M., &, Ibrahimb, M. (2010). *The usage of self-regulated learning strategies among form four students in the mathematical problem-solving context: A Case Study*. Procedia Social and Behavioral Sciences; 8 (2010), 446–452.

[9] Jacobson, R. R., & Harris, M. S. (2008*). Does the type of campus influence self-regulated learning a measured by the motivated strategies for learning questionnaire (MSLQ)*. Institute of Educational Sciences; 128 (2008), 412-431

[10] Arsal, Z. (2010). *The effects of diaries on self-regulation strategies of persevere science teachers*. International Journal of Environmental & Science Education, 5(1), 85–103.

[11] Pintrich, P. R., Smith, D. A., Garcia, T., & McKeachie, W. J (1993). *Reliability and predictive validity of the motivated strategies for learning questionnaire*. Educational and Psychology Measurement; 53(1993), 801-813.

[12] Mazumder, Q. H. and Ahmed, K. (2014). *A Comparative Study of Motivation and Learning Strategies Between Public and Private University Students of Bangladesh*. Proceedings of the 2014 ASEE North Central Section Conference, April 4-5, 2014, Oakland University, USA

CHAPTER 10:

Teaching Styles

CHAPTER OBJECTIVE

This chapter describes why teaching styles are important and compares different models of teaching styles. It also explains how they can be applied to improve quality of education.

10.1 INTRODUCTION

Much research has been done to find what the most effective ways a child can learn are, what type of environment is best for learning, and how one truly learns, which is a seemingly simple question. However, when it comes to teaching, there is little to no data on what constitutes an effective or good teacher.

There are different types of teachers with different teaching styles, just as students have different learning styles. "Teachers can be categorized as novice, experienced and experts in their field. But what makes a teacher an expert or excellent teacher is not yet clearly understood" (Mazumder & Ahmed, 2014, p. 1).

Some different models are used to define teaching styles. Following is a list of widely used teaching style models:
- Daniel D. Pratt's perspectives (2002)
- Richard M. Felder and Linda K. Silverman's components (1988)
- Anthony F. Grasha's teaching styles (1994)

10.2 PERSPECTIVES ON TEACHING STYLES

Understanding five perspectives of teaching styles provides a foundation for understanding the styles themselves. Daniel D. Pratt (2002) writes, "A perspective on teaching is an interrelated set of beliefs and intentions that gives direction and justification to our actions" (p. 6). Pratt (2002) presents five perspectives on teaching and urges teachers to use these perspectives to identify, articulate, and justify their teaching approaches rather than simply adopting one practice or another (see Figure 10.1):
- **Transmission:** Teachers focus on content and determine what students should learn and how they should learn it. Feedback is directed toward correcting students' errors.
- **Developmental:** Teachers value students' prior knowledge and direct student learning to the development of increasingly complex means of reasoning and problem solving.

- **Apprenticeship:** Teachers provide students authentic tasks in real work settings.
- **Nurturing:** Teachers focus on the interpersonal elements of student learning—listening, getting to know students, and responding to students' emotional and intellectual needs.
- **Social Reform:** Teachers tend to relate ideals explicitly to students' lives.

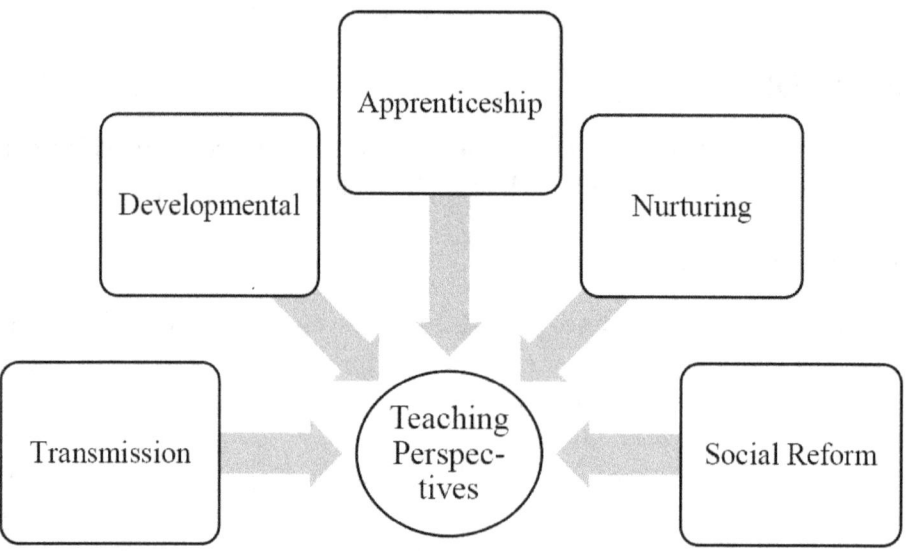

Figure 10.1: Daniel Pratt's Model

"[Perspectives] are simply philosophical orientations to knowledge, learning, and the role and responsibility of being a teacher" (Pratt, 2002, p. 14). With that in mind, each perspective is appropriate when used appropriately, but each can cause ineffective teaching. Teachers who want to improve should reflect on what they do and when those activities are warranted (Pratt, 2002). These perspectives are measurable through Collins and Pratt's (2011, as cited in Stevenson & Harris, 2014) Teaching Perspectives Inventory.

10.3 RICHARD M. FELDER AND LINDA K. SILVERMAN'S MODEL

According to Richard M. Felder and Linda K. Silverman (1988, p. 675), one's teaching style can be defined by the responses to these questions, as shown in Figure 10.2:

1) What type of information is emphasized by the instructor: concrete—factual, or abstract—conceptual, theoretical?

2) What mode of presentation is stressed: visual—pictures, diagrams, films, demonstrations, or verbal—lectures, readings, discussions?

3) How is the presentation organized: inductively—phenomena leading to principles, or deductively—principles leading to phenomena?

4) What mode of student participation is facilitated by the presentation: active—students talk, move, reflect, or passive—students watch and listen?

5) What type of perspective is provided on the information presented: sequential—step-by-step progression (the trees), or global—context and relevance (the forest)?

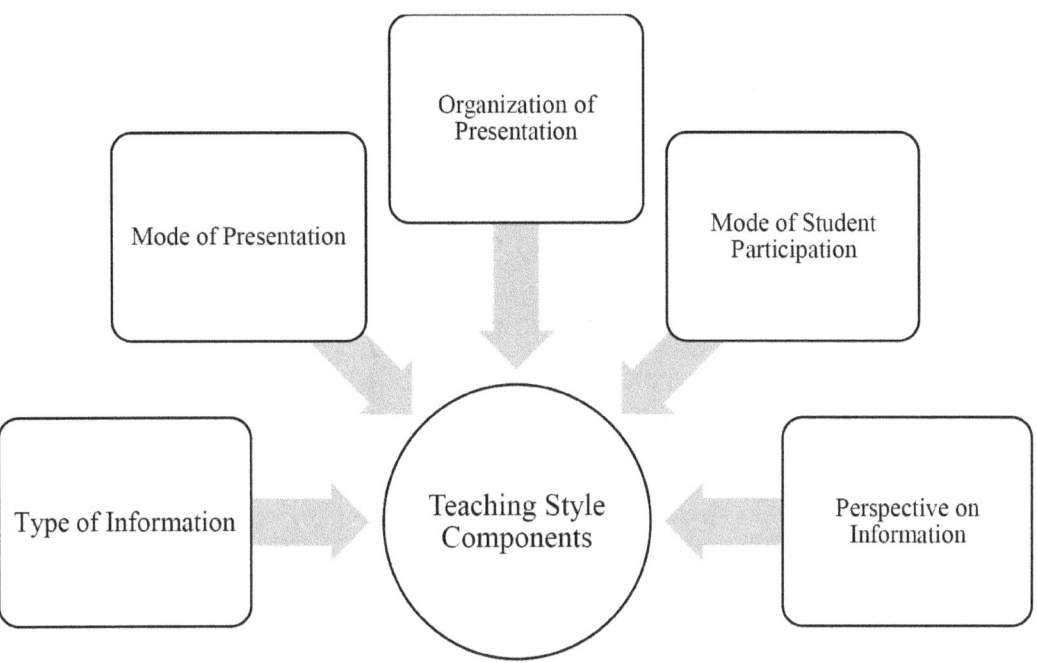

Figure 10.2: Felder and Silverman's Model

10.4 ANTHONY F. GRASHA'S TEACHING STYLES

Anthony F. Grasha (2002, as cited in Mazumder & Ahmed, 2014) explored various topics concerning teaching style, including its assessment and its effect on the classroom, in *Teaching with Style*. He also wrote that no two teachers will implement teaching guidelines the same way, and this defines teaching styles.

There are five specific teaching style categories: expert, formal authority, demonstrator or personal model, facilitator, and delegator (see Table 10.1). Grasha's (1994) observations indicated that college teachers used some styles more frequently. Therefore, his clusters of learning activities for each style suggest that there are dominant and secondary combinations of styles. "The primary or dominant styles are like the foreground in a painting. They are easily seen and central to understanding the artist's vision. The other qualities are like the background" (Grasha, 1994, pp. 142–143). Lecturing displays expert and authority styles more than other styles. "But teaching styles are more than interesting qualities. They also serve an important function in the classroom" (Grasha, 1994, p. 143).

Table 10.1: Grasha's (1994) Teaching Styles

Styles	Description	Advantages	Disadvantages
Expert	Has knowledge students require, focuses on information transmission and students	Expertise	May intimidate or neglect to convey cognitive processes
Formal authority	Has status because of role, focuses on establishing expectations and giving feedback	Clear expectations	Rigid approaches
Personal model	Teaches by example and modeling	Being hands-on	Students may feel inferior if they cannot follow the teacher's standards
Facilitator	Develops personal relationships by being supportive and fostering students' personal responsibility	Flexibility and willingness to innovate to meet students' needs	Time-consuming, ineffective when being directive is necessary
Delegator	Develops students' ability to work independently and acts as a resource consulted when students want help	Fosters students' autonomy	May make students anxious

If teachers want to choose their style of teaching, they must consider three factors (Grasha, 1994):

- Students' ability to fulfill course demands
- Teachers' need for direct control
- Teachers' willingness to maintain relationships with students

Although it is difficult to change teaching styles, there are still some methods to overcome resistance to change (Grasha, 1994):

- Adopt a new attitude on control; for instance, lecturing and discussing have these elements of control that can be established in other teaching styles:
  o Respect for the teacher's authority
  o Strict time management
  o Specific outcomes
  o Clear teacher and student roles
  o Students' accountability for learning
- Use control within small groups.
- Adopt a new attitude on students' abilities.
- Create options for teaching material, such as:
  o Write goals to achieve in a future class meeting.
  o Write how you will achieve those goals using two or more of the teaching styles.

10.5 CONNECTING LEARNING STYLE AND TEACHING STYLE

According to Felder and Silverman (1988), a learning style model identifies how students obtain and process information, and an aligned teaching style model identifies teaching methods based on how they address features of learning styles. As Felder and Silverman (1988) illustrate:

- The content component aligns with the sensory/intuitive learning style dimension.
- The presentation component aligns with the visual/auditory learning style dimension.
- The organization component aligns with the inductive/deductive learning style dimension.
- The student participation component aligns with the active/reflective learning style dimension.
- The perspective component aligns with the sequential/global learning style dimension (see Chapter 8 for definitions of these learning style dimensions).

This is not the only learning style model with an associated teaching style model. Research based on Grasha's (1994) model found a group of students' learning styles matched their professor's teaching style. The students preferred instruction that facilitated, modeled, and provided expertise, and the professor incorporated those preferences by facilitating students' collaboration. Dinçol, Temel, Oskay, Erdoğan, and Yılmaz (2011) also analyzed another group of students whose learning style differed from their professor's teaching style, but the effect of the mismatch on academic performance was not statistically significant.

10.6 TEACHING TECHNIQUES TO ADDRESS ALL LEARNING STYLES

Because of the variety of learning styles and debate over whether teaching style and learning style must align, a wise approach is to use learning activities that appeal to students of diverse learning styles (Clark & Latshaw, 2012). Allow time for independent reflection and for hands-on experimentation to reach reflective and active learners, respectively. Give practical examples for sensing learners and concepts and theories to intuitive learners. Also, the content of the course may determine the appropriate teaching style because accounting, for instance, focuses on technical data and mathematics, making traditional lectures valuable (Clark & Latshaw, 2012). A majority of instructors Cellucci, Peters, Kennedy, and Woodruff (2016) surveyed prefaced in-class case studies with discussion of applicable theories, concepts, and current events and concluded them with discussion about their relevance to the course information and their takeaways. This combination appeals to learners who like abstract concepts and those who like practical applications. Finally, a university that reformed its chemistry courses to address learning styles found students had better outcomes and satisfaction. The reforms included more group work and weekly quizzes (Dubetz et al., 2008). Instructors should not hesitate to combine teaching styles to improve educational quality.

10.7 REFERENCES

Cellucci, L. W., Peters, C., Kennedy, M. H., & Woodruff, E. (2016). Cases in the classroom: Part C. *Journal of Case Studies, 34*(2), 1–10.

Clark, S. D., & Latshaw, C. A. (2012). Effects of learning styles/ teaching styles and effort on performance in accounting and marketing courses. *World Journal of Management, 4*(1), 67–81.

Dinçol, S., Temel, S. Oskay, Ö. Ö., Erdoğan, Ü. I., & Yılmaz, A. (2011). The effect of matching learning styles with teaching styles on success. *Procedia - Social and Behavioral Sciences, 15,* 854–858.

Dubetz, T. A., Barreto, J. C., Deiros, D., Kakareka, J., Brown, D. W., & Ewald, C. (2008). Multiple pedagogical reforms implemented in a university science class to address diverse learning styles. *Journal of College Science Teaching, 38*(2), 39.

Felder, R. M., & Silverman, L. K. (1988). Learning and teaching styles in engineering education. *Engineering Education, 78*(7), 674–681.

Grasha, A. F. (1994). A matter of style: The teacher as expert, formal authority, personal model, facilitator, and delegator. *College Teaching, 42*(4), 142–149.

Mazumder, Q. H., & Ahmed, K. (2014). *The effects of teaching style and experience on student success in the U.S.A. and Bangladesh.* Paper presented at the American Society for Engineering Education Annual Conference and Exposition, Indianapolis, IN.

Pratt, D. D. (2002). Good teaching: One size fits all? *New Directions for Adult and Continuing Education, 93*, 5–16.

Stevenson, C. D., & Harris, G. K. (2014). Instruments for characterizing instructors' teaching practices: A review. *NACTA Journal, 58*(2), 102–108.

CASE STUDY: THE EFFECTS OF TEACHING STYLE AND EXPERIENCE ON STUDENT SUCCESS IN THE U.S.A. AND BANGLADESH

Quamrul H. Mazumder, University of Michigan–Flint, and Kawshik Ahmed, University of Michigan–Flint
© American Society for Engineering Education, 2014
Indianapolis, IN

ABSTRACT

In order to understand the characteristics of teachers and factors that may contribute to student success, faculty members from Bangladesh and the USA were compared to determine if there were similarities or differences in their perceptions of teaching styles and their final outcomes. Participating faculty from the USA and Bangladesh performed a self-assessment of their teaching styles using The Grasha-Riechmann teaching style survey. The current investigation explored a number of research questions such as whether teaching style depends on age, gender, number of years teaching, academic rank or highest degree earned. Statistical analysis, using independent samples t tests, Kruskall Wallace tests, and chi-squared, were conducted to answer the research questions. The second area of investigation involved looking for differences between a developing country and a developed country with regard to the characteristics mentioned above.

In addition to analysis of the above research questions, interactions between variables were considered, to determine any effect on each other. No significant difference was found in teaching styles based on age or gender; however, some interactions were observed based on level of education attained by the teacher, as well as number of years teaching. Notwithstanding, the results of this study showed no significant differences in teaching styles based on the age, gender, degree earned, number of years teaching, or academic rank.

INTRODUCTION

For years academicians have been exploring different approaches to improve quality of education and improve overall learning processes. Almost every factor has been analyzed such as students, parents, and socio-economic conditions, as well as school curriculum and standardized testing. But very little attention has been given to factors affecting the quality of instruction provided in the classroom. We have examined and revamped curriculums, standardized testing, and methods of teaching; but there has been very little mention of the teachers themselves. Yet teachers are the ones who are with the students for most of their learning years, which amounts to approximately 15,000 hours of schooling [1]. It is important to realize that teachers do matter, but what is ironic, is that there is no reliable or objective way of identifying excellent teachers [2]. There are different types of teachers with different teaching styles as students have different learning styles. Teachers can be categorized as novice, experienced and experts in their field. But what makes a teacher an expert or excellent teacher is not yet clearly understood. Is it their age, or could it be the number of years they spend teaching, gender or perhaps their level of education? Very few studies have been conducted that focus on the teacher, with data obtained directly from the classroom and/or the students. According to Brophy, "teachers are not merely reactors to whatever motivational patterns their students had developed before entering their classrooms, but rather are active socialization agents capable of stimulating the general development of student motivation to learn and its activation in particular situations." [3].

BACKGROUND

There have been numerous studies done over the years regarding teaching styles and academic achievement; this study explores a few of these studies to gain better insight into the methods used to correlate teaching styles with learning effectiveness. One of these investigations explores the interactions between variables that affect a student's capacity to learn. This study was conducted by Hattie et al, 2003, in the New Zealand school systems, and spans over 300 classrooms. Hattie observed that the student accounts for 50% of the learning experience, but what is important here, is what that student brings to the table in terms of achievement, and how he/she is influenced by their environment, including the school, principal, peers, home, and teachers. How are the parents contributing at home to improve this scenario and what levels of expectation and encouragement are the students receiving at home to improve their academic achievement? Peer pressure has an effect on the students' interest in publicly embracing learning. A student's peers may also have an effect on his or her learning; if pride in learning is not one of the values of the student's peers; he or she may not consider success in education to be important, either. [1] The school interaction accounts for only about five percent of the involvement with the student. It includes the finances of the school, the size of the school and the size of the classrooms. The school administrator's involvement includes the type of climate or environment he or she creates at the school. Does he/she promote student responsiveness or is it an atmosphere of bureaucratic control? All of the above items interact with one another, and influence the learning atmosphere and academic achievement of the student. The most important factor in the learning process is the extent and quality of student-teacher interaction in the classroom and beyond.

Amanda Ripley describes six characteristics that define an exceptional teacher or what constitutes a good teacher. Time after time, it was found that an excellent teacher would *set high expectations* for their students and they would constantly try to find ways to improve their effectiveness by *reevaluating methods and techniques* they are using. In addition, a successful teacher would persistently recruit students and their families to participate in the learning process. They would maintain the students focus by *checking their understanding* to ensure they are contributing to the student grasping the subject matter. An excellent teacher will exhaustively and purposefully plan for the next session or even year. Lastly, a teacher who rises above the norm will work relentlessly, ignoring the combined factors contributing to less resources and low achievements such as socio-economic background of students, reduced funding at the institution, and bureaucracy.

A more comprehensive description of teaching styles can be found in Dr Grasha's book, *Teaching with Style* [4]. In it, he examines a variety of subjects regarding teaching style, from how to assess teaching styles, to how the classroom climate is affected by the teaching style of the instructor. He touches on virtually every topic imaginable that could affect the academic outcome of a student. Dr. Grasha also pointed out that, although two teachers may read the same exact guidelines, and attempt to follow the same instructions, of "how to present information in the classroom" the final result will be very different, due to "the unique ways in which we understand, interpret and execute such guidelines." Furthermore, this is what he claims defines the styles of teachers.

Studies have shown that people prefer to learn in different ways or they may have different learning style preferences. Dunn & Griggs found that factors that affect these differences could include age, culture, religion, nationality, etc. Studies have found that when students learn using their learning styles preferences, their achievement results are significantly higher than when they don't utilize their preferences. Their strengths are measured on a test, indentified and transferred to a computer program that generates a personalized prescription for each student for how they should focus their study habits. In addition, the authors suggest the use of a learning instrument to identify the learning styles of adolescents, mainly because many of their behaviors are misinterpreted; therefore, their traits and preferences are usually misunderstood as well [5].

Guild reported, "Every educational decision is evaluated based on its impact on individual students' learning." [6]. She suggests that there is a link between culture and learning style, and educators need to familiarize themselves with the various patterns of style preferences. Furthermore, she also brings our attention to the fact that "if instructional decisions were based on an understanding of each individual's culture and ways of learning, we would never assume that uniform practices would be effective for all". Teachers who understand and embrace these differences will be able to "offer opportunities for success to all students.

Rezler suggested that teachers need to find out the learning preferences of their students in order to capture the attention of the entire class and to be able to "match these preferences with suitable learning conditions" [7]. A Learning Preference Inventory (LPI) was used to identify the learning preferences of students so that the teaching style may be adjusted to accommodate their needs.

In chapter 3 of her book, Irene Sanchez also emphasized the need for identifying learning preferences between Hispanic and Native American students, then adjusting the teaching methods to accommodate the student's learning preference. In today's diverse classroom, teaching methods need to provide more instructional classroom activities to tap into the higher level of cognition of these minority students. [8]

METHODS

The current study used the forty question Grasha-Riechmann teaching style survey to determine teaching styles of 45 faculty members from two different universities. Of these faculty members, 23 of them were from Khulna University, Bangladesh, and 22 from the

University of Michigan Flint (UMF). Using the responses to survey questions about their individual teaching styles, a score was issued for each of the following five categories; (1) Expert, (2) Formal authority (3) Personal Model, (4) Facilitator and (5) Delegator. They were numbered from highest to lowest, with (1) being the highest and (5) being the lowest. These scores were recalculated by assigning a ranking to each variable as shown in Table 1 and summed into a final category, entitled Total Score of Teaching Style. The total score calculation was necessary as individual faculty had multiple teaching styles with strong bias towards a particular style.

Table 1: Values Used in Teaching Score Calculation

Expert Rating	Recoded Numerical Value	Authority Rating	Recoded Numerical Value	Personal Model Rating	Recoded Numerical Value
4-4.99	9=High	4-4.99	7=High	4-4.99	5=High
3-3.99	6=Moderate	3-3.99	5=Moderate	3-3.99	3=Moderate
2-2.99	3=Low	2-2.99	3=Low	2-2.99	1=Low

Facilitator Rating	Recoded Numerical Value	Delegator Rating	Recoded Numerical Value
4-4.99	3=High	4-4.99	2=High
3-3.99	2=Moderate	3-3.99	1=Moderate
2-2.99	1=Low	2-2.99	0=Low

The teaching styles data was calculated by assigning each category a value and adding them together for each participant. Parametric tests were conducted to compare two variables at a time. An independent samples t-test was also conducted to test the following hypotheses (H_0)

1. The Teaching Style does not differ based on the type of degree earned.
2. The Teaching Style does not change based on age (under 45, 45+).
3. The Teaching Style does not change based on gender (Male vs. Female).
4. The Teaching Style does not differ based on number of years teaching.
5. The Teaching Style does not differ based on the academic rank of the instructor (Lecturer, Adjunct, Assistant Professor, Associate Professor, and Professor).

RESULTS

The Kruskal Wallis test was used to compare the independent variable of degree earned (Bachelor, Masters of Arts, Masters of Science, Doctor of Philosophy, Doctor of Philosophy 1 & 2), to the dependent variable teaching style, to determine if there was a difference in the styles based on degree attained. Figure 1 shows the teaching style score of faculty with different academic degrees. Teachers with a Bachelor or Bachelor of Pharmacology had an average ranking of between 24.83 and 29.83, whereas teachers with a PhD and PhD 1&2 had an average ranking of between 21.94 and 24.00. No significant difference was found [$H(5) = 3.901$, $p > .05$] indicating that the groups did not differ significantly from one another. Type of degree attained did not seem to influence the teaching style, which was determined through a self-assessment survey, the Grasha-Riechmann teaching style survey.

Figure 2 shows a comparison between numbers of years teaching experience and teaching style scores. There was no correlation between number of years of teaching experience and score.

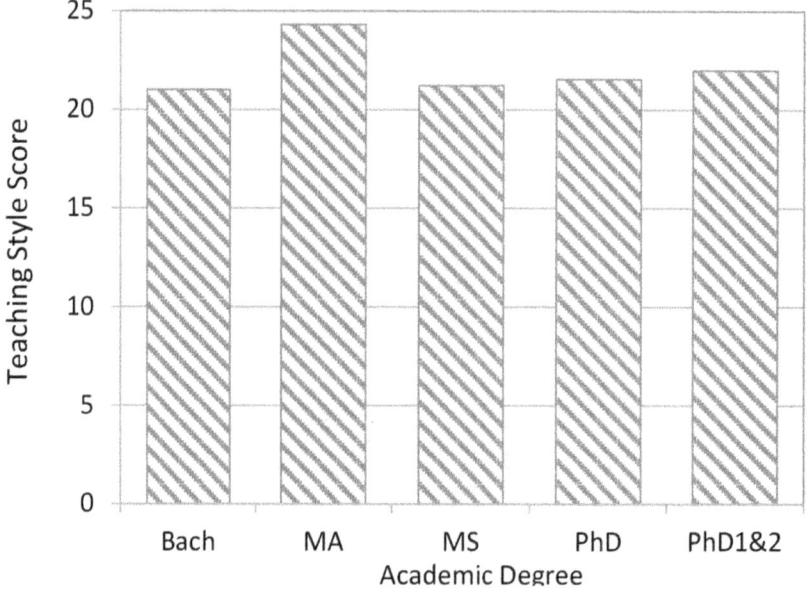

Figure 1: Teaching Style Score of Faculty with Different Degrees

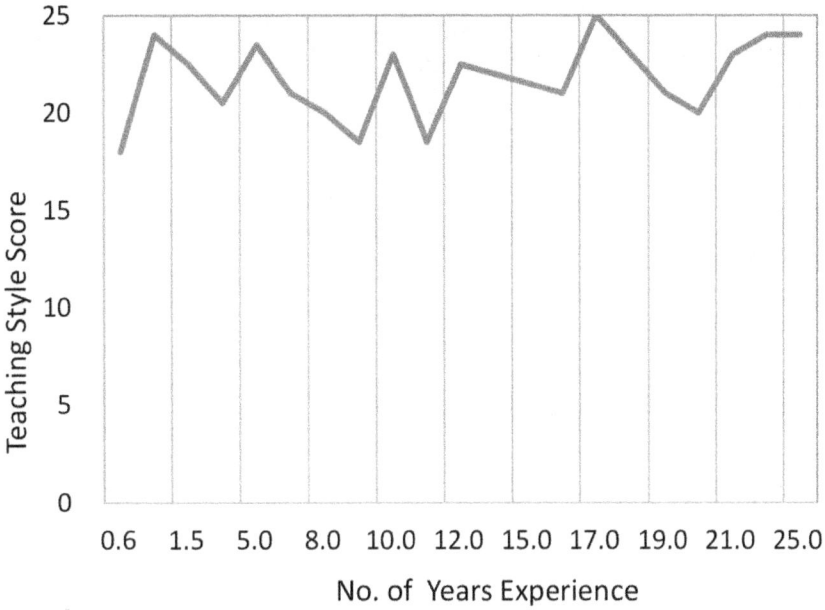

Figure 2: Teaching Style Score Based on Number of Years' Experience

Figure 3 shows the relationship between highest degree and number of years of teaching experience showing that faculty with PhD degrees has largest number of years of teaching experience.

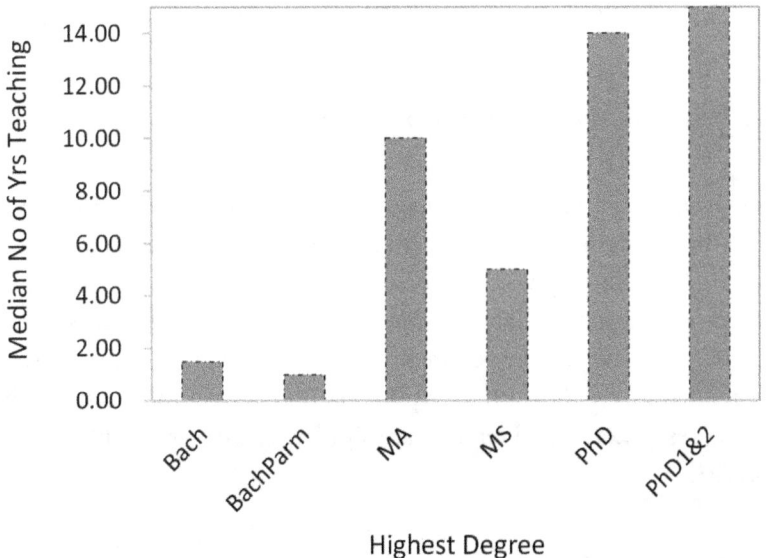

Figure 3: Relationship between Number of Years Teaching and Highest Degree

Highest Degree	Means	Std. Deviation	t	df	Significance
Bachelors Degree	21.00	6.25	-	2	-
Bachelor of Pharmacology	23.00	4.35	-0.455	4	-0.124
Master of Arts	24.33	3.05		4	
Master of Science	21.22	2.11	2.004	10	1.33
PhD	21.53	2.35		23	
PhD 1&2	22.00	n/a	-0.192	2	-2.097

Table 2: Statistical Analysis of Teaching Scores Based on Academic Degrees

Age	N	Mean	Standard Deviation	t	df	Significance (2-tailed)	Mean Difference	Std.Error Difference
Below 45	32	21.62	3.07					
45 and Above	13	22.00	1.91	0.407	43	0.686	-0.37	0.92
Gender								
Male	37	21.70	2.93					
Female	8	21.87	2.03	0.157	43	0.876	-0.17	1.094

Table 3: Statistical Analysis of Teaching Score Based on Age and Gender

Independent samples t-test between faculty with age below and above 45 did not show any significant difference, t (43) =0.407, p=.686. The sample means show that the mean teaching style scores of faculty with age below 45 were similar to the mean teaching style scores of faculty with age 45 or above. The observed difference between the means was 0.375. Another test conducted between male and female faculty members also did not show any significant difference, t (43) =0.157, p=.876. The sample means show that the mean teaching style scores of males and females are similar. The observed difference between the means was 0.1723.

Years of Teaching Experience	N	Means	Standard Deviation	t	df	Significance (2-tailed)	Mean Differenc	Std.Error Difference
10 or Less years	25	21.52	3.28					
More than 10 yrs	20	22.00	2.02	0.572	43	0.570	-0.480	0.838
Academic Rank								
Junior	23	21.21	3.35					
Senior	19	22.10	1.852	1.029	40	0.310	-0.887	0.862

Table 4: Statistical Analysis of Teaching Score Based on Experience and Rank

An independent samples t-test did not reveal any statistically significant difference between number of years of experience and teaching score, t (43) =0.572, p=.57. The sample means show that the mean teaching style scores obtained by people with 10 or fewer years of teaching experience was similar to the mean teaching style scores obtained by people with more than 10 years of teaching experience. The observed difference between the means was 0.48.

Independent samples t-test between academic rank also did not show any statistically significant difference, t (40) =1.029, p=.31. The sample means show that the mean teaching style scores obtained by juniors is similar to the mean teaching style scores obtained by seniors. The observed difference the means was 0.89.

Comparative statistical analysis between Bangladeshi and USA faculty teaching styles are presented in Table 5 and 6. Significant correlation between professors was observed who rated themselves as delegator, facilitator, formal authority and experts (p < 0.05) as shown in Table 6.

Review of the above analysis shows the Expert category resulted in p< .05, which means the null hypothesis is rejected. Therefore, we must go to table number 5 to compare the means of teachers' ratings in the Expert Category M .05 (Bangladesh), and M 1.75 (USA). For the group labeled Formal Authority it was found that p< .05, which means the null hypothesis is rejected. We will compare the means in Table 5 under the group Formal Authority to find that M 1.60 (Bangladesh) and M 3.00 (USA). In the group Personal Model, no significant correlation was observed (p>0.05, 0.219). If we look at the group labeled Facilitator, we find that p<.05, so we must therefore compare the Means of this group in Table 5, M 8.6 (Bangladesh), and M 18.99 (USA). For the group labeled Delegator, we have significant results in that p< .05, so we will be rejecting the null hypothesis and comparing the Means of the group in Table 5 M 9.3 (Bangladesh) and M 23.60 (USA).

Teaching Style	Mean Score (Bangladesh/USA)	N	Correlation	Sigma
Delegator	9.30/ 23.60	40	0.305	0.190
Facilitator	8.60/ 18.99	40	0.096	0.687
Personal Model	4.00/5.15	40	0.360	0.118
Formal Authority	1.60/ 3.00	40	0.371	0.108
Expert	0.05/ 1.75	40	0.970	0.000

Table 5: Paired Sample Statistics Between Bangladesh and USA

Teaching Style	Mean	t	df	Sigma (2-tailed)
Delegator	-14.30	-8.814	19	0.000
Facilitator	-10.35	-8.073	19	0.000
Personal Model	-1.15	-1.272	19	0.219
Formal Authority	-1.40	-2.833	19	0.011
Expert	-1.70	-3.747	19	0.001

Table 6: Paired Sample t-test between Bangladesh and USA

It is important to point out that the data collected in this study was based solely on each teacher's self- assessment of their own teaching styles, and may contain some error, as some of them may not have accurately assessed their styles. The study also did not include any ratings from students, parents, peers or administrators regarding individuals teaching style. However, it is obvious that there are many different types of teaching styles; some of which may be difficult to describe, because teachers who embrace certain styles may demonstrate characteristics that are inherent to their personality. As Curry pointed out in his study, there is too much confusion in the definition surrounding the conceptualization of learning styles and too much variation in the instrumentation used to measure cognition and various learning styles. The same is true of teaching styles – using a self-administered survey to determine whether a professor is an expert or a Delegator is only their own perception of how they view themselves. This assumption could lead to some very confounding results. This makes it very difficult to mimic all of the styles of teaching. Still, studies have shown that teachers who demonstrate certain characteristics tend to have students who perform much better academically. Some of these teaching characteristics include: setting high standards for their students, holding them accountable for their performance, re-evaluating, self-assessing, showing compassion, and monitoring – all of the characteristics that define metacognitive strategies. Although these strategies account for a good portion of the academic success of the student, having a good teacher only accounts for part of the equation. A student has to provide part of the equation as well, by having the right attitude, being motivated to learn, and being disciplined in his/her study habits. However, the number of years a professor has been teaching, and the level of degree held, may also have an effect on student success.

When comparing how the teachers rated themselves in Bangladesh versus the United States as Experts, Formal Authority, Personal Model, Facilitator or Delegator we observed an interesting phenomenon. What was observed was that in all of the cases where $p<.05$, the teachers in the US rated themselves significantly higher than the teachers in Bangladesh. As the scale goes down below personal model, it seems that teachers from the USA rated themselves more in the role of delegator or facilitator than those in Bangladesh. It is possibly due to a difference in education norms between the two countries, or it could possibly indicate that teachers in the USA do not see their roles the same as teachers in Bangladesh. When the means of the two teaching styles are compared in the Expert and Formal Authority Category, there is not as great a difference as seen in the two previously mentioned categories. To determine the actual meaning behind these results will require additional testing to validate the differences observed.

SUMMARY AND CONCLUSION:

In this study, when we compared the teachers' academic ranking to how they rated their own personal teaching style, an interesting interaction between some of the variables was discovered. It was observed that teachers with less experience teaching and holding a lower academic rating than some of their counterparts, rated themselves at the same level or higher than teachers holding a senior level position with a higher level degree. This could be due to the teacher being more enthusiastic about their profession or it could be a misconception based on the ego of the instructor, believing they are far more superior than is actually the case. One way to resolve this deficiency in the study would be to have the students rate their professors' teaching styles and to correlate the results with students' test scores or final grades. However, in addition to teaching style, number of years teaching, and the degree earned, a teacher's job satisfaction may have an effect on student performance as well.

The current study showed that teachers had higher performances in years 1, 5, 10, and 17, with lower performances in years 3, 9, 11, and 20. The specific reasons for this variation in performance are not known at this time and can be investigated in a future study. Teaching style and the number of years teaching account for just a small fraction of what makes a good teacher, and further studies should be conducted, to address additional areas that have been discussed in this paper, such as gender, age, and the level of the degree earned. An analysis of the reliability of the instruments used in collecting the data for this study is highly recommended as well.

REFERENCES

[1] Hattie, J. (2003). Distinguishing expert teachers from novice and experienced teachers. Teachers make a difference, what is the research evidence? University of Auckland, *Australian Council for Educational Research*.

[2] Ripley, A. (3/14/2012). What makes a great teacher. Retrieved from http://www.theatlantic.com/magazine/archive/2010/01/what-makes-a-great-teacher/7841/

[3] Brophy, J. (1986). *On Motivating Students*. East Lansing, Mich.: Institute for Research on Teaching, Oct. 1986. (ED 276 724).

[4] Grasha, A PhD. (2002). *Teaching with style: a practical guide to enhancing learning by understanding teaching and learning styles*. San Bernadino, CA: Alliance Publishing 31-34.

[5] Dunn, R., & Griggs, S. A. *Multiculturalism and Learning Style: Teaching and Counseling Adolescents*. New York: Praeger, 1995.

[6] Guild, P. (1994). The culture/learning style connection. *Educational Leadership*, 51(8), 16–21.

[7] Rezler, A. G., &Rezmovic, V. (1981). The learning preference inventory. *Journal of Allied Health*, 10, 28–34.

[8] Sanchez, I. M. (1996). An analysis of learning style constructs and the development of a profile of Hispanic adult learners." Unpublished doctoral dissertation, Department of Education, University of New Mexico, 1996.

CHAPTER 11:

Student Satisfaction

CHAPTER OBJECTIVE

The primary objective is to understand how different factors affect student satisfaction and to describe assessments of student satisfaction using different conceptual frameworks. Information in this chapter is also intended to provide fundamentals to institutions and faculty concerning improvement of student satisfaction. This chapter provides a case study of student satisfaction to determine what its contributing factors are.

11.1 INTRODUCTION

Quality of education is an important issue of higher education development, and improving it is the ultimate goal of higher education around the world. Providing students high-quality service is an important facet of educational quality. Due to growing demands from students, student satisfaction is a factor that decides what support and funding educational programs receive. Some researchers and administrators use satisfaction as evidence for program success. Therefore, researchers have found that student satisfaction can consistently predict many desirable student outcomes, such as persistence and intellectual growth. The influence of satisfaction on performance results in the improvement of student success.

To know the quality of education being provided to students, their level of satisfaction, achievement, and absorption should be analyzed carefully because these people represent the nation's future. It is true that the higher education industry is competitive and constantly changing because it tries to adapt to the world's realities and satisfy students' increasing expectations. (Butt & ur Rehman, 2010). From students' point of view, high quality of education provides better learning opportunities. Aldridge and Rowley (1998, as cited in Butt & ur Rehman, 2010) "suggest that the levels of satisfaction or dissatisfaction strongly affect the student's success or failure of learning" (p. 5446). Higher education institutions are learning and fulfilling students' needs and expectations (Deshields et al., 2005, as cited in Butt & ur Rehman, 2010).

11.2 WHAT IS STUDENT SATISFACTION?

Student satisfaction is more important in evaluating quality of education programs than other sophisticated assessments. Student satisfaction can be defined as the attitude toward certain study and living environments of higher education. Satisfaction has also been linked to student motivation and retention. It can evaluate program effectiveness. The primary goal of most universities is to provide higher education service to satisfy the students, their direct customers. Due to this, the institutions must have comprehensive knowledge of factors related to students' satisfaction (Aldemir & Gülcan, 2004). Students are the essential part of assessing the quality of higher education.

Learning satisfaction, a related concept, refers to the joy of individuals during learning (Long, 1985, as cited in Topală, 2014). In addition, learning satisfaction can be identified as the "level of coherence between the individual's expectations and his actual experience" (Martin, 1988, as cited in Topală, 2014, p. 228). Students' satisfaction is related to student involvement and student interaction with faculty and peers (Astin, 1993, as cited in Topală, 2014). In addition, it can emerge from learning activities that consider learning preferences (Deci, Ryan, & Williams, 1996, as cited in Topală, 2014). If the situation meets the individual's expectation, the individual feels satisfied. If the situation is less than his or her expectations, this makes him or her feel unsatisfied (Flammger, 1991, as cited in Topală, 2014). In other words, satisfaction is the difference between expectations and reality of performance (Aldemir & Gülcan, 2004).

Students' satisfaction mainly depends on the quality of education provided to them. Satisfaction of students is measured through their personal experience within the educational institutions. Satisfaction results from the interaction of demographic characteristics, faculty performance, learning facilities, and reputation of the college (Butt & ur Rehman, 2010). There are plenty of conceptual frameworks and theories related to student satisfaction based on certain assessment factors. Some of the models for the evaluation of student satisfaction are explained below.

11.3 FACTORS AFFECTING SATISFACTION

People decide to purchase a product using their valuation of its marketing, but their satisfaction depends on whether the product met their needs. Applying this to college students, if institutions know what features enhance satisfaction, they can improve their services (El-Hilali, Al-Jaber, & Hussein, 2014). To gain competitive advantage, universities need to describe the ways they support achievement of students' goals (Petruzzellis & Romanazzi, 2010, as cited in El-Hilali et al., 2014). Along with improving the university's competitiveness, making students aware of support efforts could improve their satisfaction.

Many higher education institutions are likely to improve their service quality through five main dimensions: "reliability, assurance, empathy, responsiveness and tangibles" (Zeithaml, Bitner, & Gremler, 2009, as cited in El-Hilali et al., 2014, p. 421), as shown in Figure 11.1. The first dimension, reliability, equates to the service being what the college promised (Parasuraman, Zeithaml, & Berry, 1988, as cited in El-Hilali et al., 2014). Correcting this dimension is crucial when colleges make mistakes so that they regain students' trust (Danish, Malik, & Usman, 2010, as cited in El-Hilali et al., 2014). Reliability is the most critical component of service quality (Alexandris & James, 2002, as cited in El-Hilali et al., 2014). The second dimension, assurance, indicates employees' knowledge and courtesy, which fosters students' confidence and trust (Parasuraman et al., 1988, as cited in El-Hilali et al., 2014). Empathy can be viewed "as giving an individualized attention to students" (El-Hilali et al., 2014, p. 421). Empathy is important because students always seek a customized way to achieve their aims. To provide satisfying services to students, educational staff ought to serve students and solve their problems promptly, which explains the responsiveness component (Zeithaml et al., 2009, as cited in El-Hilali et al., 2014). Because the last three components greatly rely on the personnel, their interpersonal skills and reactions to customers form the foundation of satisfaction with service (Danish et al., 2010, as cited in El-Hilali et al., 2014).

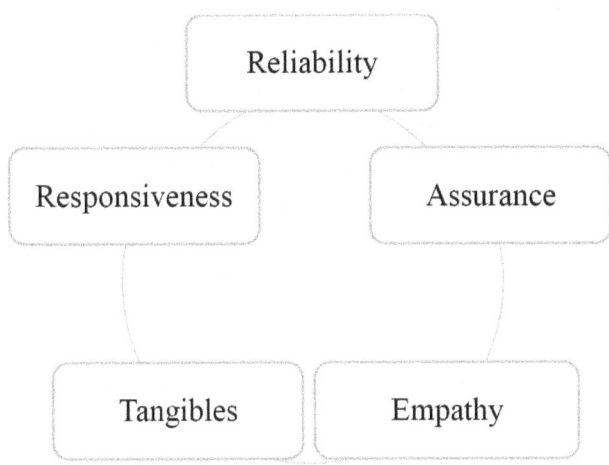

Figure 11.1: Five Dimensions of Service Quality for Student Satisfaction

In the education industry, it is not possible to evaluate the service before receiving it (Padma, 2006, as cited in El-Hilali et al., 2014). However, tangibles can assist in forming an opinion. These include employees' appearance and physical facilities and greatly affect satisfaction (Hill & Epps, 2010, as cited in El-Hilali, 2014). Brand image also affects the students' satisfaction, achievement, and absorption capacity. Teaching is the top satisfaction determinant partly because it requires changing methods to reflect the subject (Palmer, 1993, as cited in El-Hilali et al., 2014). Methods along with support services are vital in quality knowledge delivery (Petruzzellis & Romanazzi, 2010, as cited in El-Hilali et al., 2014). The caliber of advising and programs enhances satisfaction and effectiveness in careers (Hagen & Jordan, 2008, as cited in El-Hilali et al., 2014). Tuition fees also influence satisfaction. Therefore, all university attributes play a critical role in students' choosing of a certain university.

Tangibles were the most significant factor that influenced the students' perception of satisfaction in El-Hilali et al.'s (2014) study. The types of offered programs, teaching methods, and college's reputation are other factors that contributed to students' satisfaction. The variety of programs as well as their content mattered in enhancing achievement and absorption (El-Hilali et al., 2014).

11.4 NOEL-LEVITZ STUDENT SATISFACTION INVENTORY

The Student Satisfaction Inventory is among the most widely used satisfaction assessments in higher education, and it is comprehensive because it covers 12 dimensions (Letcher & Neves, 2010). This inventory has 79 items phrased as expectations students have of the school and a 7-point scale, where 1 is "not at all important" and 7 is "very important" (Schreiner, 2009, p. 2). The second part of the instrument asks students to rate on a 1–7 scale their satisfaction with the fulfillment of each expectation. For example, it includes items about advising, instructional effectiveness, responsiveness, and campus climate, which was a significant predictor of student retention in Schreiner's (2009) study. Because this study found different factors influenced satisfaction to different degrees based on students' length of time spent at the college, breaking down Student Satisfaction Inventory results by class level makes it easier for colleges to decide how to address retention issues. Two pairs of researchers used this inventory to agree that four attributes contribute most to satisfaction: campus climate, service quality, instructional excellence, and quality computer labs (Elliott & Healy, 2001; Elliott & Shin, 2002; as cited in Letcher & Neves, 2010). Because the instrument is comprehensive and valid, higher education administrators should consider using it.

11.5 ALDEMIR AND GÜLCAN'S SURVEY ON STUDENT SATISFACTION

Aldemir and Gülcan's (2004) survey is based on primary aspects of student satisfaction Harvey (2001) identified, as shown in Figure 11.2: institutional factors, extracurricular factors, student expectations, and student demographics. Based on his previous research, Harvey (2001, as cited in Aldemir & Gülcan, 2004) stated that many universities conduct surveys based on their services, focusing on teaching, learning support and environment, and external aspects.

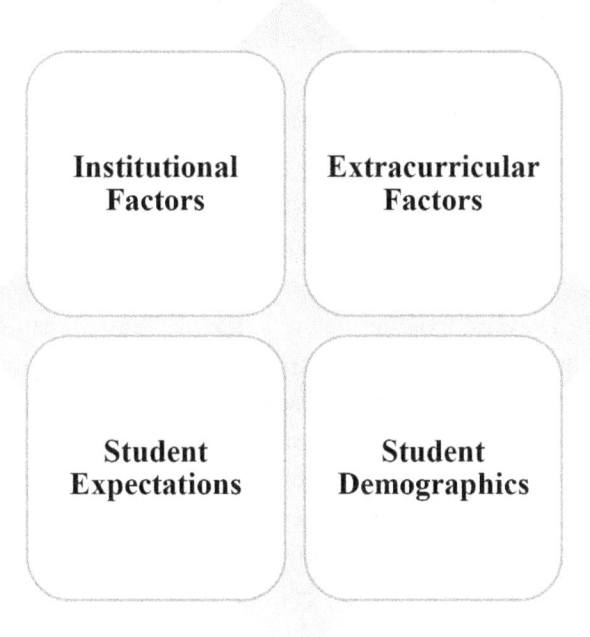

Figure 11.2: Four Factors of Student Satisfaction

The institutional factors include two components, namely academic aspects and the administration's management style. The academic aspects include educational quality, interaction of students and teachers, evaluation of instructors by students, curriculum design, and textbooks. Management aspects include practices followed by administrators of the institution. Extracurricular activities include social, health, sporting, and cultural activities provided by the institution to students. These activities also include transportation and residential facilities of students on campus (Aldemir & Gülcan, 2004). According to Aldemir and Gülcan (2004), student expectations include those related to participation in administration, to which fields students can get jobs in after graduation, to ability to pursue education or employment abroad in the future, and to efforts faculty make to prepare students for the job market. Demographics, such as age, sex, attendance, and grade point average, also influence the students' satisfaction with universities. There may be several other factors to consider because satisfaction is both a psychological and a social concept.

Assessing causal relationships and quantitatively assessing management philosophy is challenging. However, Aldemir and Gülcan (2004) developed a 63-question survey for students based on the four factors. They allowed responses of yes, no, and "I have no idea" to see the satisfaction level generally and see the overall strength of satisfaction (Aldemir & Gülcan, 2004, p. 114). Faculty influenced respondents' satisfaction in more than one way, so the authors recommended that universities recruit and retain high-quality instructors.

Another finding was male students were less satisfied than female students (Aldemir & Gülcan, 2004).

11.6 STUDENT OPINION SURVEY

The American College Testing Service created the *Student Opinion Survey* with a 5-point Likert scale on items relating to satisfaction with admissions, rules, registration, academics, and facilities (Kelso, 2008). Students also rate how important each factor is to them (Letcher & Neves, 2010). The instrument also has a space where students can give written, qualitative comments. The State University of New York is one of the universities that use it, usually every 3 years, and it has found that sense of belonging, advising, and intellectually challenging course material are most important to satisfaction (Kelso, 2008). Northwestern State University in Louisiana focused on the academic portion of the survey to enhance quality, specifically of class size, grading, and instructor availability. Now all public universities in Louisiana measure satisfaction with the survey. Based on these accounts and more, the *Student Opinion Survey* appropriately and validly measures higher education service quality. Kelso's (2008) administration of the survey led him to conclude that colleges must improve based on student feedback and that their staff must complete customer service training. Table 11.1 summarizes the assessments.

Table 11.1 Overview of the Assessments

Assessment	Discipline	Researchers
Noel-Levitz Student Satisfaction Inventory	All disciplines	Letcher and Neves, 2010; Schreiner, 2009
Aldemir and Gülcan's survey	All disciplines	Aldemir and Gülcan, 2004
Student Opinion Survey	All disciplines	Kelso, 2008

11.7 REFERENCES

Aldemir, C., & Gülcan, Y. (2004). Student satisfaction in higher education: A Turkish case. *Higher Education Management and Policy, 16*(2), 109–122.

Butt, B. Z., & ur Rehman, K. (2010). A study examining the students satisfaction in higher education. *Procedia - Social and Behavioral Sciences, 2*, 5446–5450.

El-Hilali, N., Al-Jaber, S., & Hussein, L. (2015, April). Students' satisfaction and achievement and absorption capacity in higher education. *Procedia - Social and Behavioral Sciences, 177*, 420–427. doi:10.1016/j.sbspro.2015.02.384

Kelso, R. S. (2008). *Measuring undergraduate student perceptions of service quality in higher education*. Doctoral dissertation, University of South Florida. Retrieved from http://scholarcommons.usf.edu/etd/328

Letcher, D. W., & Neves, J. S. (2010). Determinants of student satisfaction. *Research in Higher Education Journal, 6*(1), 1–26.

Schreiner, L. A. (2009). *Linking student satisfaction and retention*. Coralville, IA: Noel-Levitz.

Topală, I. (2014). Attitudes towards academic learning and learning satisfaction in adult students. *Procedia - Social and Behavioral Sciences, 142*, 227–234.

CASE STUDY: STUDENT SATISFACTION IN PRIVATE AND PUBLIC UNIVERSITIES IN BANGLADESH

Mazumder, Q. H. (2013). *International Journal of Evaluation and Research in Education,* 2(2), 78–84. Reprinted with permission.

ABSTRACT

To compare and contrast the quality of higher education in public and private universities of Bangladesh, a study was conducted, to evaluate student satisfaction in these institutions. The study used a modified Noel-Levitz student satisfaction survey, consisting of twenty-two questions which measured student satisfaction levels in four different areas: faculty, curriculum, resources, and campus environment. The survey also measured the students' overall level of satisfaction with the institution. Data collected from different private and public universities showed overall satisfaction level to be higher among private university students than public university students. The data also indicated that students from private universities are more satisfied than those of public universities. Finally, comparison of data from male and female students showed higher level of satisfaction among female students.

INTRODUCTION

The Private Universities Act of 1992 was passed in Bangladesh. This has allowed for the rise of many private universities in Bangladesh creating more options, as well as competition amongst universities. This is beneficial to students, the public, and the nation. However, there is no regulatory agency with power to control quality and costs. One of the public perceptions is that in Bangladesh, private universities are using business models to maximize profit and therefore, effecting quality of education. On the other hand, public universities are resistant to change their legacy system of education and therefore unwilling to improve the quality. The perception of higher education stakeholders is that some private universities provide better educational services than public universities [1]. Yet it remains to be determined whether student satisfaction levels are higher in private universities. Determining whether student satisfaction levels are higher in private universities, and in which categories (professor, curriculum, university resources and extracurricular activities), is useful for two reasons. One, it may determine whether higher costs at private universities are actually justified. Two, it may provide a framework for other universities to follow. The previous studies available in the literature mainly focused on quality management in general and within institutions, though at least one study noted the lack of quality management in distance education programs [2]. The study presented in this paper attempts to evaluate level of quality in higher education using student satisfaction levels within, and across, universities.

As early as the 1980s, principles of Total Quality Management (TQM) were adopted from the business world, and incorporated into institutions of higher education. In regards to TQM, students were thought of as the customers. However, many educators did not welcome TQM, as "the customer is always right" [3]. In the late 1990s, it became clear that, regardless of what educators thought about treating students as customers, reform in higher education was needed. There was also more demand amongst students to be treated as customers [4]. Though quality assurance (QA) measures have a place in post-secondary education, they often fail to produce meaningful results due to the "lack of rigorous theoretical foundations ... [and] demands of satisfying external agendas," leading to differences between the "rhetoric" and "reality." It is clear that more research into student satisfaction levels is needed, as most post-secondary institutions use quality assurance methods to monitor issues of accountability rather than student concerns. The student feedback questionnaire (SFQ) has been used to improve the quality of teaching, to assess the staff, and to meet standards of quality assurance [5].

The Noel-Levitz Student Satisfaction Inventory (SSI) is one of the popular and valid instruments used to assess students' perception of teacher quality and other quality factors in institutions of higher education. Then these perceptions of quality and measures of student satisfaction are used to improve services. The Noel Levitz SSI is widely utilized in North America [6]. In addition, the importance–satisfaction gap is a beneficial feature of the SSI, because it allows universities to ascertain how much a particular level of satisfaction or dissatisfaction actually matters to students. The addition of the importance–satisfaction measurements to the SSI constitutes the reasoning for many researchers, including the author of this study on public and private universities, to use it above other Student Satisfaction Inventories [7].

Because of the importance-satisfaction measurements, institutions can "identify aspects of the students' experience where the institutions are failing to meet their expectations" [8]. Noel-Levitz's 2000 study also recommends that there are "four areas of interaction between importance and satisfaction," including "high importance/low satisfaction," which suggests an area commanding prompt attention, "high importance/high satisfaction," an area which could be beneficial in marketing the institution, "low importance/high satisfaction," an area in which resources might be reallocated to an area with "greater need," and "low importance/low satisfaction," an area which should continue to be monitored [9]. The importance-satisfaction gap has been criticized due to the fact that gap scores sometimes do not effectively predict overall student satisfaction, and because the gap scores in each area may lead to recommendations that are counterproductive [10]. However, they are still useful for managers [11]. In many cases, the SSI is used only to measure satisfaction within a university, not to compare and contrast one university with other universities. This is useful in that administrators can focus on strengths and weaknesses of their institution; however, by assessing the experiences of students at other universities, administrators may be able to improve their competitiveness. There are some studies that have compared and contrasted student satisfaction levels across institutions, by type of institution. Among these are the National Student Satisfaction Reports of 2002 and 2003 [12]. Another study assesses the difference in satisfaction levels and quality control between a campus-based program and a distance education program within a university [13]. One study is particularly relevant to this study of the difference between satisfaction levels at public and private universities in Bangladesh, analyzing the satisfaction levels of students at ten private universities in Bangladesh, and finding that students correlate "faculty credentials, ... campus facilities, research facilities and cost of education ... with quality education," but that the cost of these private universities is still unreasonable, despite the higher quality of the education [14]. A limited number of studies were performed to evaluate the quality of higher education in Bangladesh as reported in the available literature. Challenges and opportunities related to higher education quality improvement based on a survey of university faculty showed training to improve curriculum and faculty motivation to be two most important factors [15]. These barriers can be eliminated by providing systematic and regular training on teaching and learning methodologies. Comparative analysis of learning styles of students of Bangladesh and USA resulted no significant difference between them as the differences were based on major field of study [16] pursued by individual student. A study on globalization of engineering curriculum in USA explored the existing quality issues and how to address them effectively [17]

The current study compares and contrasts student satisfaction levels at two different private and public universities in Bangladesh, to determine whether the higher costs at private universities are justified, and in what ways these public and private universities might improve.

RESEARCH METHOD

The study was performed using the Noel Levitz Student Satisfaction Inventory (SSI), which was found to be internally and externally reliable. Six additional questions were added at the end of the survey, to evaluate students' overall satisfaction and expectations, and to solicit comments about the strength and areas of improvement needs of the university. The first step consisted of the computation of mean of scores in four categories (professor, curriculum, university resources and extracurricular activities) for both the Chittagong Veterinary and Animal Sciences University (CVASU), a public college, and Ahsanullah University of Science and Technology (AUST), a private college. Results were then analyzed using OneWay ANOVA.

Analysis was performed to determine the mean satisfaction rating and the mean importance rating using the satisfaction-importance pairs. One-way ANOVA was performed in order to examine the relationship between the mean scores for importance and satisfaction for professors, curriculum, universities and extra-curricular activities from students in different universities. Paired samples t-tests were performed between importance and satisfaction ratings for each group of survey questions. The survey included 21 questions divided into four different categories: professor, curriculum, university resources, and extracurricular activities. In the survey questions, seven are related to professors, five are related to curriculum, six are related to university services, and three are related to extracurricular activities. A seven point Likert scale was used on two dimensions for each of the questions as follows: (1) not important at all, (2) not very important, (3) somewhat unimportant, (4) neutral, (5) somewhat important, (6) important, (7) very important, and N/A

– not applicable. One of the dimensions was importance, and the other dimension was satisfaction level of the students. For example, one of the questions asked whether professors are fair and unbiased in their treatment of individual students. Students were asked to rate how important the professors' fair and unbiased treatment was to them, and their level of satisfaction with it.

Each student's responses to questions were averaged for each of the four categories for importance and satisfaction. For example, the average of responses to the first seven questions was used as importance and satisfaction measures of students' attitude toward the professor, resulting in four different average values for level of satisfaction for each student. Average values falling between zero and seven were used in the analysis of the data. The statistical analysis compared the relationship between importance and satisfaction for each category. Comparative analysis was performed between public and private universities, and between male and female students. At the end of the survey questions, comments from student were collected using six additional questions: the additional questions includes a) how the university was able to meet expectations, b) overall satisfaction with the university, by percentage of 0 to 100 (%), c) whether the student will recommend this university to others, d) whether the current university was their first choice for admission, e) what was the best experience at the institution, and f) what would the student like to see changed. The last two questions were free response questions, and were used in order to determine the strengths and weaknesses of the university.

RESULTS AND DISCUSSION

The results of the current study are summarized along with comprehensive discussion. The anlaysis results are presented using appropriate figures and tables for proper interpretation [2], [5].

ANALYSIS OF THE DATA

The analysis presented in this paper is based on 216 survey responses, out of which 96 responses were from a public university, and 120 from a private university. Data collected from Chittagong Veterinary and Animal Science University (CVASU), a public university and Ahsanullah University of Science and Technology (AUST), a private university located in Dhaka, the capital of Bangladesh. A few students choose not to respond to some questions, thereby showing different n- values in the analysis. Data was collected from first year to final year students in an effort to represent a wide range of students with different levels of experience at the universities. The data sets included 62 first year students, 45 second year students, 33 third year students, 76 fourth year students, with 13 not reporting their year level. Out of 216 students, 159 were male and 47 were female students, with 10 not reporting gender.

LIMITATIONS OF THE STUDY

It is important to note that there were some limitations to this study. One is that the methodology was influenced by lack of complete data. When students failed to rate a particular question in each category, the response was not included. Scale scores not reported were recognized as null value and were not included in computation. As the number of null responses were small, the influence on overall result was negligible. Another limitation is the sample size of number of universities. While care was taken to survey diverse students from a number of different public and private universities, inclusion of data from more universities could improve validity of the results.

RESULTS

Statistical analysis was performed using SPSS software, and the results are presented in Tables 1–5 in the following section.

Table 1. Importance and Satisfaction in Public and Private Universities

Criteria		University CVASU (Public) AUST (Private)	Mean	95 % Confidence Interval for Mean		F	Sig.
				Lower Bound	Upper Bound		
Professor	Importance	CVASU	5.81	5.59	6.02	0.08	0.768
		AUST	5.85	5.66	6.04		
	Satisfaction	CVASU	3.54	3.31	3.76	87.83	0.000
		AUST	5.02	4.81	5.23		
Curriculum	Importance	CVASU	5.65	5.41	5.88	6.39	0.012
		AUST	6.03	5.84	6.22		
	Satisfaction	CVASU	3.84	3.59	4.09	55.66	0.000
		AUST	5.03	4.83	5.23		
Campus Resources	Importance	CVASU	6.19	6.00	6.38	4.48	0.035
		AUST	5.90	5.71	6.09		
	Satisfaction	CVASU	3.99	3.75	4.22	25.03	0.000
		AUST	4.84	4.60	5.07		
Extra-curricular Activities	Importance	CVASU	5.60	5.33	5.87	0.22	0.639
		AUST	5.69	5.43	5.94		
	Satisfaction	CVASU	3.22	2.93	3.50	34.03	0.000
		AUST	4.40	4.12	4.68		

The relationship between importance and satisfaction of 216 students is presented in Table 1 for all four categories. Among all four categories, campus resources were considered to be most important (mean=5.90 and 6.19), followed by curriculum (mean=5.88 and 6.03), professor (mean=5.81 and 5.85), and extracurricular activities (mean=5.60 and 5.69). Students' response showed lower levels of satisfaction in all four categories: Professors (mean=3.54 and 5.02), curriculum (mean=3.84 and 5.03), campus resources (mean=3.99 and 4.84) and extracurricular activities (mean=3.22 and 4.40). The role of professors was rated as important, with scores ranging between 5.59 and 6.04, with a maximum possible score of 7.0. However, the level of satisfaction with professors was lower (mean=3.31 and 3.76) in public universities, contrasted with private universities (mean=4.81 and 5.23). The difference between importance and satisfaction was calculated to determine whether there is an agreement between them. If students reported a category as very important, are they also highly satisfied? The difference between importance and satisfaction was greater among public university students.

Table 1 shows the results of one-way ANOVA for importance and satisfaction of each group of survey questions (professor, curriculum, campus resources, and extracurricular activities) for both public and private universities. Results showed no significant differences in importance of professor and extracurricular activities between public and private universities (for professor, p=0.768, for extra-curricular activities, p=0.639). However, significant differences were observed in curriculum (p=0.012) and campus resources (p=0.035). Students at both universities felt these categories to be equally important to them. However, significant differences were observed in level of satisfaction between public and private universities in all four categories (professor: F=87.38, p =0.000; Curriculum: F=55.664, p = 0.000; Campus resources: F= 25.038, p = 0.000;

Table 2. Overall Student Satisfaction in Public and Private Universities (N=216)

Criteria	Name of University	Mean	95% Confidence Interval of Mean		F	Sig.
			Lower Bound	Upper Bound		
How Well the Expectations were met	CVASU (public)	2.33	2.65	2.93	23.02	0.000
	AUST (private)	2.79	2.48	2.68		
Overall Satisfaction	CVASU (public)	54.55	51.68 %	59.41 %	17.01	0.000
	AUST (private)	66.70	63.03 %	70.38 %		

Two of the six free response questions at the end of the survey were analyzed using ANOVA, as shown in Table 2. These questions were an important determinant of quality and student satisfaction, as responses were sought about how well the universities were able to meet their expectations, and their level of overall satisfaction. There was a significant difference observed in the responses to these two questions, between public and private universities. However, the level of overall satisfaction was higher in private universities than public universities.

Table 3. Importance and Satisfaction between Male and Female Students (N=206)

Criteria		Gender	Mean	95 % Confidence Interval for Mean		F	Sig.
				Lower Bound	Upper Bound		
Professor	Importance	Male	5.83	5.65	6.00	0.27	0.603
		Female	5.73	5.47	5.99		
	Satisfaction	Male	4.43	4.21	4.64	0.09	0.765
		Female	4.36	4.06	4.66		
Curriculum	Importance	Male	5.88	5.70	6.05	0.28	0.596
		Female	5.78	5.43	6.12		
	Satisfaction	Male	4.52	4.30	4.73	0.31	0.576
		Female	4.64	4.34	4.93		
Campus Resources	Importance	Male	6.04	5.88	6.19	0.20	0.655
		Female	5.96	5.65	6.27		
	Satisfaction	Male	4.42	4.21	4.63	2.66	0.104
		Female	4.77	4.45	5.08		
Extra-curricular Activities	Importance	Male	5.63	5.41	5.84	0.35	0.557
		Female	5.76	5.39	6.12		
	Satisfaction	Male	3.83	3.58	4.08	2.87	0.092
		Female	4.27	3.85	4.68		

Comparison between importance and satisfaction of male and female students at both public and private universities are presented in table 3. The number of respondents was 206 compared to 216 total responses, as 10 students did not respond to the gender question. Among all four categories, campus resources were considered to be most important by both male (6.04), and female (5.96), students followed by curriculum. Satisfaction level was highest for curriculum (male: 4.52, Female: 4.64) followed by campus resources (male: 4.42, Female: 4.77). Student satisfaction level was third for professors' contribution to the learning process (male: 4.43, Female: 4.36). In general, female students are slightly more satisfied than the male students. Difference between importance and satisfaction level was highest for male students in extracurricular activities category (1.80), and lowest for female students in curriculum category (1.14). This can be interpreted as, female students are more satisfied with the curriculum, and male students are less satisfied with extra-curricular activities.

Results of one-way ANOVA for importance and satisfaction of each group of survey questions (professor, curriculum, campus resources, and extracurricular activities) between male and female students is presented in Table 3. No significant difference in importance and satisfaction was observed among the four categories. There was also no significant difference in how well the universities were able to meet students' expectations. However, the overall satisfaction level showed a significant difference (p=0.007). The female students were more satisfied than the male students in both public and private universities. Students at both universities felt these categories to be equally important to them. However, significant differences were observed between level of satisfaction between public and private universities in all four categories (professor: F=87.38, p =0.000; Curriculum: F=55.664, p = 0.000; Campus resources: F= 25.038, p = 0.000; Extracurricular activities: F = 34.03, p = 0.000).

Table 4. Overall Student Satisfaction between Male and Female (N=215)

Criteria	Gender	Mean	F	Sig.
How Well the Expectations Met	Male	2.57	2.01	0.158
	Female	2.74		
Overall Satisfaction	Male	60.03	7.50	0.007
	Female	69.15		

Two of the six free response questions at the end of the survey were analyzed using ANOVA, as shown in Table 4. These questions were an important determinant of quality and student satisfaction, as responses were sought about how well the universities were able to meet their expectations, and their level of overall satisfaction. There was a significant difference observed in the results from both of these two questions, between public and private universities. However, the level of overall satisfaction was higher in private universities than public universities.

Table 5. Paired Sample t-test Between Importance and Satisfaction

	Criteria	Mean	t	DOF	Significance (2 tailed)
Public	Professor	2.29	14.76	96	0.000
	Curriculum	1.84	10.20	96	0.000
	Campus Resources	2.22	14.28	96	0.000
	Extracurricular Activities	2.46	11.95	95	0.000
Private	Professor	0.86	8.91	117	0.000
	Curriculum	1.03	9.06	117	0.000
	Campus Resources	1.13	8.87	117	0.000
	Extracurricular Activities	1.35	7.81	117	0.000

Paired sample t- tests between importance to satisfaction for each category of survey questions (professor, curriculum, campus resources and extracurricular activities) are summarized in Table 5. The analysis was performed for both a public (CVASU) and a private university (AUST) to determine whether any significant difference exists. As shown in Table 5, significant differences were observed in all four categories, in regards to satisfaction levels between public and private universities. Based on the results in the previous tables, students of private universities appear to be more satisfied than those of the public universities.

CONCLUSION

A survey was conducted among 216 students from one public university and one private university in Bangladesh, using a modified Noel-Levitz student satisfaction survey. The survey questions were grouped in four different categories, as professor, curriculum, campus resources and extracurricular activities. The twenty-two question survey used a seven point Likert scale, with two different responses for each question. Students were asked to rate the importance of each of the four categories and their satisfaction with current level of university services.

The survey also included questions to measure whether the students' expectations were met, and their overall satisfaction with the university, measured as a percentage. Paired sample t-test and ANOVA results revealed that students from Chittagong Veterinary and Animal Sciences University (public) and Ahsanullah University of Science and Technology (private) hold similar opinions about the importance of professors, curriculum, campus resources, and extra-curricular activities. However, students at the private university were more satisfied than at the public university, in all four categories. Female students expressed higher levels of satisfaction than the male students in both public and private universities. One of the reasons may be the expectations of male students are higher than the female students.

ACKNOWLEDGEMENTS

The author would like to thank Dr. Gourging Ch. Chanda of Chittagong Veterinary & Animal Sciences University and Dr. M. Shahabuddin, Dean, Ahsanullah University of Science and Technology, Bangladesh for their support in collection of the survey responses from the students.

REFERENCES

[1] M.A. Ashraf. "Quality Education Management at Private Universities in Bangladesh: An Exploratory Study." *Jurnal Pendidik dan Pendidikan*, Vol. 24, 2009, pp. 17-32.

[2] M.A. May. "A Comparative Study of Student Satisfaction with the Provision of Student Services in Traditional and Web-Based Environments." Doctoral Dissertation, Kent State University Graduate School of Education, Ohio, 2002

[3] S. Griffith. "Using the National Survey of Student Engagement as a Tool to Help Determine Influences of Overall Student Satisfaction with the College Experience and Help Define Student Centeredness." Doctoral Dissertation, The University of Toledo, Ohio, 2011.

[4] A. Levine & J. Cureton. *When Hope and Fear Collide: A Portrait of Today's College Student*. San Francisco: JosseyBass Publishers, 1998.

[5] D.C.S. Law. "Quality assurance in post-secondary education: the student experience," *Quality Assurance in Education*, vol. 18, 2010, pp. 250-251.

[6] J. T. E. Richardson. "Instruments for Obtaining Student Feedback: a Review of the Literature." *Assessment and Evaluation in Higher Education*, vol. 30, 2005, pp. 387-415.

[7] M. K. Roszkowski, "The Nature of the Importance-Satisfaction Relationship in Ratings: Evidence from theNormative Data of the Noel-Levitz Student Satisfaction Inventory," *Journal of Consumer Satisfaction, Dissatisfaction, and Complaining Behavior*, vol. 16, 2003, p. 212.

[8] J. T. E. Richardson. "Instruments for Obtaining Student Feedback: a Review of the Literature." *Assessment and Evaluation in Higher Education*, vol. 30, 2005, pp. 387-415.

[9] USA Group Noel-Levitz, Inc. *Student Satisfaction Inventory*. Iowa City, Iowa: USA Group, 2000.

[10] K. M. Elliot and M. A. Healy. "Key Factors Influencing Student Satisfaction Related to Recruitment and Retention." *Journal of Marketing for Higher Education*, vol. 10, 2001, pp. 1-11.

[11] A. Yuksel and M. Rimmington. "Customer-Satisfaction Measurement." *Cornell Hotel and Restaurant Administration Quarterly*, vol. 39, 1998, pp. 60-70.

[12] USA Group Noel-Levitz, *National Student Satisfaction Report*, Iowa City, Iowa: USA Group, 2002.

[13] M.A. May. "A Comparative Study of Student Satisfaction with the Provision of Student Services in Traditional and Web-Based Environments." Doctoral Dissertation, Kent State University Graduate School of Education, Ohio, p. 8,2002.

[14] M.A. Ashraf. "Quality Education Management at Private Universities in Bangladesh: An Exploratory Study." *Jurnal Pendidik dan Pendidikan*, vol. 24, pp. 17–32, 2009.

[15] Mazumder, Quamrul H, Karim, Rezaul Md., Bhuiyan, I. Serajul Higher Education Quality Improvement in Bangladesh, Paper no: AC2012-5127, 119th ASEE Annual Conference, June 10-13, 2012, San Antonio, TX, USA

[16] Mazumder, Quamrul H, Karim, R. Md." Comparative Analysis of Learning Styles of Students of USA and Bangladesh, Paper no: AC2012-5075, 119th ASEE Annual Conference, June 10-13, 2012, San Antonio, TX, USA

[17] Mazumder, Quamrul H., "A Comparative Analysis and Evaluation of Different Approaches of Globalization of Engineering Curriculum in the USA" *International Journal of Modern Engineering*, Volume 10, No. 1, Spring/Summer 2009

[18] J. C. Obiekwe. "Identifying the Latent Structures of the Noel-Levitz Student Satisfaction Inventory (SSI): The Community, Junior, and Technical College Version." presented at the Annual Meeting of the Association for the Study of Higher Education, Sacramento, California, 2000.

CHAPTER 12:

Ethics

CHAPTER OBJECTIVE

The primary goal of this chapter is to motivate students toward ethics and ethics education in higher education. Ethics plays a key role in being successful in professional education and at any workplace because it helps in making beneficial decisions and handling dilemmas effectively. This chapter touches on the importance of moral notions and ethical values in the curriculum of higher education. It also describes various theories based on students' perception of ethics.

12.1 INTRODUCTION

Universities should make an effort to change the curriculum and program design without reducing the quality of education. Social ethics is an important topic to learn in life that is taught primarily at the elementary and secondary school levels. The lack of programs discussing ethics directly in higher education poses a problem that the introduction of the study of ethics in all levels of higher education can solve. Instructors of ethics need to develop a way to motivate students to behave in an ethical manner, and students need motivation to make good choices. Academic dishonesty is an increasing problem in higher education, which because of the link between academic dishonesty in higher education and professional work leads to unethical behavior in the work environment. Therefore, universities need to train tomorrow's workers with higher ethical standards for building ethical behavior and ethical environments (Anitsal, Anitsal, & Elmore, 2009). Ethics instruction is essential to adequately prepare engineering students to address unique ethical issues for engineers due to emerging technologies, for instance. Along with teaching courses and providing other services, faculty should impart the knowledge of ethics to students. The faculty should also have high moral and ethical standards and maintain academic integrity in their scholarly work. Ethical obligations can be supported by theories of moral decision-making and the fundamental standards of ethics in one's field.

12.2 WHAT IS ETHICS?

Ethics is the guidelines governing the conduct of an individual or group. Personal ethics differs from a code of ethics for a group; personal ethics may conflict with the ethics of a group to which one belongs. For example, when teaching ethics in a class with a blend of religions, this will create a challenge of conflicts in ethics. Ethics helps students improve their individual behavior and decision-making skills to make a moral judgment of what is right and what is wrong in the ethical context (Balakrishnan & Tarlochan, 2015, p. 18). Here, individuals' national culture plays an important role in establishing ethical standards. Higher education institutions play a vital role in inspiring younger generations to be ethical and preparing them for promising futures.

Besides training in academic skills and providing quality education, higher education institutions should impart ethical values in students to make them recognize the necessity of ethics in life. The main objective of the institutions of higher education should be the creation of a new learning environment with quality education and ethical standards. To initiate this process, the institutions of higher education need to revisit the previous ethical practices and adopt the code of ethics from those practices. They also need to train the students to maintain ethical behavior in their way of life and motivate them to work with ethical responsibilities. Ethics helps elevate the status of professions. Engineers, for example, need to act ethically and resolve conflicts related to responsibilities toward society and their profession. People may think society and science are distinct, but social context affects the development of new technology and knowledge. The converse is true because science has affected morality (Johnson, 2010). Therefore, students going into science-related fields will face ethical conflicts in their careers. Becoming a reflective professional results from understanding the results of workplace activities on the public (Perlman & Varma, 2001). Therefore, hard sciences and social sciences, including ethics, belong side by side in the curriculum. Thus, this chapter explains three theories and their application to engineering students to understand students' perception of ethics.

12.3 STUDENTS' PERCEPTION OF ETHICS

Lau, Caracciolo, Roddenberry, and Scroggins (2012) examined college students' perception of ethics by analyzing five important factors, as shown in Figure 12.1: education's impact, attitude toward cheating, technology's impact, ethics' importance, and campus climate. Some but not all previous research showed the positive effect of ethics education on students (Shurden, Santandreu, & Shurden, 2010; Bloodgood, Turnley, & Mudrack, 2010; as cited in Lau et al., 2012). To measure the factors, the authors gave an online survey of 22 questions about demographics, majors perceived to have the highest ethical standards, and degree of agreement with the effect of the five factors. The analysis provided enough evidence to show that ethics instruction and instructors are useful in building students' ethical behaviors. By measuring perception of cheating in nonmajor classes and in college generally, Lau et al. (2012) found that cheating occurs less in nonmajor college classes than in high school, that technology access makes students more tolerant of cheating, and that students feel no pressure to report cheating. Even so, students said that they hold others to the same level of ethics they hold themselves to and that higher education institutions should teach ethics.

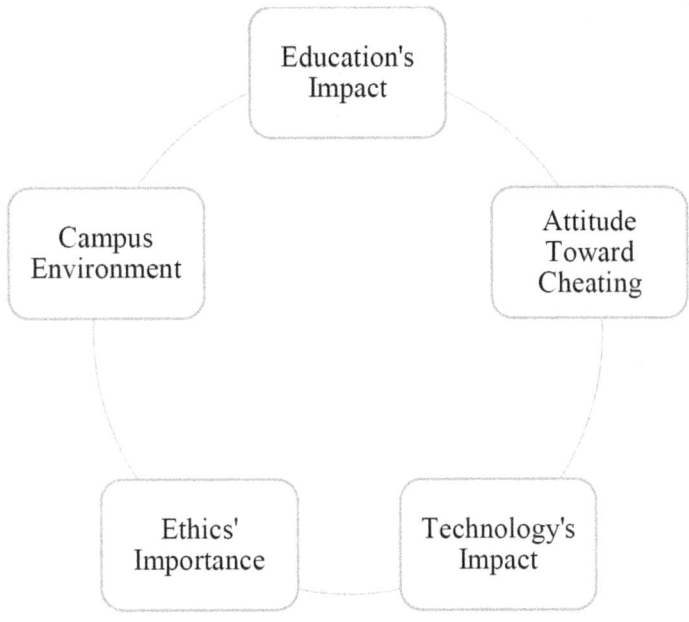

Figure 12.1: Factors of Students' Perception of Ethics

12.4 FOUR COMPONENT MODEL OF MORALITY

Morality is related to a significant percentage of the skills and characteristics of an ethical worker (Hamad, Hasanain, Abdulwahed, & Al-Ammari, 2013). The effort to develop previous researchers' ideas about the causes of moral behavior led to the creation of the Four Component Model of Morality, as shown in Figure 12.2. Psychologically speaking, these constructs cause moral behavior (Rest, 2009):

- Moral sensitivity, which represents the understanding of the situation as a moral dilemma
- Moral judgment, which refers to judging the available actions
- Moral motivation, which refers to the prioritization of the moral concerns over others
- Moral character, which refers to implementation of moral actions

A deficiency in any of the four leads to a moral failure. For instance, someone who is unaware of a personal bias against women lacks moral sensitivity and thus behaves immorally toward them (Rest, 2009).

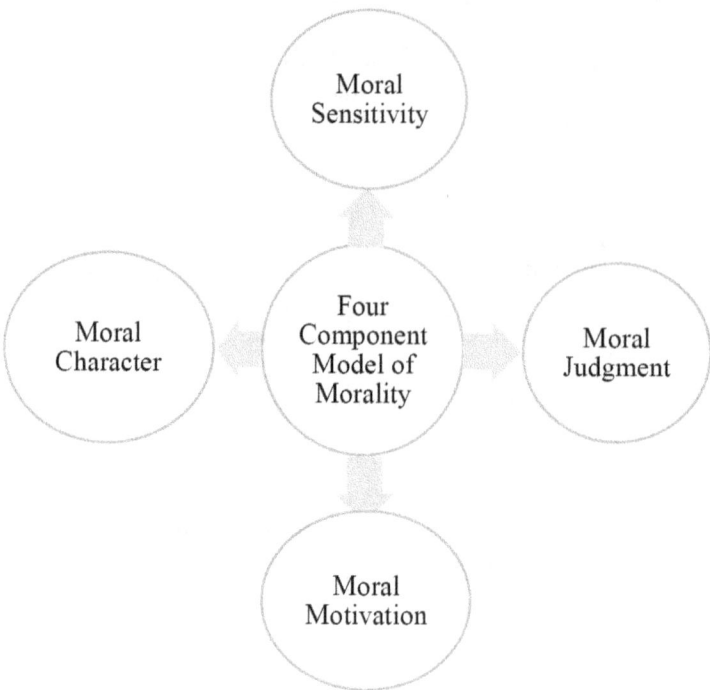

Figure 12.2: Four Component Model of Morality

12.5 THEORY OF VIRTUE-BASED ETHICS

Virtue-based ethics is defined as the right action being what action a virtuous person would take in the situation (Troesch, 2014). Rules do not motivate this action. Instead, the person's core nature prompts the action for its inherent value. Acts of virtue show one's moral character. This theory also recognizes that virtuous feelings, not just virtuous actions, make up strong character (Aristotle, as cited in Troesch, 2014). Scholars have written that virtue-based ethics could develop students' liking of ethics instruction, which currently is lacking (Troesch, 2014).

12.6 THEORY OF DEONTOLOGICAL OR RULES-BASED ETHICS

Ethics can also be studied from a deontological theory approach. Kant (as cited in Troesch, 2014) wrote about behaving only in ways that one wants to be laws that all must follow. His view is that right behavior's rules are universal, are inviolable, are created through reason, and are always applicable. This theory is reflected in codes of ethics, which tend to use prescriptive words, such as *shall*. Individuals who do not question such codes or other rules do not question the ethics of their behavior. This approach is easy to apply in teaching ethics (Troesch, 2014).

12.7 APPLICATION OF ETHICAL THEORIES TO ENGINEERING EDUCATION

Traditionally, undergraduate engineering ethics education has assumed that because scientific and engineering knowledge are different from ethical knowledge, students will understand ethics only if it is taught with a problem-solving and objective approach, the way engineering is taught (Troesch, 2014). Although engineering students can learn and apply the rules of professional ethics and are capable of considering ethics from multiple perspectives, they find the information trivial, which could prevent them from applying it optimally (Newberry, as cited in Troesch, 2014). The importance of engineering ethics is not fully realized in higher education despite the subject's applicability to many issues faced by engineers in their personal and professional lives. Thus, there is a need to include ethical responsibilities in the engineering curriculum along with the traditional technical material. In fact, the Accreditation Board for Engineering and Technology requires engineering programs to include ethics education (Balakrishnan & Tarlochan, 2015). Balakrishnan and Tarlochan (2015) investigated Malaysian students' attitude toward ethical issues and their ethical education. They found that students had a poor attitude toward the issues because faculty put less emphasis on ethics education. Engineering educators may need to be aware of the more general issues of academic ethics.

Fostering ethical development of engineering students has proved ineffective in some cases. Finelli et al.'s (2012, as cited in Hamad et al., 2013) study was meant to provide descriptive data to help identify ethics education practices that encourage engineering undergraduates' ethical development effectively. Data collection tools were the Student Engineering Ethical Development survey, which Finelli et al. (2012) created to measure students' characteristics and ethics-related experiences, and the Defining Issues Test Version 2 to measure development of moral judgment (as cited in Hamad et al., 2013). The result was that students' ethical knowledge was lower than expected. A main finding of the study by May and Luth (2012, as cited in Hamad et al., 2013) was that students had no significant difference in moral judgment after experiencing an ethics course.

Incorporating ethics education has had a limited effect, so other researchers have investigated how to make the effect positive. The main concern of Balakrishnan and Tarlochan's (2015) study was how to teach ethics to achieve the objective of producing socially responsible engineers. Therefore, Balakrishnan and Tarlochan (2015) made a few recommendations for teaching ethics, as shown in Figure 12.3 and explained here. First, enhance teaching of socioethical issues by adding their relationship with sustainability and technological advancements. Second, allow engineers to share their experiences with students, especially concerning how to use a code of ethics. Third, discuss examples and case studies of problems in engineering ethics. Finally, use community-based learning to foster students' sense of responsibility (Balakrishnan & Tarlochan, 2015).

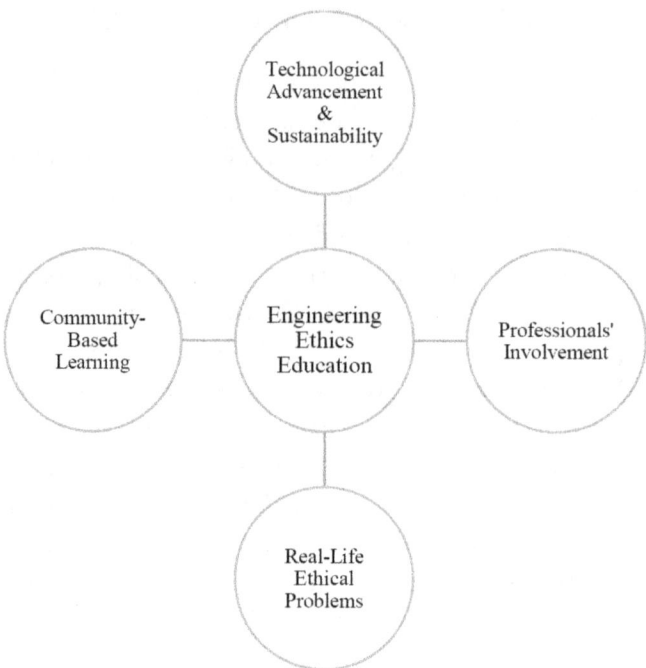

Figure 12.3: Model of Effective Engineering Ethics Education

The three main delivery methods of engineering ethics courses Hamad et al. (2013) lists are stand-alone courses, embedded courses, and team-taught courses. The stand-alone approach is disadvantageous because it overburdens the engineering curriculum (Cruz & Frey, 2000, as cited in Hamad et al., 2013). The embedded approach incorporates an ethical component into existing engineering courses. Its major disadvantage is faculty's unwillingness to discuss ethics in technical courses (Li & Fu, 2010, as cited in Hamad et al., 2013). The approach of team teaching delivers the course through a group of multidisciplinary professors (Cruz & Frey, 2000; Graber & Pionke, 2006; as cited in Hamad et al., 2013). This approach is advantageous because it provides insight from professors with diverse expertise, but finding such professors is difficult (Li & Fu, 2010, as cited in Hamad et al., 2013). Table 12.1 summarizes the ethical theories.

Table 12.1 Overview of the Theories

Name of the Theory	Discipline	Researcher
Four component model of morality	All disciplines	Rest, 2009
Theory of virtue ethics	All disciplines	Troesch, 2014
Theory of deontological or rules-based ethics	All disciplines	Troesch, 2014

12.8 REFERENCES

Anitsal, I., Anitsal, M. M., & Elmore, R. (2009). Academic dishonesty and intention to cheat: A model on active versus passive academic dishonesty as perceived by business students. *Academy of Educational Leadership Journal, 13*(2), 17–26.

Balakrishnan, B., & Tarlochan, F. (2015). *Engineering students' attitude towards engineering ethics education.* Paper presented at Institute of Electrical and Electronics Engineers Ethics Global Engineering Education Conference, Tallinn, Estonia. doi:10.1109/EDUCON.2015.7095944

Hamad, J. A., Hasanain, M., Abdulwahed, M., & Al-Ammari, R. (2013). *Ethics in engineering education: A literature review.* Paper presented at 2013 Institute of Electrical and Electronics Engineers Frontiers in Education Conference, Oklahoma City, OK. doi:10.1109/FIE.2013.6685099

Johnson, D. G. (2010). The role of ethics in science and engineering. *Trends in Biotechnology, 28*(12), 589–590.

Lau, L. K., Caracciolo, B., Roddenberry, S., & Scroggins, A. (2012, March). College students' perception of ethics. *Journal of Academic and Business Ethics, 5,* 1–13.

Perlman, B., & Varma, R. (2001). *Teaching engineering ethics.* Paper presented at American Society for Engineering Education Annual Conference and Exposition, Albuquerque, NM.

Rest, J. R. (2009). Background: Theory and research. In J. R. Rest & D. Narváez (Eds.), *Moral development in the professions: Psychology and applied ethics* (e-book ed., pp. 1–26). New York, NY: Taylor & Francis.

Troesch, V. (2014). *A phenomenological approach to teaching engineering ethics.* Paper presented at 2014 Institute of Electrical and Electronics Engineers International Symposium on Ethics in Science, Technology and Engineering, Chicago, IL. doi:10.1109/ETHICS.2014.6893434

CASE STUDY: STUDENT PERCEPTION OF ETHICS IN BANGLADESH, INDIA AND USA

Quamrul H. Mazumder, University of Michigan–Flint, and Raghava Mahankali, University of Michigan–Flint
© 2016 American Society of Engineering Education
New Orleans, LA

ABSTRACT:

Ethics is an important attribute that students must develop to succeed in their academic career and profession. To improve the ethics perception in students, it is essential to integrate ethics in the curriculum. A survey questionnaire was used to investigate the students' perception of ethics in three different countries. The objective was to evaluate students' perception of ethics using 5 factors: 1) the impact of education and faculty on ethics; 2) students' attitude towards cheating; 3) the impact of technology; 4) the importance of ethics and 5) the ethical campus environment. A total of 138 responses were collected from 4 different universities in three countries. Analysis of the data showed how the student's perception on ethics is relevant in shaping their own ethical behavior. Students' perception on cheating showed that they tend to cheat less in colleges when compared to high schools. The faculty and educational services of the institutions also impacted the ethics perception of students. Students reported ethics to be important and they hold themselves to the same ethical perceptions to their peers. Initially this study made a hypothesis that there is no significant difference observed in ethical standards among students in Bangladesh, India & the USA. But later the analysis of the survey results showed certain difference in students' perception of ethics in three different countries. The results proved the students of the United States to be more ethical compared to the other two countries. College students reported the environment to be more ethical due to higher ethical standards of the faculty.

INTRODUCTION:

Although classroom instructions on ethics education affects students' perceptions and ethical behaviors, it may not be sufficient to change the attribute. The primary concern of this instruction should enhance the ethicality of the students to make decisions individually1. Hence, the improvement of ethics education in the engineering curriculum is necessary.

Students' perception of ethics and ethical behavior may be necessary to introduce ethics education in their curriculum. Yet there are certain factors which are needed to be addressed to improve the ethical responsibility in students. This study emphasizes understanding the factors affecting the students' perception of ethics. The survey administered in this study helps to analyze these factors among students of three different countries: Bangladesh, India & the USA. This analysis helps to understand the levels of ethicality in students from each one of them.

There is a difference among analyzing ethical concepts, making ethical decisions and the implementation of ethical behavior. Even if the ethics education and training influence some individuals, it may not always result in improved ethical behavior. Williams and Dewett (2005) questioned the ability of universities to teach ethics in an engineering curriculum and suggested that improvement and better organization of teaching ethics is important as it can enhance the ethical behavior of students2. In order to address the factors mentioned in this study, certain ethical issues like students' attitude towards cheating, the impact of increasing usage of technology, and the role of faculty in reducing this impact on academically productive behaviors of students should be monitored.

LITERATURE REVIEW:

Ethics can be defined formally as "the discipline dealing with what is good and bad with respect to moral duty and obligation" [3]. Ethics education is essential in an engineering curriculum to assist the students in facing issues of ethical dilemma in professional practice. Every engineer has to exhibit his ethicality in the aspects of safety, testing procedures, or in the ways of designing reliability and durability[4]. Desplaces, Beauvais, Melchar and Bosco (2007) reported that proper ethics education can influence the ability of an individual to make important ethical decisions in their profession[5]. They found that ethical codes and students' perception of these ethical codes can affect how they perceive, maintain, and act according to the ethical standards set at their place of work or study. However, just the proper code of ethics alone does not influence an individual's view[6].

According to Shurden (2010) the importance of teaching and ethical behavior of faculty also reinforces the development of positive perception of students in terms of ethics over time[7]. To properly evaluate students' views on ethical issues, a survey was utilized to form the conclusion that teaching ethics has an impact on students' personal beliefs and behaviors throughout the course of their lifetime[6]. However, Bloodgood et al. (2010) suggested that teaching ethics can have an adverse impact on students who obtain a high score on Machiavellianism[1]. Machiavellianism can be defined as the "implementation of cunning activities and cheating in general conduct. It focuses on personal gain disregard of morality". This type of trait, such as Machiavellianism, can create a much larger impact on behaviors of students than simply teaching ethics [1].

The difference of ethics education at different institutions around the world is reported by comparing the countries such as South Africa. This comparison stated that students remain uncommitted to their studies, disrespectful to their teachers, and are devoid of self-disciplinary actions which lead to poor behavior in the classroom in certain countries. This is due to the low level of commitment by teachers not enforcing proper disciplinary action and exhibiting unprofessional conduct themselves[8]. Another element of the problem lies in unsupportive parents who are often illiterate and are unable or unwilling to involve in their children's education. The combination of both factors and lack of discipline leads to a low ethical environment due to there being no consequence for unethical behavior[8]. Due to the vast amount of data on the internet, cheating can impact student's academics. The students who spend more time watching television and participating in extracurricular activities tend to cheat more when compared to the students who spend time on learning[9].

Anitsal and Elmore (2009) argued that cheating within one's academic career can lead to an unethical behavior in the work environment[10]. Teaching ethics at the college level can be beneficial due to the fact that it can develop the ability to analyze situations from an ethical perspective[1]. A properly designed ethics course would require students to critically think towards the issues and consequences that can arise from unethical behavior. Teaching ethics within the engineering curriculum can improve judgment when it involves ethical decisons[4]. The main issue of ethics education is understanding how much instruction is required for each student due to the difference in each of their ethical habits[1]. Awareness of higher education is low in India when compared to Western Countries. There is such a sector in India which provides collection of statistical information on higher education. Moreover, shortage of accreditation policies and quality faculty leads the students to become more unethical and does not defend them from fraud and abuse activities. As a result, there is aneed to introduce qualified people and incentives in institutions to ensure quality of education[11].

According to Luthar and Karri (2005), the requirement of incorporating ethics education in engineering education is still being questioned,[12] although most students thought that receiving ethical education and/or training would benefit them later on in the workplace[13]. According to the proposed ABET criteria, engineering ethics and its concepts can be inculcated in the mainstream engineering courses[14]. Rossouw (2002) suggested that education on ethics can aid students in improving their moral reasoning skills[15]. The ethical codes listed by many engineering societies are a good reference for ethical teaching within engineering programs. However, they cannot be used to train students entirely in recognizing and resolving ethical dilemmas that they may face in their day to day jobs[16].

RESEARCH METHODOLOGY:

PROBLEM OBJECTIVE:

The objective of this research is to understand the students' perception of ethics by conducting the survey on certain ethical factors among the students of three different countries. The main purpose of the study is to improve the ethical behavior students by including ethics education in engineering curriculum. This study is performed by certain hypotheses mentioned below.

HYPOTHESES:

To assess the ethical standards of students, four hypotheses were tested.
H-1: There is no significant difference in ethical standards among students of Bangladesh, India & USA.
H-2: There is no significant difference between male and female students.

H-3: There is no significant difference between public and private university students.

H-4: There is no significant difference between undergraduate and graduate students.

METHOD:

The survey used was initially developed by The Institute for Global Ethics. This non-profit organization was contracted by the Maricopa Community College District in Arizona to create a survey that could be utilized to evaluate the values and ethics of a particular populace. The survey was revised and utilized by a research group at Longwood University in Virginia. The questionnaire was revised and tested among a small group in advance by Longwood University in Virginia and then the modified version of the survey was approved by a Human Subjects Research Review Committee before its final distribution and implementation. This modified survey questionnaire was distributed among 300 students in Bangladesh, India & USA in this current study. The number of responses received was 138 or 46%. The United States, India, and Bangladesh were selected because of previous relations of the researchers with the universities. India was included in this study in order to create more diversity and to compare more than two nations' ethical standards. The reliability of the survey instrument used in this study is limited as it is not conveyed by the original survey developers in their study.

QUESTIONNAIRE:

The survey questionnaire used in the research consisted of 14 questions with five factors assessing perceptions of students towards ethics using a five-point Likert scale. A copy of the survey questionnaire is included in Appendix One of this paper. The first factor is, "Impact of Education and Faculty on Ethics". The questions of this factor focused on the ability of faculty to include ethics as a part of the curriculum and a part of their classroom, as well as the ability of faculty to enforce an ethical standard. However, these questions did not provide any information related to the impact of ethics education. The second factor, "Attitude towards cheating", stresses on questions about the personal attitude towards cheating and how cheating affects particular students and their classmates. The third factor, "Impact of Technology", pertained to the ease of cheating when technology is involved and used in the classroom. But the survey analyzed this factor narrowly with only 2 questions.

The fourth factor, "Importance of Ethics", asked students how they see ethics within their own lives and how important it is to them. Even though this factor is a broad aspect, the number of questions were limited due to the tangibility of the study. The fifth factor, "Ethical Environment on Campus", concentrated on the ethics of faculty in the eyes of the students and if other peer students exhibited ethical behavior. The survey questionnaire contained cheating as one of the unethical behaviors and therefore, it was part of the study. There is no evidence that the results will help students behave more ethically when practicing the engineering profession. A separate study is required to understand the issue.

PARTICIPANTS:

As presented in Figure 1, the sample consists of 138 students participated in the survey where 63 were from Bangladesh, 29 from India and 46 from the USA. From the total number of participants, 109 students were from public universities and 29 students were from the private universities. Among the participants, 84 were male students and 54 were female students as shown in Figure 2. The population included 75 undergraduate students and 63 graduate students.

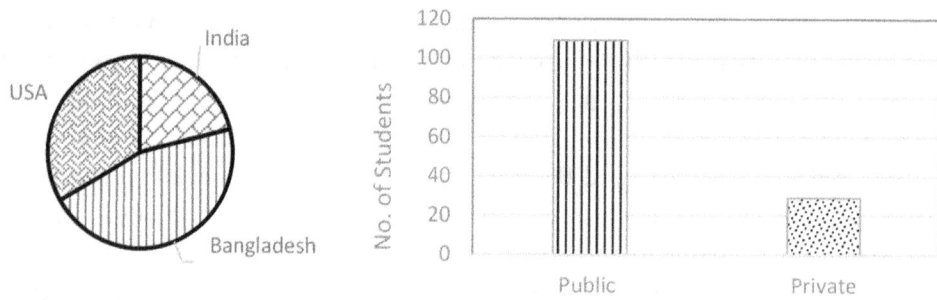

Figure 1: Distribution of Survey Respondents

Institution	Male	Female
Private	73	36
Public	11	18
Total	84	54
Percent	60.9	39.1

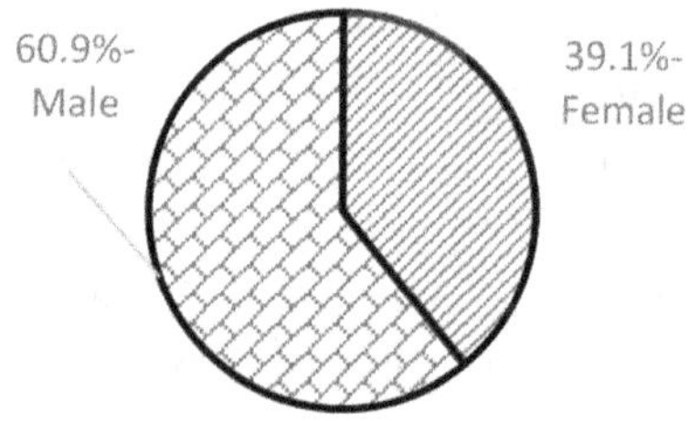

Figure 2: Gender of Participants

DATA ANALYSIS:

A statistical analysis of the survey responses was performed by using Independent sample t-test to determine the mean values of all 5 factors. Statistical analysis software SPSS-22 was used for the descriptive analysis and Independent t-test18. Independent t-test is used to evaluate the hypothesis listed in the previous section. The hypotheses require evidence of any significant difference between different groups and therefore, statistical analyses were performed to determine whether any significant difference exists.

RESULTS:

Descriptive statistics for students of Bangladesh, India & the USA are presented in Table 1 to evaluate hypothesis one. The mean values of Bangladesh, India & the USA are higher for Impact of Education (Bangladesh = 3.36 < India 3.59 < USA 3.88), Attitude towards cheating (Bangladesh = 3.21 < India = 3.50 > USA 3.25) and ethical campus environment (Bangladesh = 3.39 >India = 3.35 >USA = 2.89). USA students appear to be more ethical compared to Bangladesh and India.

Table 1: Descriptive Statistics for different countries (H-1)

Factors	Country	N	Mean	Std. Dev	Std. Error
Impact of Education	Bangladesh	63	3.36	1.13	0.14
	India	29	3.59	0.86	0.16
	USA	46	3.88	0.88	0.13
Attitude towards cheating	Bangladesh	63	3.21	1.12	0.14
	India	29	3.50	1.29	0.23
	USA	46	3.25	0.96	0.14
Ethical campus environment	Bangladesh	63	3.39	1.07	0.1
	India	29	3.35	1.13	0.21
	USA	46	2.89	0.94	0.13

The 2-tailed test uses half of alpha value (0.05) to test the significance in one part, and a half to test significance in the other part. A 95% confidence interval shows that 95% of the population distribution is in the Confidence Interval (C.I). The lower and upper limits give an indication of how much uncertainty the mean has and estimates how the mean varies from sample to sample. The standard error difference is the Standard Deviation of sample means over all possible samples. The t-statistic is a ratio of the departure of an estimated parameter from its standard error. An F-test is used to identify the model that best fits the population from which the data was sampled. The mean difference measures the absolute difference between the mean values in two groups. When the equal variance is assumed it shows that two distributions of the samples have population size and, if not assumed, it shows that how widely individuals of a group varies.

Independent t-test results presented in table-2 showed significant differences between three countries. The level of significance for Bangladesh, India & USA for impact of education was ($p=0.009 < 0.05$), Attitude towards cheating ($p=0.01 < 0.05$) and ($P=0.04 < 0.05$) for ethical campus environment. The statistical analysis results rejects hypothesis (H1) as there is a significant difference between Bangladesh, India & USA in their ethical standards ($p = 0.009, 0.001, 0.002, 0.04 < 0.05$).

Table-2: Independent t-test for different Countries (H-1)

	Equal variances	F	Sig. ($p<0.5$)	t	df	Sig. (2-tailed)	Mean Difference	Std. Error Difference	95% C.I Lower	95% C.I Upper
Impact of education on ethics	assumed	11.38	**0.009**	-1.58	93.4	0.20	-0.34	0.22	-0.78	0.09
	not assumed			-1.66	84.78	0.17	-0.34	0.20	-0.75	0.07
Attitude towards	assumed	5.96	**0.01**	-2.30	90	0.02	-0.61	0.26	-1.15	-0.08
	not assumed			-2.26	77.28	0.02	-0.61	0.26	-1.14	-.074
Impact on technology	assumed	12.05	**0.002**	-0.01	90	0.64	-0.01	0.23	-0.49	0.45
	not assumed			-0.04	73.15	0.63	-0.01	0.23	-0.48	0.44
Ethics campus environment	assumed	4.241	**0.04**	-1.74	90	0.15	-0.34	0.195	-0.73	0.03
	not assumed			-1.70	78.18	0.14	-0.34	0.197	-0.74	0.04

Descriptive statistics for male and female students are presented in Table 3 to evaluate hypothesis two. The mean values of male and female students of Bangladesh, India & USA are higher for the impact of education (3.69 < 4.69), Impact of technology (3.10 < 3.28), Importance of ethics (3.95 < 4.35) and ethical campus environment (3.10 < 3.38). The results demonstrate that female students' ethical standards to be higher than male students.

Table 3: Descriptive Statistics for Male and Female (H-2)

Factors	Gender	N	Mean	Std. Dev	Std. Error
Impact of Education	Male	84	3.69	1.01	0.11
	Female	54	4.69	1.03	0.14
Impact of technology	Male	84	3.10	1.13	0.12
	Female	54	3.28	1.04	0.14
Importance of ethics	Male	84	3.95	0.93	0.10
	Female	54	4.35	0.62	0.85
Ethical campus environment	Male	84	3.10	1.09	0.17
	Female	54	3.38	1.08	0.148

Independent t-test results presented in table-4 showed significant differences between male and female students. The level of significance for male and female students for impact of education was ($p=0.01 < 0.05$), attitude towards cheating ($p=0.03 < 0.05$) and ($P=0.03 < 0.05$) for impact of technology. The statistical analysis results reject hypothesis (H2) as there is a significant difference between male and female students ($p= 0.017, 0.032, 0.036$).

Table 4: Independent t-test for Male and Female (H-2)

	Equal variances	F	Sig.	t	df	Sig. (2-tailed)	Mean Difference	Std. Error Difference	95% C.I Lower	95% C.I Upper
Impact of education on ethics	assumed	5.85	**.017**	2.32	136	0.22	0.41	.17	0.06	.76
	not assumed			2.26	103.57	0.25	.412	.18	.051	.77
Attitude towards cheating	assumed	4.66	**.032**	1.48	136	.140	.33	.22	-.11	.77
	not assumed			1.44	101.41	.153	.33	.23	-.12	.79
Impact of technology	assumed	4.46	**.036**	.20	136	.83	.037	.17	-.31	.39
	not assumed			.21	128.02	.83	.037	.17	-.30	.37

Descriptive statistics for students of public and private universities are presented in Table 5 to evaluate hypothesis three. The mean values of students of public and private universities in Bangladesh, India & the USA are higher for impact of technology (3.17 < 3.18), the importance of ethics (4.16 > 3.91) and ethical campus environment (3.18 < 3.35). The results showed students of public universities are more ethical than private universities.

Table-5: Descriptive Statistics for Public and Private Universities (H-3)

Factors	Type of University	N	Mean	Std. Dev	Std. Error
Impact of technology	Public	109	3.17	1.10	0.10
	Private	29	3.18	1.11	0.20
Importance of ethics	Public	109	4.16	0.81	0.07
	Private	29	3.91	0.93	0.17
Ethical campus environment	Public	109	3.18	1.08	0.10
	Private	29	3.35	1.13	0.21

Independent t-test results presented in table-6 showed significant differences between students of public and private universities. The level of significance for students of public and private universities in Bangladesh, India & the USA for impact of education was (p=0.01 < 0.05) and (P=0.009 < 0.05) for impact of technology. The statistical analysis results reject the hypothesis (H3) as there is a significant difference between students of public and private universities (p = 0.017, 0.009 < 0.05).

Table-6: Independent t-test for Public and Private Universities (H3)

	Equal variances	F	Sig.	t	df	Sig. (2-tailed)	Mean Difference	Std. Error Difference	95% C.I Lower	Upper
Impact of education on ethics	assumed	5.85	.017	-.60	136	.54	-.13	.21	-.55	.29
	not assumed			-.76	65.80	.45	-.13	.17	-.47	.21
Impact of technology	assumed	2.75	.009	.86	136	.38	.18	.21	-.23	.60
	not assumed			.92	48.82	.35	.18	.19	-.21	.58

Descriptive statistics for undergraduate and graduate students are presented in Table 7 to evaluate hypothesis four. The mean values of undergraduate and graduate students in Bangladesh, India & USA are higher for impact of education (3.77 > 3.36), the impact of technology (3.12 < 3.24), the importance of ethics (4.07 < 4.15) and ethical campus environment (3.07 < 3.39). The results showed graduate students to be more ethical than undergraduate students.

Factors	Highest Degree	N	Mean	Std. Dev	Std. Error
Impact of Education	Undergraduate	75	3.77	1.06	0.17
	Graduate	63	3.36	0.86	1.13
Impact of technology	Undergraduate	75	3.12	1.10	1.17
	Graduate	63	3.24	1.11	1.022
Importance of ethics	Undergraduate	75	4.07	0.81	0.88
	Graduate	63	4.15	0.93	0.756
Ethical campus environment	Undergraduate	75	3.07	1.08	0.10
	Graduate	63	3.39	1.13	1.07

Table-7: Descriptive Statistics for Undergraduate & Graduate Students (H-4)

Independent t-test results presented in table-8 showed significant differences between undergraduate and graduate students. The level of significance for undergraduate and graduate students for impact of education was (p=0.01 < 0.05), impact of technology (p=0.01 > 0.05) and (P=0.009 < 0.05) for ethical campus environment. The statistical analysis results rejects hypothesis (H4) as there is significant difference between undergraduate and graduate students (p = 0.001, 0.012, 0.009 < 0.05).

Table -8: Independent t-test for Undergraduate & Graduate Students (H-4)

	Equal variances	F	Sig.	t	df	Sig. (2-tailed)	Mean Difference	Std. Error	95% C.I Lower	95% C.I Upper
Impact of education on ethics	assumed	10.73	.001	2.64	13	.002	.43	.16	.10	.75
	not assumed			2.58	115.07	.011	.43	.16	.10	.76
Impact of technology	assumed	6.48	.012	-.81	136	.415	-.14	.17	-.49	.20
	not assumed			-.83	134.86	.404	-.14	.17	-.48	.19
Ethical campus environment	assumed	7.11	.009	-3.48	136	.001	-.77	.22	-.21	-.33
	not assumed			-3.54	135.83	.001	-.77	.21	-1.2	-.34

CONCLUSION:

The purpose of this study was to comprehend the ethical standards of students at undergraduate and graduate levels, male and female, in both public and private universities in Bangladesh, India, and the USA. The survey results were used to test four hypotheses. Each hypothesis resulted in significant differences in the ethical standards of students. Factors like the impact of education on ethics, impact of technology, and ethical campus environment were higher for students at public universities than private universities. Additionally, graduate students showed higher mean values compared to undergraduate students in an impact of technology, importance of education on ethics, and ethical campus environment. Moreover, significant differences were also observed between genders, where female students showed higher ethical standards than male students in the impact of ethics on education, attitude towards cheating and impact of technology. Overall, students in the USA are more ethical when compared to Bangladesh and India. The survey responses were collected from one public university in USA, one public university in Bangladesh and three private universities in India. Due to challenges associated with data collection process, the sample size may not be adequate to draw a strong conclusion. However, the results from this study will be used for a further study in the future. The study was based on a limited number of students and will be extended to a larger population to better understand the ethical standards of college students. Although the current study results may not draw a conclusion about the ethics of the students in these three countries, it focused on important aspect about the importance of integrating ethics in the curriculum to improve students' perception of ethical behavior.

ACKNOWLEDGEMENT:

The author would like to thank Dr. Burhan Uddin, Professor of Bangladesh Agricultural University for his support in collecting data for this study.

REFERENCES

1. Bloodgood, J., Turnley, W., and Mudrack, P. (2010). Ethics Instruction and the Perceived Acceptability of Cheating. Journal of Business Ethics, 95(1), 23-37.
2. Williams, S. D. and T. Dewett: 2005, 'Yes You Can Teach Business Ethics: A Review and Research Agenda', Journal of Leadership and Organizational Studies 12(2), 109–120.
3. Merriam-Webster Dictionary (2015). Retrieved on October 1, 2015. http://www.merriam- webster.com/dictionary/ethics.
4. Harris, C. E., Davis, M., Pritchard, M. S. and Rabins, M. J. (1996), Engineering Ethics: What? Why? How? And When? Journal of Engineering Education, 85: 93–96. doi: 10.1002/j.2168-9830. 1996.tb00216.x

5. Desplaces, D., Beauvais, L., Melchar, D., and Bosco, S. (2007). The Impact of Business Education on Moral Judgement Competence: An Empirical Study. Journal of Business Ethics, 74(1), 73-87.
6. Linda K. Lau, Brandon Caracciolo, Stephanie Roddenberry, Abbie Scroggins, Longwood University: March 2012. "College students' perception of ethics".
7. Shurden, S., Santandreu, J., and Shurden, M. (2010). How Student Perceptions of Ethics Can Lead to Future Business Behavior. Journal of Legal, Ethical and Regulatory Issues, 13(1), 117-127.
8. Weeks, F. (2012). How does a culture of learning impact on student behavior? Journal of Social Sciences, 8(3), 332-342.
9. Kitahara, R., Westfall, F., and Mankelwicz, J. (2011). New, Multi-Faceted Hybrid Approaches to Ensuring Academic Integrity. Journal of Academic and Business Ethics, 3, 1-12
10. Anitsal, I., Anitsal, M., and Elmore, R. (2009). Academic Dishonesty and Intention to Cheat: A Model on Active versus Passive Academic Dishonesty as Perceived by Business Students. Academy of Educational Leadership Journal, 13(2), 17-26.
11. Bhatia, K., & Dash, M. K. (2011). A demand of value based higher education system in india: A comparative study. Journal of Public Administration and Policy Research, 3(5), 156-173.
12. Luthar, H. K. and R. Karri: 2005, 'Exposure to Ethics Education and the Perception of Linkage between Organizational Ethical Behavior and Business Outcomes', Journal of Business Ethics 61, 353–368.
13. Verschoor, C. C.: 2003, 'Is Ethics Education of Future Business Leaders Adequate?' Strategic Finance August, 20–23.
14. Herkert, J.R. 1997. "Engineering Ethics Education Finally Reaches a Critical Mass." *The Institute* (News Supplement of *IEEE Spectrum*) (December).
15. Rossouw, G. J.: 2002, 'Three Approaches to Teaching Business Ethics', Teaching Business Ethics 6(4), 411–433.
16. Selby, M. A. (2015, June), Assessing Engineering Ethics Training Paper presented at 2015 ASEE Annual Conference and Exposition, Seattle, Washington. 10.18260/p.23579
17. Kidder, R., Mirk, P., and Lodges, W. (2002). Maricopa Values & Ethics Survey. Tempe, AZ: Institute for Global Ethics.
18. SPSS user manual for SPSS22 Software, IBM SPSS Statistics 22 Information Center- IBM Corporation - Chicago, IL; 60606-U.S.A.1989, 2013.

Appendix 1

University: _____ Degree: Bachelors/Masters University Type: Public/Private Gender: Male/Female						
Factor-1 Impact of Education and Faculty/ Instructors on Ethics						
Q1	Faculty and instructors help students develop values in their classes.	SD	D	NA nor D	A	SA
Q2	Faculty and instructors incorporate ethics training into their classes.	SD	D	NA nor D	A	SA
Q3	Faculty and instructors should enforce ethical standards onto their students.	SD	D	NA nor D	A	SA
Factor -2 Attitude towards cheating						
Q4	I have never cheated on my school work while in high school.	SD	D	NA nor D	A	SA
Q5	I have never cheated on my school work while in college.	SD	D	NA nor D	A	SA
Q6	When I see other students cheat I feel compelled to report them.	SD	D	NA nor D	A	SA
Q7	It is acceptable for me to cheat in a non-major class. (Negative correlation)	SD	D	NA nor D	A	SA
Factor-3 Impact on Technology						
Q8	It is easier to cheat in an online or hybrid class than a regular class.	SD	D	NA nor D	A	SA
Q9	It is easier to cheat when technology is involved, e.g., Blackboard, calculator, etc.	SD	D	NA nor D	A	SA
Factor -4 Importance of Ethics						
Q10	Ethics is very important to me.	SD	D	NA nor D	A	SA
Q11	I hold myself to the same ethical standards that I hold others to.	SD	D	NA nor D	A	SA
Factor -5 Ethical Environment on Campus						
Q12	I don't think that our students abide by the University's Honor Code.	SD	D	NA nor D	A	SA
Q13	I consider the faculty and instructors in my major to be ethical human beings. (Negative correlation)	SD	D	NA nor D	A	SA
Q14	By the time people reach college age it is too late to teach them about ethics.	SD	D	NA nor D	A	SA

SD = Strongly Disagree, D = Disagree, NA nor D = Neither Agree / Disagree, A = Agree, SA = Strongly Agree

CHAPTER 13:

Quality in Online Learning

CHAPTER OBJECTIVE

The main purpose of this chapter is to explain the quality and standards of online learning. This chapter defines the quality of online learning and explains the view of students toward online education. In addition, it discusses ways to assess online education.

13.1 INTRODUCTION

The Internet has become a powerful platform for delivering college-level courses and even degrees. Online learning removes the need to go to a campus at certain times and days, which has increased access to education for people with disabilities, international students, and nontraditional students. Some of these programs do not lead to a degree but may still be of high quality, and they encourage lifelong learning. They are still developing and taking on new forms, as are their quality standards, so there are ways to improve the quality of online learning.

13.2 INTRODUCTION TO MASSIVE OPEN ONLINE COURSES

Massive open online course (MOOC), a term introduced in 2008, refers to an online, open-registration course that targets a large audience, and this is one way to deliver online education (Tsironis, Katsanos, & Xenos, 2016). See Table 13.1 for a comparison of online courses and MOOCs. Like many online courses, MOOCs provide a forum for discussions with students and professors. A MOOC is typically free and offered by a professor from a reputable university. It usually consists of several small video lectures, written assignments, online discussions, and an exam and a completion certificate at the end.

Table 13.1: Differences Between Online Courses and MOOCs

Characteristics	Online Courses	MOOCs
Cost	Require tuition and fees	No or low fees
Prerequisites	May/May not have	None
Scale	Limited	Large audience
Lecturer's participation	Assignments, assessment, and quality assurance	Limited individual support
Course operators	Distance education operators or reputable universities	Reputable research universities
Certifications	Conservative	Liberal
Quality assurance	Follows quality assurance process	None

One MOOC provider is Udacity, which gained an enrollment of over 1.5 million students by 2014. It began with courses in math and computer science and now also offers courses in business and public health (Mitra, 2016). Two other large MOOC providers are Coursera and edX. Coursera provides about 2,000 courses to about 24 million users (Coursera, 2017), and edX offers more than 1,350 courses with more than 3 million students enrolled (edX, 2017).

The MOOC movement is significant and global trends have given it a push. The large audience for MOOCs is the evidence for their popularity. They have the potential to get education to millions who may not have the opportunity to learn in any other way.

13.3 SIGNIFICANCE OF ONLINE EDUCATION

In general, it is not technology that affects learning; it is the method of education that affects learning. Switching from one medium to another, without a change in how we teach, has very little impact on education. The number of students taking at least one online course is increasing and is expected to continue to grow. The following facts show the importance of online learning.

Per a 2015 survey by Allen and Seaman (2016), the number of students taking one online course increased by 7% between 2012 and 2014 to reach 20.5 million students. Of that number, about 14% took only online courses in 2014 (Allen & Seaman, 2016). Table 13.2 shows the prominence of online courses.

Table 13.2: Percentage and Number of Students Taking All Their Courses Online: Fall 2014

Institution Type	Percentage of Online Students	Number of Students
Public	48.4%	1,382,872
Private nonprofit	22.1%	632,341
Private for-profit	29.5%	843,579
Total	100%	2,858,792

Note. Allen and Seaman, 2016, p. 47.

Even though online education for college students has been made available at 69% of institutions in the past 20 years, it remains burdened by negative stereotypes—for example, that its instructors are inferior and that its content is not as demanding as its counterpart of face-to-face courses (Allen & Seaman, 2016). The 2015 survey of online learning reveals that online learning has been gaining its dominance over the past decade, yet 28.6% of academic leaders think that online learning outcomes are less rigorous than face-to-face learning outcomes (Allen & Seaman, 2016). That number jumps to 51.2% among academic leaders of colleges without online courses (Allen & Seaman, 2016). The same attitude applies to faculty per the survey, which states that only 29% of faculty believe online education is legitimate and valuable (Allen & Seaman, 2016).

13.4 ADVANTAGES AND DRAWBACKS OF ONLINE EDUCATION

The Internet has grown in popularity and has increased its reach to all corners of the world with positive information about e-learning. The advantages are abundant, from flexibility in choosing which degree a student would like to pursue to the low cost of attendance when compared with traditional schools.

Some of the advantages include:

- **Course availability:** Many courses are available online. Everyone can find a course online with ease, from nursing to engineering. Learners can find degrees, from a certificate course to a doctorate degree, online.
- **Low cost of attendance:** Online courses are cheaper than traditional classroom programs. Even though some of the courses have a cost close to that of traditional degree courses, the costs of commuting and, of course, materials are lower. Online courses may also take less time to complete or enable students to keep their jobs, increasing their cost savings (Al-Musa & Al-Mobark, 2005, as cited in Al-Qahtani & Higgins, 2013).
- **Comfortable learning environment:** The learning environment can more easily be changed according to individuals' needs. The class takes place in any location that has Internet access, so students can learn while traveling or in a library, for example. Resources can be provided on demand rather than taking up an entire class's time (Akkoyunlu & Soylu, 2006, as cited in Al-Qahtani & Higgins, 2013).
- **Convenience and flexibility:** Online courses give students flexibility in planning their time for studying and for completing assignments at their convenience. There may be deadlines but no set class meeting time, which facilitates work–life balance (Al-Musa & Al-Mobark, 2005, as cited in Al-Qahtani & Higgins, 2013).
- **Enhanced interaction:** Shy students or ones who communicate better through writing than face-to-face conversation may more readily interact with classmates online (Hameed, Badii, & Cullen, 2008, as cited in Al-Qahtani & Higgins, 2013).
- **Cultural awareness:** The ability for students all over the world to enroll in many online courses can also expose students to different cultures. Table 13.3 covers both advantages and disadvantages of online learning.

Table 13.3: Advantages and Disadvantages of Online Education

Advantages	Disadvantages
Flexibility of geographic place and time	Lack of face-to-face interaction among students and instructors
Asynchronous and synchronous communication and interaction	Students' incomplete attention
Travel and other costs saved	Extra dedication and motivation are required
24/7 accessibility to course and study material and ease of interaction	Skills and resources are required to understand and follow the course
Autonomy of learners	Difficulties in concentration
Collaborative work	Deviation from regular studies
Multimedia learning content	Comparatively higher dropout rate

Even though there are several significant advantages, there are still some drawbacks that learners must understand before jumping into an online course. Some of them can be lack of accreditation, having no face-to-face interaction, required high self-discipline, and ease of distraction.

Having less face-to-face interaction with classmates and faculty can prevent students from learning from one another. Learners tend to underestimate the negativity of this aspect (Heritovo, 2016). Also, online learning courses typically need a greater amount of effort than traditional classes. Sometimes for several courses students need to work more than what they would have in traditional classes, in part because students cannot immediately get answers to questions they ask faculty.

Students registered for online courses need to manage time for studying for tests and reading the materials. They need time management and organization skills to keep up with deadlines. Online courses are typically harder in regard to time management than typical classroom classes are (Heritovo, 2016). Traditional higher education programs, unlike e-learning, typically require students to consult their advisers for assistance in plotting their path. Deviating from the path could stop academic progress and lead to lost financial aid (Heritovo, 2016).

In summary, institutions and professors should understand and thoroughly analyze the benefits and consequences of online education. Students should evaluate the course and the curriculum of the online program, keeping in mind the benefits and drawbacks of e-learning. Students could become constrained in their ability to perform well academically if they are not prepared to meet expectations and apply their knowledge.

13.5 WHAT IS QUALITY IN ONLINE EDUCATION?

Quality is the main principle that enables institutions to commit to the course and students, to make the public aware of their fine educational value, and to attain full enrollment. The objectives are to organize the courses so that they are meeting the market demands and to help the institutions develop better strategic plans for market share capture and build up institutional recognition for long-term reliability among present and prospective stakeholders.

Per the Online Learning Consortium (n.d.) there are five pillars of quality of online education. A simple summary of the model appears below.

Learning effectiveness is the main purpose of any educational system. In the education world, learning is defined as acquiring knowledge and skills through study and experience. The instructional designer should create the online course in a way to at least meet the industrial standards or to be better than them. This can be achieved by following educational integrity and by maintaining rapport with the faculty the same way as in traditional programs. The effectiveness of the learning can be measured through students' outcomes (Online Learning Consortium, n.d.).

Another pillar is faculty satisfaction, which is a measure of the happiness of the faculty with their teaching experience online. Faculty satisfaction can be achieved by ensuring there is support given to the faculty for preparation and course delivery. The improvement of the faculty's contribution and efficiency can be measured by postcourse surveys. In general, repeated teaching can improve the faculty's effectiveness in online learning. Also, institutions should study and improve the online teaching experience and value it as much as face-to-face teaching (Online Learning Consortium, n.d.).

The next pillar is scale. In short, scale is a measure of cost-effectiveness and commitment to quality with respect to capacity. It describes the providers continuously updating their services. Scalability controls educational resources while providing development opportunities to students and faculty in leadership, partnerships, policy, scalability, and marketing (Online Learning Consortium, n.d.).

The fourth factor of quality is student satisfaction. In any education system, a main goal is student satisfaction, which considers the role and experiences of the online student. Student satisfaction is based on the experiences of students in online learning. It also includes the interaction with instructors and the level of peer-to-peer interaction. The satisfaction is measured by postcourse surveys and from testimonials. The outcomes of the course can also measure student satisfaction (Online Learning Consortium, n.d.).

The final factor of quality is access. Students who are interested in learning the topics of their choosing can access online courses from all parts of the world. The students can do this at any time and with ease and resources. Focus groups and student surveys can measure ease of access (Online Learning Consortium, n.d.).

13.6 WHY IS QUALITY IN ONLINE LEARNING COMPLEX?

Quality in online education is not just about online content delivery or simply adding videos. It is more about student and faculty involvement, meeting student needs, and many other factors.

The main difficulty in assessing the quality of online education is there are few standards for how an online course should be taught. Online students have specific priorities, some of which tend to be well suited for the online course format. They indicate the same concerns with quality.

For any course, elements of how the course is designed and supported are important to students. This was proved in a survey of more than 3,100 students from 31 institutions (Ralston-Berg, Buckenmeyer, Barczyk, & Hixon, 2015). Respondents reported that course design standards represented in the Quality Matters rubric were important to their skills attainment. Quality Matters is a peer review and improvement program with eight research-based standards to improve online and hybrid course design, and its rubric assigns 1 to 3 points to show the importance of each standard (Ralston-Berg et al., 2015).

The Quality Matters rubric and the surveyed students value clearly defined, easily accessible, and fully relevant assignments, in other words, instructional excellence (Ralston-Berg et al., 2015). These do not require technology, but they require attention and consistency. Educational institutions have started shifting their focus to these components of instructional quality, but more improvement is needed.

Ethics is another concern in quality online learning. Ethics is what students should do, and ethical concerns emerge when students' interests conflict, meaning principles that respect everyone's rights are necessary. E-learning's ethical concerns arise from instructional and communication ethics (Toprak, Özkanal, Aydin, & Kaya, 2010).

13.7 PRINCIPLES OF EFFECTIVE ONLINE ASSESSMENT OF STUDENTS

Online assessment is not much different from assessment of normal face-to-face classroom courses. After all, both types of courses aim to provide education and skills to students. Principles that ought to be followed in online student assessment include (Palloff & Pratt, 2003, as cited in Palloff & Pratt, 2009):

- Use learner-centered assessments with self-reflection on the course.
  - Online courses should be student centered and student focused, so it follows that assessment within the course should be the same.
  - For an online course, students should take responsibility for learning activities such as online discussions; participation in collaborative activities is important for the assessment.
- Incorporate grading rubrics for evaluating participation in discussions, projects, assignments, and collaboration (see Table 13.4). These need to be of high quality and clear to the students.

Table 13.4: Sample Rubric

Criteria	Points for Evaluating Criteria				Comments
	Not performed (0)	Basic performance (1)	Average performance (2)	Distinguished performance (3)	
Use of relevant course concepts or materials					
Use of professional, personal, and other experiences					
Responds to fellow learners					
Supports points with resources beyond course textbook					

Note. Palloff and Pratt (2009).

- Embrace collaborative assessments through online comments by students on how to make assignments better.
    - Collaboration gives the chance for discussion among the student community that can provide the opportunity to test out new ideas by sharing thoughts and developing a constructive model through discussions and interactions.
    - Using peer review forms (see Table 13.5) and getting the students involved in assessments improve their performance.
    - Peer comments can answer these questions:
        - What can be improved in my performance?
        - What is needed to be employed and to make me a better team player?
        - How well did I contribute to the group's workload?
- Model expectations for student feedback to encourage development of this skill.
    - Students could then in turn provide constructive feedback that can support improvement of the course.
    - Students should be encouraged to learn professional communication and develop it by providing constructive feedback. The instructor is seen as a reference for providing the feedback, and it is his or her responsibility to make the students understand the effective way to use the feedback skills. In the end, these skills can be effectively used for other courses, too.
- Incorporate assessments that fit the learning objectives and context.

Table 13.5: Sample Feedback Form for Peer Review

Criteria	Evaluation Points			
	Weak	Average	Good	Excellent
Clarity				
Citations				
Evidence				
Grammar and mechanics				
Overall effect on the reader				

Note. Palloff and Pratt (2009).

- Create assessments that are clear and feasible.
    - By having continuous assessments, it is easy to understand the continuous progress of the student.
    - Usage of traditional assessments, such as essays and presentations, would show the skills of the learners and their abilities to solve problems and demonstrate skills.
- Do not allow cheating and plagiarism.
    - Prevent it by providing randomized, open-book, or timed tests.
    - Prevent it by using authentic assessments.
    - McNett (2002, as cited in Palloff & Pratt, 2009) said that deadlines are the most common reason learners cheat and plagiarize.
    - Plagiarism also results from improper knowledge and by accident. Many institutions are using several plagiarism-detecting tools, and the reports generated are helpful in reminding students of the need to paraphrase and add citations.

13.8 EFFECTIVE ASSESSMENT OF ONLINE COURSES

There are thousands of online degree courses available on the Internet; the first factor to consider before pursuing an online degree is accreditation. A course program with accreditation is more legitimate than one with no accreditation. A degree from an unaccredited institution may be worthless (Heritovo, 2016). The below list is a basic assessment model that can be used to understand the value of an online course or degree in greater detail. In this assessment model there are several factors to look into. The factors include analyzing the interaction of faculty and students, evaluating the skills gained by the students during the course, assessing course materials, and others (Morrison, 2015). The main five steps to assess online course quality are as follows.

1. Assess the quality of the basic elements. Some of the basic course elements are institutional and faculty support, learning resources, online course organization, instructional design, assessment and evaluation of student learning, innovative teaching, and usage of technology (Morrison, 2015). Some of the institutions always have a tool or framework in place for understanding the basic online course quality. If the institution doesn't have one, there are many tools available to evaluate the basic course elements.
2. Assess course materials. This can also include assessment of course artifacts provided and understanding the usage of the course material. Consider the students' feedback on the course material offered. Course material consists of video lectures, the reference books offered, presentation slides, assignments, case studies, and all the helpful resources provided during the course (Morrison, 2015).

3. Analyze the course from students' perspective. This is a tricky but helpful part of evaluating quality. There are numerous ways to consider quality from this perspective, but the important factor is whether the student is benefiting from the course. Compare the feedback from course iterations, and respond as required for the effectiveness of the course (Morrison, 2015).
4. Evaluate peer-to-peer interaction and student–faculty interaction during the course. This is a main pitfall of many courses because communication is critical for e-learning. Students, if connected to peers and faculty, will be able to contribute more during the course time. This boosts their motivation and learning satisfaction to the next level. An online course with much interaction would have more benefits for the students than one with less interaction. Student–faculty interaction is much needed to keep the students on track to achieve the course goals and to have positive feed back on the course (Morrison, 2015).
5. Assess evidence of student learning. The true evidence for benefiting from the course is student learning through the course design pattern and expectations. If the level of skill of students expected after course completion does not match actual outcomes of the course, then it is easy to say that the course failed in reaching its objective. The course structure needs to be changed for the betterment of the course (Morrison, 2015).

The basic assessment model is about ensuring the students benefit from the online courses and to make students motivated to understand which online courses will enhance their knowledge to a higher level. A proper assessment can also help students understand their level of knowledge gained from the course and can help them strengthen their own skills. In addition to that, it can help students stay focused and motivated, which in turn moves the faculty to be involved with the course. To achieve improvements, interactive, online course faculty should be well equipped with the effective tools available in an online course, such as discussion boards and videos, and give better support and feedback to students that can in turn help in developing the communication between students and faculty that can help students be more involved in the course. By using a guided assessment and understanding the requirements of the students, administrators and faculty can improve the online education system, with a resulting exponential increase in the system's popularity.

13.9 FROM STUDENTS' PERSPECTIVE

In and across the Internet world, there are few differences found between online and face-to-face faculty from students' perspective, except that online instructors are unavailable to meet the students directly to understand the students' views and clarify concepts. Student feedback from 1,500 past, present, and future e-learners was published by Learning House and Aslanian Market Research. Online students responded to questions about academic rigor and faculty engagement, and then the researchers compared the responses with those of students in traditional classes (Magda, 2014, para. 4).

The results showed 30% of online students said faculty gave examples to clarify challenging concepts compared with 22% of freshman students in face-to-face classes. For the latter, detailed feedback tended to come from faculty faster, however (Learning House & Aslanian Market Research, 2014). Magda (2014) reports, "In other areas, including 'explaining course goals' and 'teaching in an organized way,' online students provided similar faculty ratings compared to students taking exclusively or predominately face-to-face courses" (para. 7). These findings challenge the belief that online courses are inferior in rigor because these students conveyed virtually no difference between face-to-face and online teaching. Magda (2014) concludes, "Although some remain biased against online education, it may just take time for perceptions to catch up to this reality" (para. 8).

Buzasi (2010) also obtained students' feedback on online education. The advantages and disadvantages of online education are clear. The main concern of students regarding online education is the absence of face-to-face interaction in courses (Buzasi, 2010). Even though video lectures would help students, they are not as useful as face-to-face learning.

Several courses, such as psychology, require face-to-face interaction. Without this live interaction, the courses would be difficult to understand because body language and other physical interpretations are important aspects to learn. To master business management and negotiation techniques and several soft skills, interacting with the instructor, analyzing other people, and being under supervision are necessary to understand better. Interaction with other peers to work on group assignments is also a technique for better understanding of the specific subject.

13.10 CONCLUSION

There are several changes happening in education systems that are causing progressive changes in online courses, such as giving more freedom to the online courses to grow continuously. Students enroll in online courses for their ease, content, and time convenience to fit their busy lives.

Online learning is considered the best way to provide learning when the learner is under constraints. Many students and professors prefer online courses over classroom courses due to their advantages. Students and professors find these easy to learn from and teach as more courses are moving to online formats. But is this the best way to educate? In online classes the social interaction between the students and professors must take place. Exploring course factors ought to be completed before taking the course. Research of online learning needs to be a priority because this way of education would help increase the quality of higher education.

13.11 REFERENCES

Al-Qahtani, A., & Higgins, S. E. (2013). Effects of traditional, blended and e-learning on students' achievement in higher education. *Journal of Computer Assisted Learning 2*(3), 220–234. doi:10.1111/j.1365-2729.2012.00490.x

Allen, I. E., & Seaman, J. (2016). *Online report card: Tracking online education in the United States*. Retrieved from https://onlinelearningconsortium.org/read/online-report-card-tracking-online-education-united-states-2015/

Buzasi, Z. (2010). *Inside of distance learning- from students' perspective*. Proceedings of the 33rd International Convention on Information and Communication Technology, Electronics and Microelectronics, Opatija, Croatia.

Coursera. (2017). *By the numbers*. Retrieved from https://about.coursera.org/

edX. (2017). *In-demand online courses from the world's best universities and institutions*. Retrieved from https://www.edx.org/sites/default/files/mediakit/file/edx_-_mediakit_-_march_2017.pdf

Heritovo, R. (2016). *Internet as an academic resource*. Retrieved from https://www.scribd.com/document/313279568/ECA-Book-INTERNET-Without-Photos

Learning House & Aslanian Market Research. (2014, December). *Equal opportunity in higher education: Understanding rigor and engagement across learning modalities*. Louisville, KY: Learning House.

Magda, A. (2014, December). Online learning quality: Perception and reality [Web log message]. Retrieved from *The Online Learning Curve*, http://www.learninghouse.com/blog/tlh-news/online-learning-quality-perception-and-reality

Mitra, S. (2016, April 12). How billion-dollar Udacity plans to make money. *Inc*. Retrieved from http://www.inc.com/linkedin/sramana-mitra/billion-dollar-unicorn-udacity-leans-industry-giants-sramana-mitra.html

Morrison, D. (2015). How 'good' is your online course?: Five steps to assess course quality [Web blog message]. Retrieved from *Online Learning Insights*, https://onlinelearninginsights.wordpress.com/2015/05/26/how-good-is-your-online-course-five-steps-to-assess-course-quality/

Online Learning Consortium. (n.d.). *Our quality framework*. Retrieved from https://onlinelearningconsortium.org/about/quality-framework-five-pillars/

Palloff, R. M., & Pratt, K. (2009). Assessment online. In *Assessing the online learner: Resources and strategies for faculty* (pp. 29–48). San Francisco, CA: Jossey-Bass.

Ralston-Berg, P., Buckenmeyer, J., Barczyk, C., & Hixon, E. (2015). Students' perceptions of online course quality: How do they measure up to the research? *Internet Learning*, 4(1), 38–55.

Toprak, E., Özkanal, B., Aydin, S., & Kaya, S. (2010). Ethics in e-learning. *TOJET: The Turkish Online Journal of Educational Technology*, 9(2), 78–86.

Tsironis, A., Katsanos, C., & Xenos, M. (with Poulin, R., & Straut, T. T.). (2016). *Comparative usability evaluation of three popular MOOC platforms*. Paper presented at Institute of Electrical and Electronics Engineers Global Engineering Education Conference. doi:10.1109/EDUCON.2016.7474613

www.ingramcontent.com/pod-product-compliance
Lightning Source LLC
Chambersburg PA
CBHW081347080526
44588CB00016B/2397